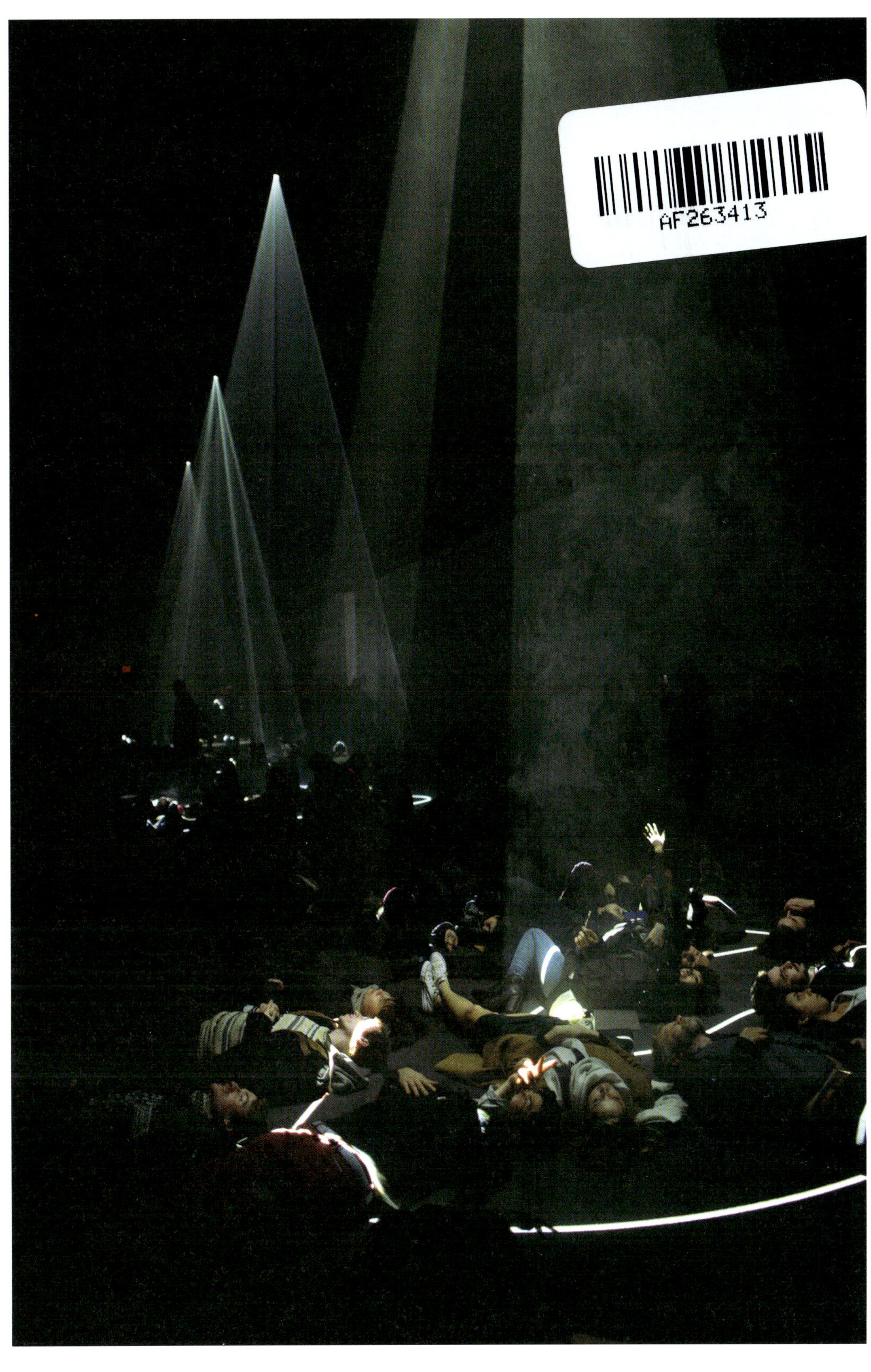

A.   Anthony McCall. From front to back: *Skirt (III)*, 2010, *You and I (II)*, 2010, *Breath (III)*, 2005, *Meeting You Halfway*, 2009. Installation view of *Anthony McCall: Solid Light Works*, Pioneer Works, New York, 2018.
B.   Anthony McCall. *Leaving (With Two-Minute Silence)*, 2009. Installation plan, 2018.
C.   Anthony McCall. *Skirt*, 2010. Footprint drawing, 2010. Charcoal on paper.

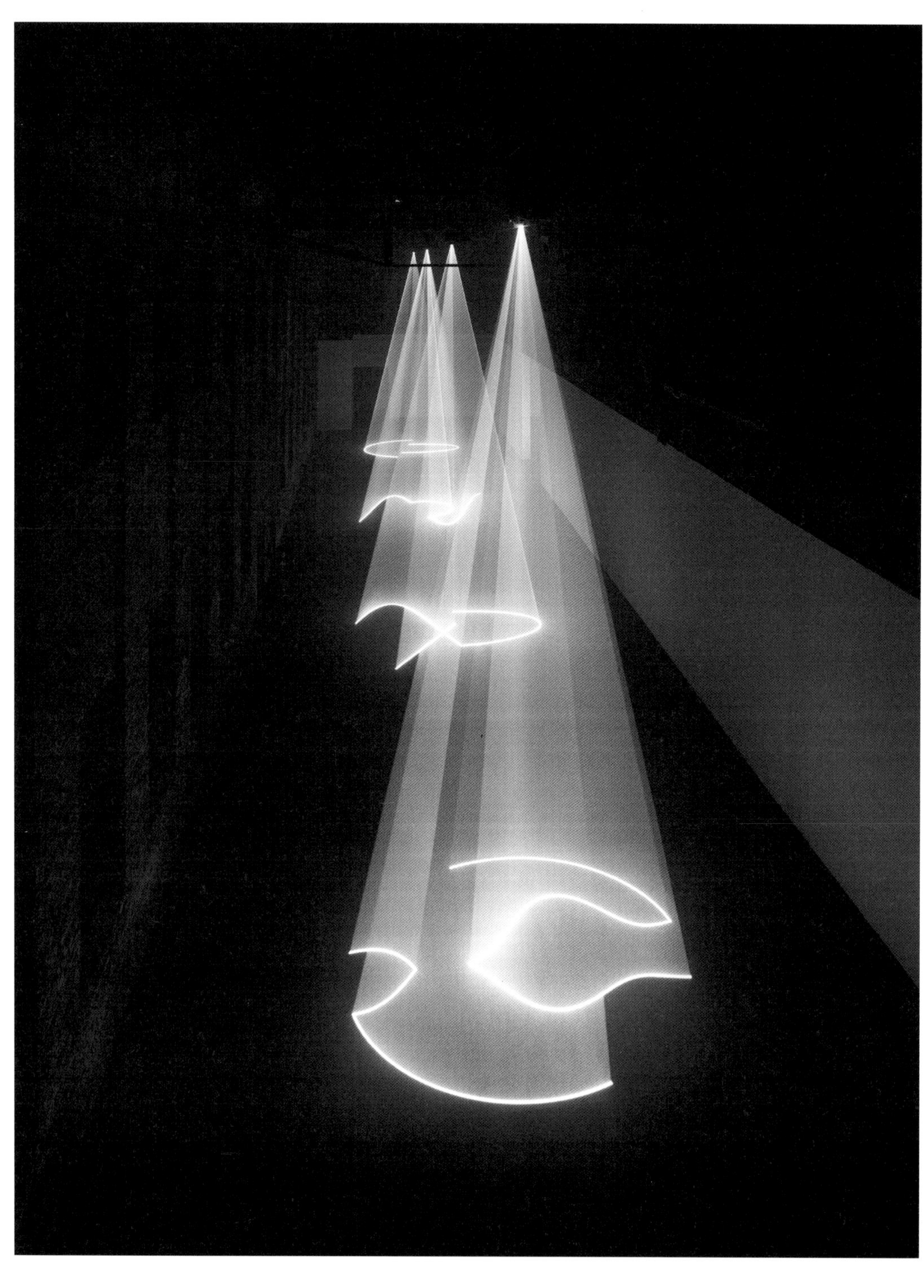

A

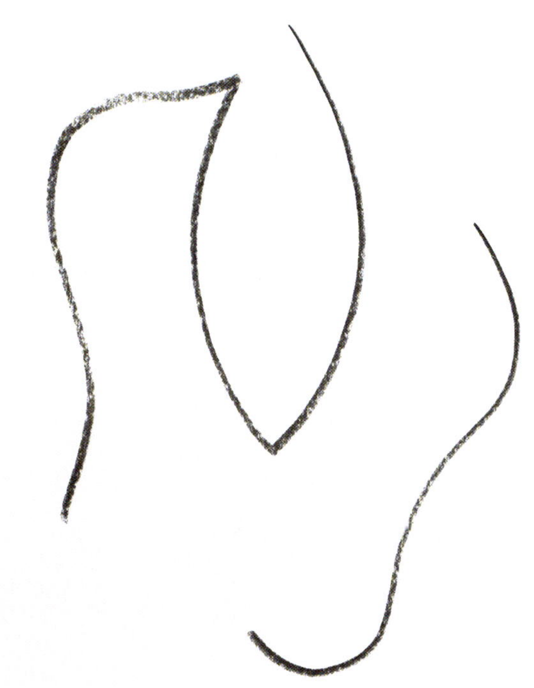

ANTHONY MCCALL
"LEAVING (WITH TWO-MINUTE SILENCE"
INSTALLATION NOTES 2018.11.01

A. Anthony McCall. *Doubling Back*, 2003. Installation drawing, 2004. Pencil on paper.

B. Anthony McCall. From left to right: *You and I, Horizontal*, 2005, *Doubling Back*, 2003. Installation view, Pioneer Works, New York, 2018.

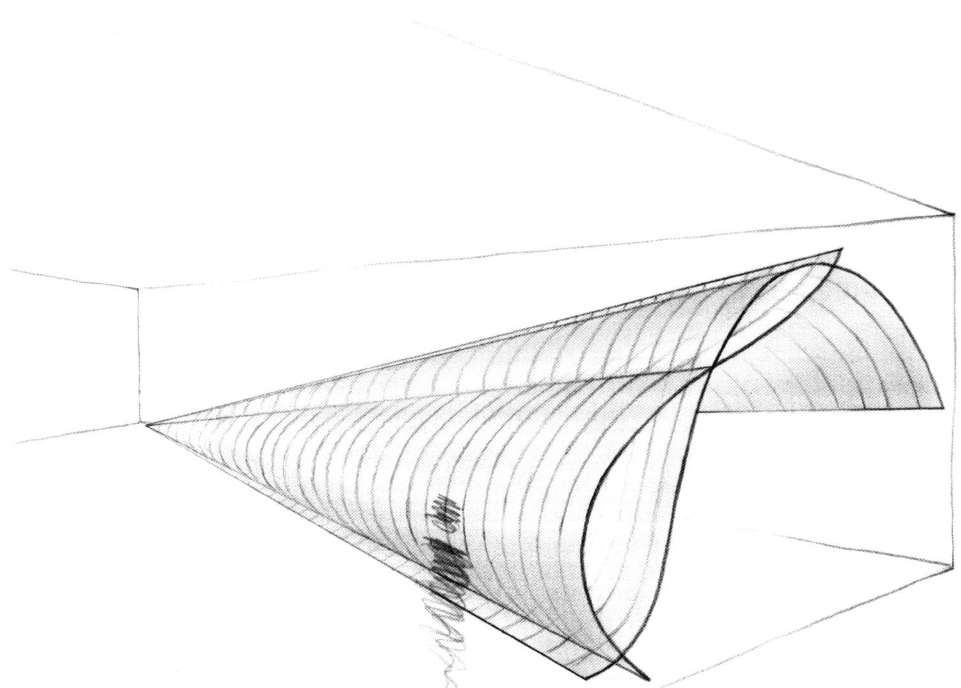

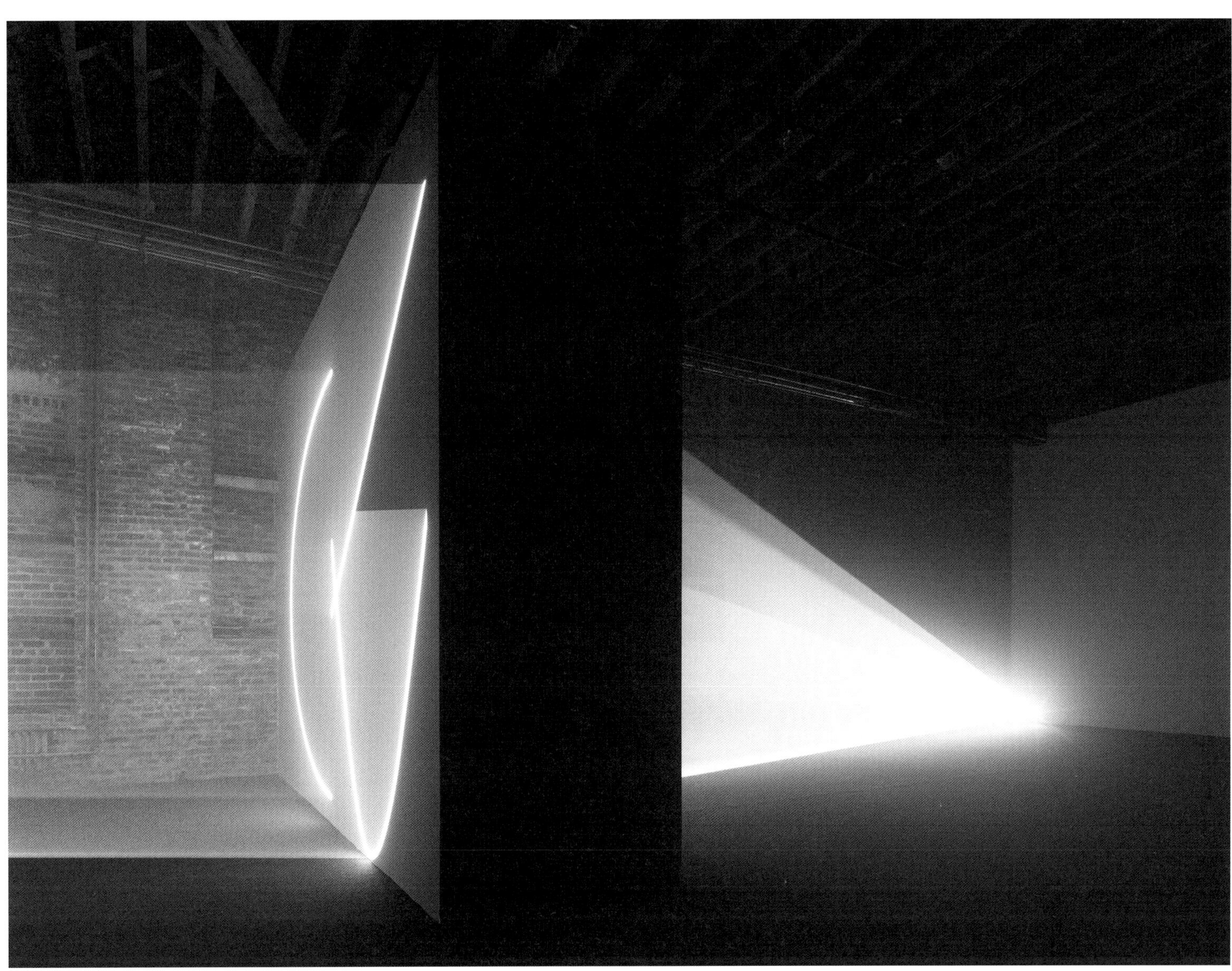

B

A. Anthony McCall. *Breath (III)*, 2005. Footprint drawing, 2015. Charcoal on paper.

B. Anthony McCall. *You and I (II)*, 2010. Footprint drawing, 2011. Charcoal on paper.

C. Anthony McCall. *You and I, Horizontal*, 2005. Footprint sequence in six parts, 2011.

A

B

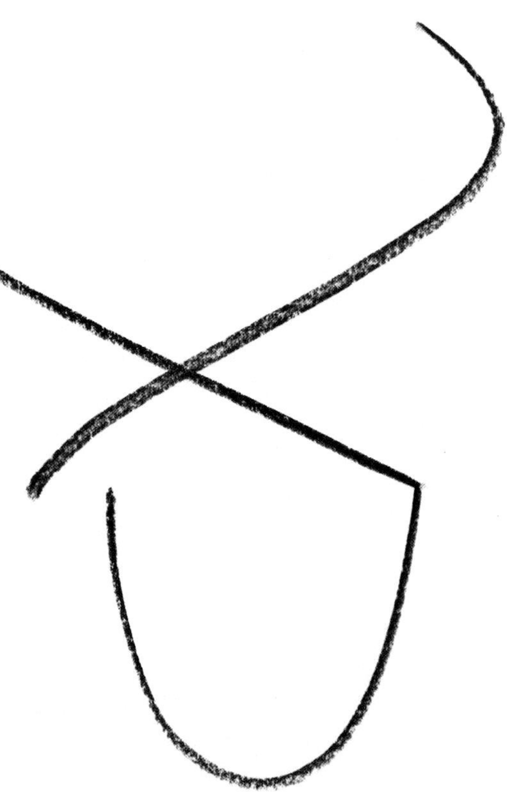

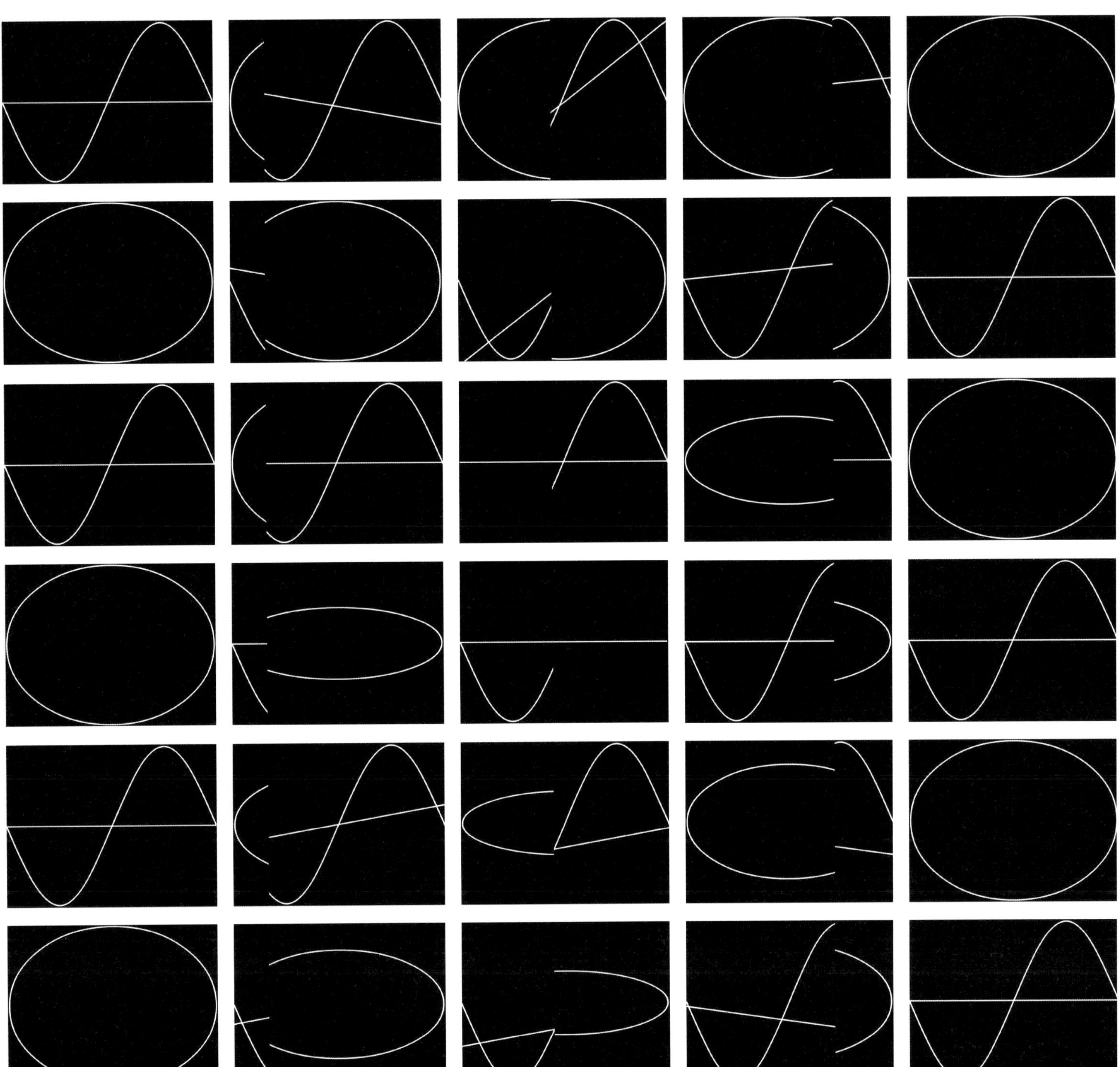

A. Anthony McCall. *Meeting You Halfway*, 2009. Notebook study, 2009.

B. Anthony McCall. *Leaving (With Two-Minute Silence)*, 2009. Notebook study, 2008.

C. Anthony McCall. *You and I, Horizontal*, 2005. Installation view, Pioneer Works, New York, 2018.

D. Visitors to *Anthony McCall: Solid Light Works*, Pioneer Works, New York, 2018.

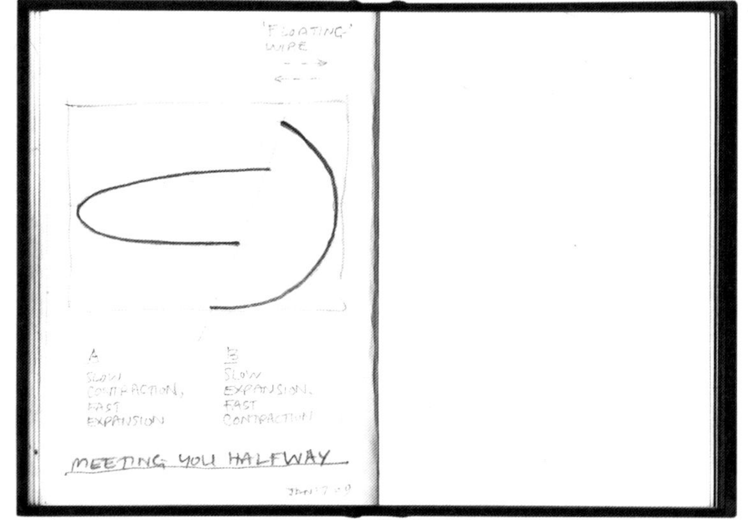

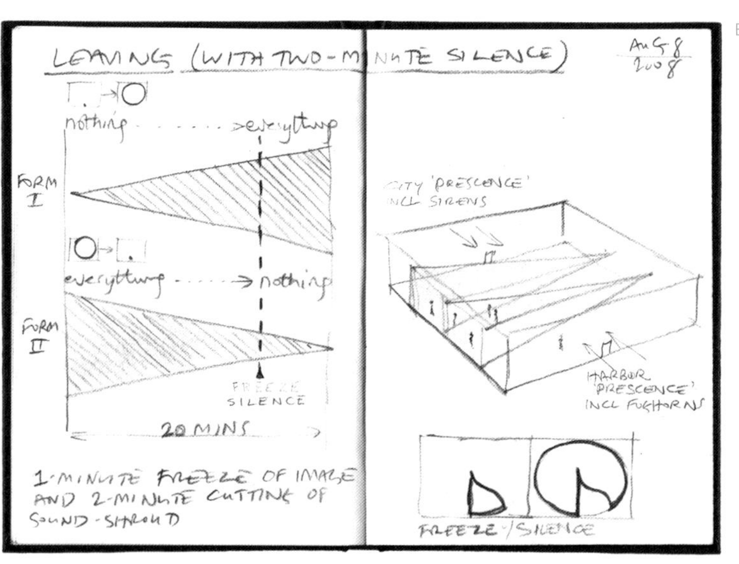

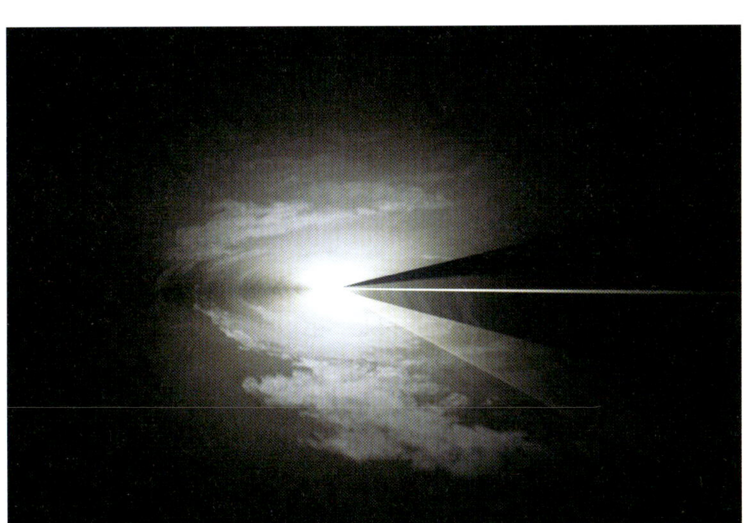

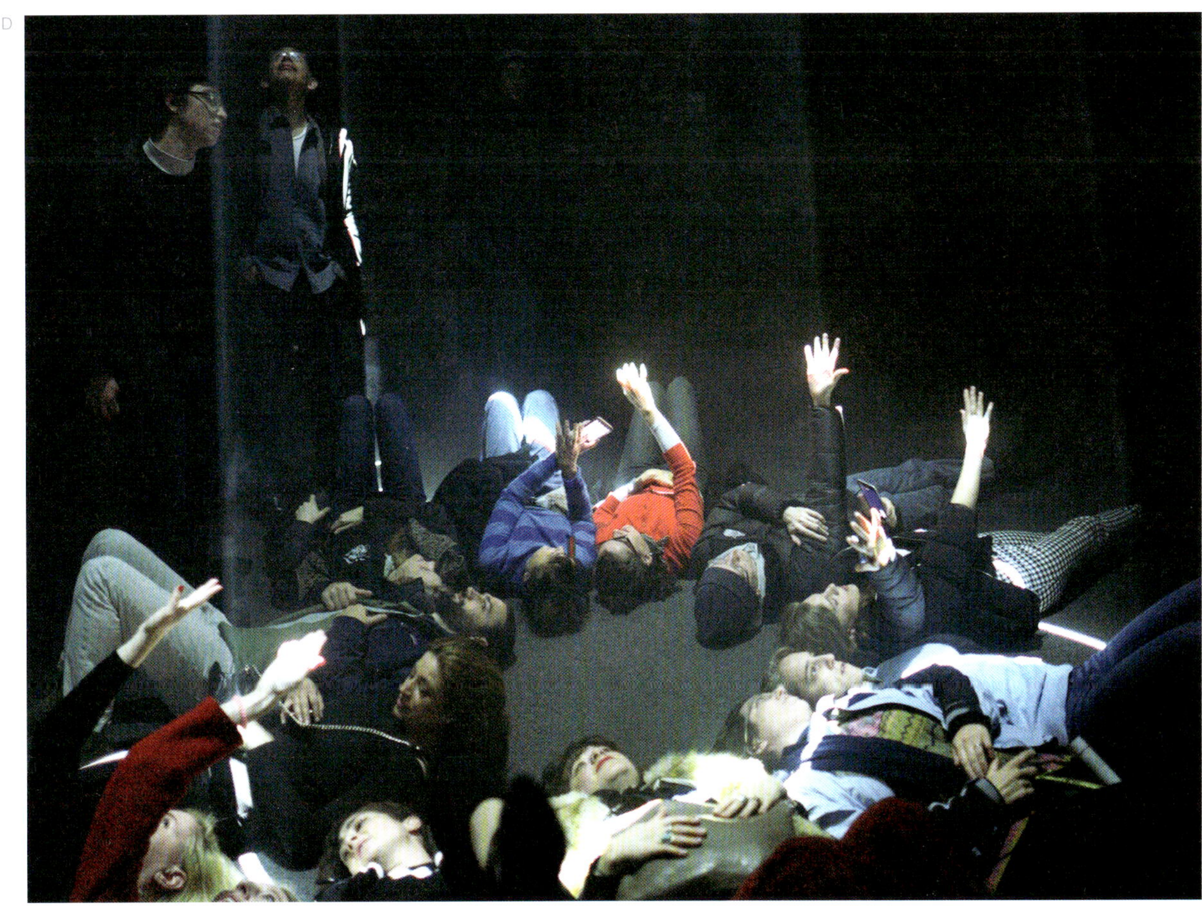

Simultaneous Soloists
Anthony McCall & David Grubbs

Pioneer Works Press

Contents

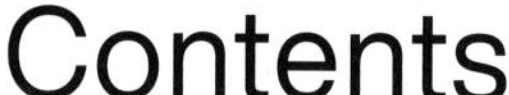

Anthony McCall. *Breath (III)*, 2005. Footprint sequence at 150-second intervals, 2011.

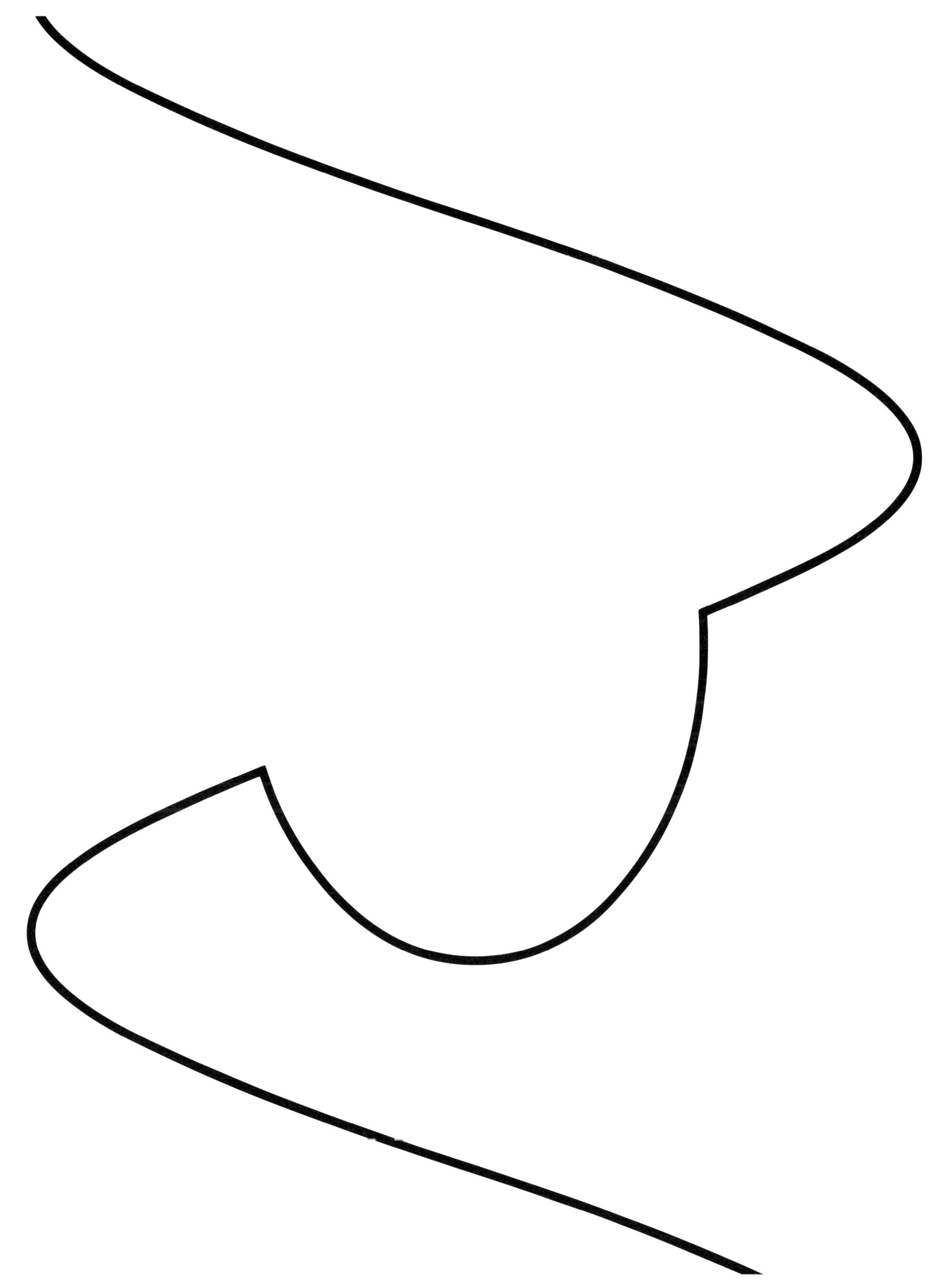

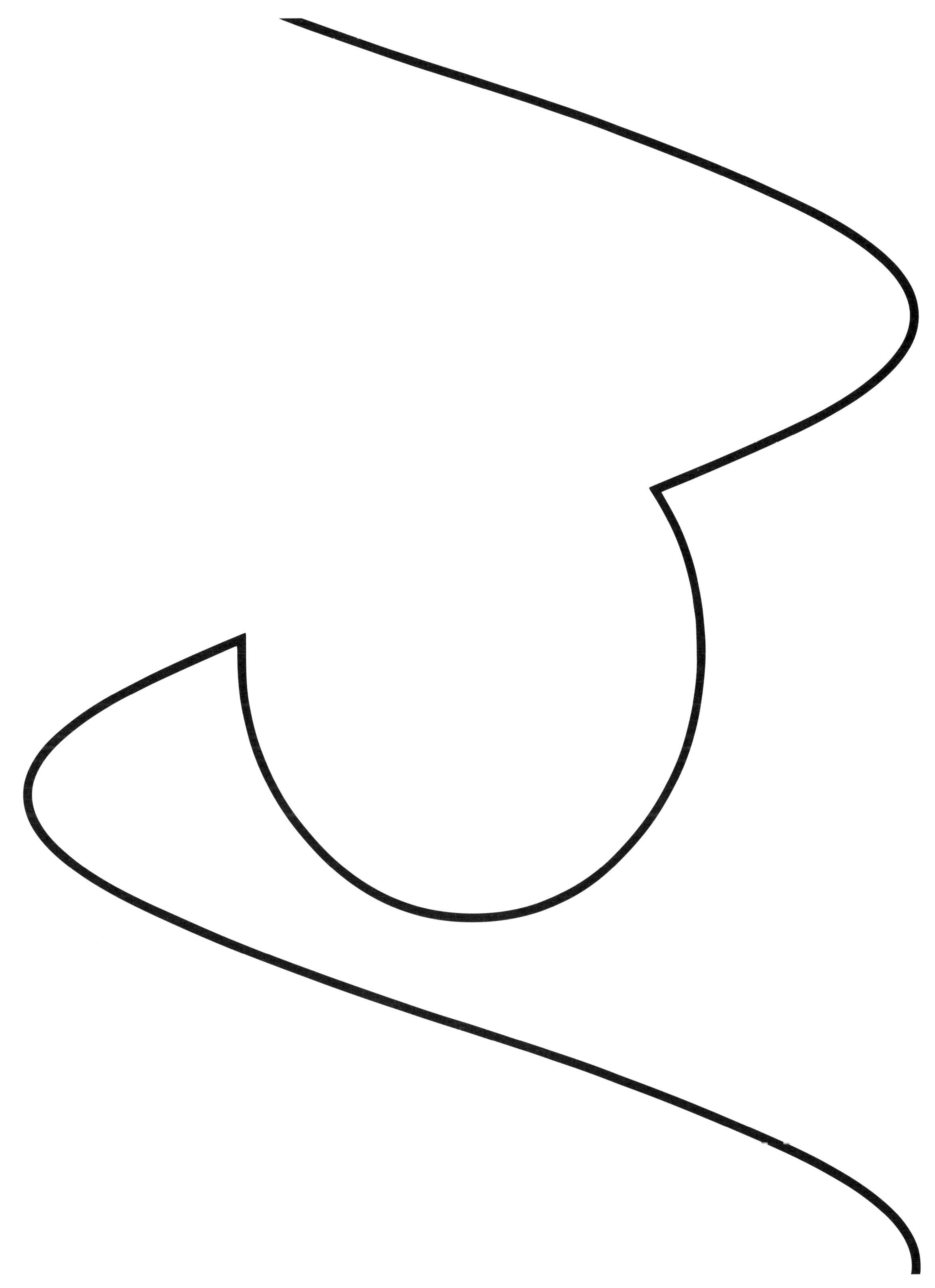

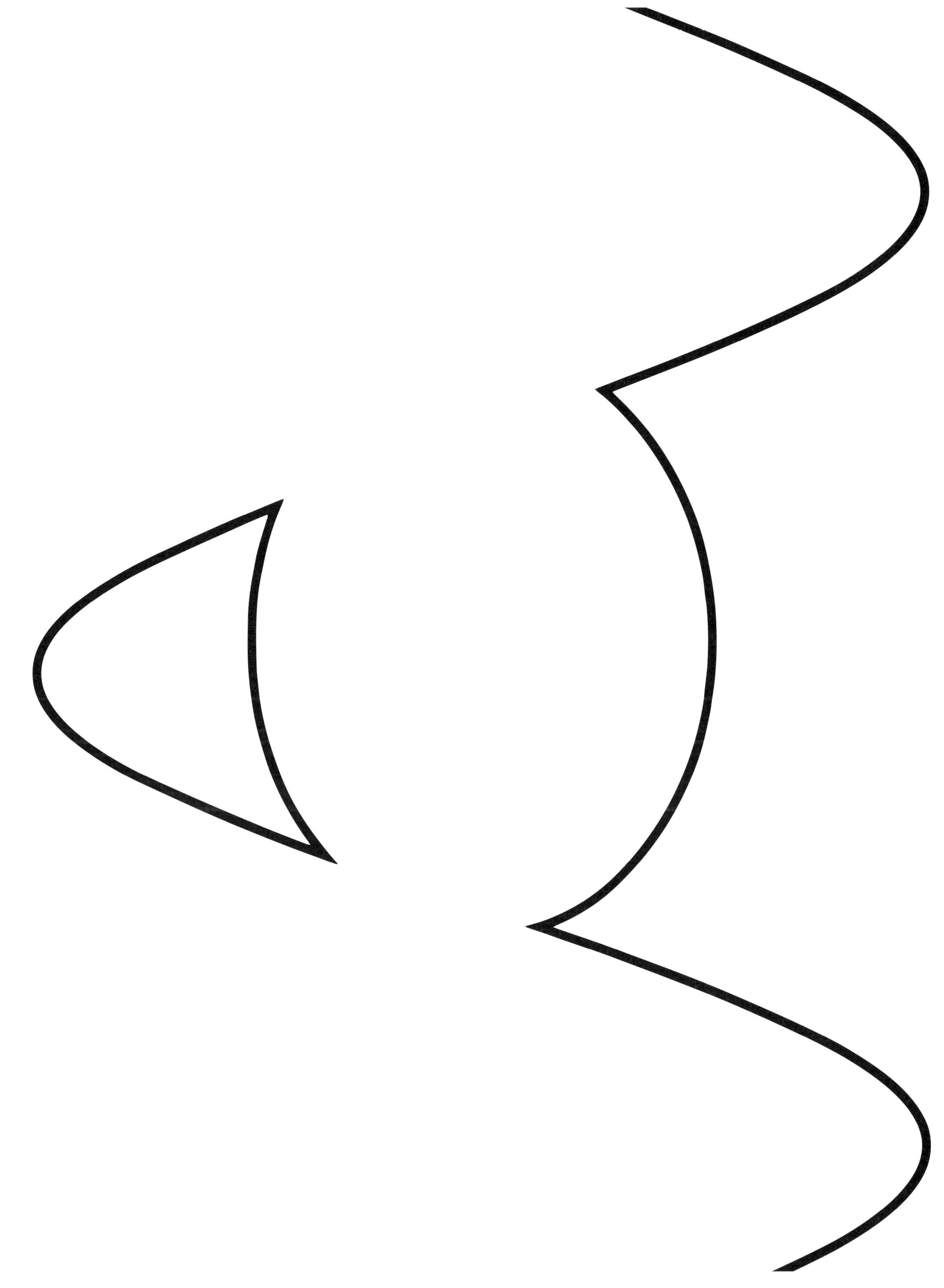

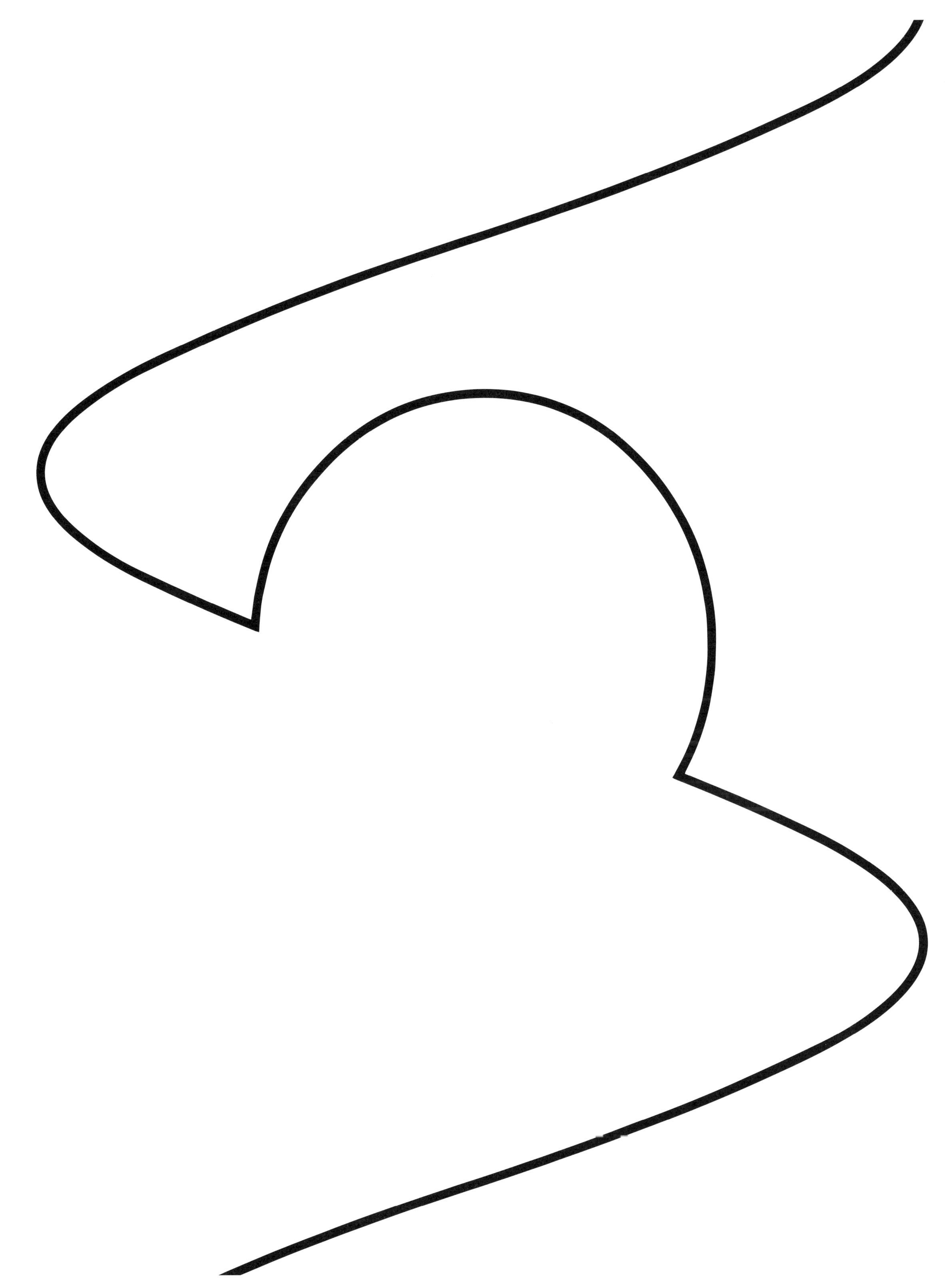

Introduction
Branden W. Joseph

1. Anthony McCall, *"Line Describing a Cone* and Related Films," *October* 103 (Winter 2003): 60.

2. Cornelius Cardew, "John Cage—Ghost or Monster?" (1972), *Leonardo Music Journal* 8 (1998): 3-4.

3. John Cage, "Composition as Process II: Indeterminacy," in *Silence* (Middletown, CT: Wesleyan University Press, 1961), 39.

4. McCall, *"Line Describing a Cone* and Related Films," 60.

In 1972, Anthony McCall attended the London premiere of John Cage and Lejaren Hiller's massive multimedia spectacle *HPSCHD* (1967-69). Presented at the Roundhouse as part of the International Carnival of Experimental Sound (ICES 72)—during which McCall staged one of his iconic *Landscape for Fire* performances—Cage and Hiller's composition involved, in addition to seven amplified harpsichords and fifty-two tape recorders, eighty-four slide projectors and a dozen film projectors. Yet, despite such a panoply of visual material, McCall's recollection most clearly foregrounded the acoustical experience. "I remember standing at the very center of the circle [of harpsichords]," he noted in 2003, "finding the place where all the different pieces being played merged into one, rapturous cacophony. Then, as I moved toward a particular harpsichord, the sound of that instrument rose, as those behind me, or to the side, diminished. One became a kind of mobile mixer, creating one's own musical experience."[1]

Amidst a rhetorical atmosphere marked by heated polemics—the composer Cornelius Cardew, one of the Roundhouse harpsichordists, had launched an infamous attack on Cage, a former associate, only a couple months earlier—McCall's precise and insightful characterization presciently highlighted *HPSCHD*'s interrelation of acoustic spatialization and autonomous listening.[2] Cage had written about the former as far back as 1958, explaining in "Composition as Process II: Indeterminacy" that "separation in space is spoken of as facilitating independent action on the part of each performer. Sounds will then arise from actions, which will then arise from their own centers rather than as motor or psychological effects of other actions and sounds in the environment."[3] The corollary, as McCall realized, was a listener who, in the process of creating their own ambulatory acoustical mix, also became a distinct center of their own, imbued with a unique perspective upon an experience that was, nonetheless, communal and shared. "It was qualitatively different from...'following' a piece of music," he explained. "Cage's placing of the spectator as central to the realization of the piece, his attitude toward musical sound and listening, and his use of space, all struck me as being extremely suggestive."[4]

Although McCall did pursue a number of sound works, such as *White Noise Installation* (1972), during this period, it would be in the development of his pioneering "solid light films" that Cage and Hiller's example would resonate perhaps most consequently. The following year, when describing the first of his sculptural film pieces, the iconic *Line Describing a Cone* (1973), McCall's words would point back to the spatial experience of *HPSCHD*. "The form of attention required on the part of the viewer," he noted, "is unprecedented. No longer is one viewing position as good as any other. For this film, every viewing position presents a different aspect. The viewer therefore, has a participatory role in apprehending the event: he or she can, indeed needs to, move around, relative to the emerging light-form."[5] All this to indicate that McCall's solid light films—often still understood and discussed as self-reflexive modernist gestures, canonic instantiations of film about film—betray an important, if often overlooked, genealogical relationship to the legacy of post-World War II experimental composition. It is thus apt that they rejoined that legacy in *Four Simultaneous Soloists*, the performance series organized at Pioneer Works by David Grubbs.

Grubbs, who had already worked closely with a number of visual artists such as Angela Bulloch and Cosima von Bonin, played a key role in reintroducing sound into McCall's contemporary practice. Interestingly, their initial collaboration, *Leaving (With Two-Minute Silence)* (2009), engaged with the spatiality of sound in a manner completely different from that of Cage and Hiller at the Roundhouse. Reproducing the atmosphere of a harbor, to one side, and a traffic-filled urban street, to the other, Grubbs's two-channel soundtrack seemed to virtually dissolve the walls of the darkened gallery into which McCall's dual light forms were cast. The effect was of a subtle, but persistent acoustical illusion of being outside in the open air. A subsequent collaboration, *Leaving (With Four Half-Turns)* (2011), conjoined an amplified live guitar performance with a single solid light projection to create something like an audiovisual duet. That McCall's works of the last decade have subtly but persistently played with certain anthropomorphic associations (twined, nearly erotic, couplings, breath-like formal transformations, and so on) only heightened the potential interplay between subject and object, musical performer and work of art.

The collaboration between Grubbs and McCall at Pioneer Works effectively multiplied the set-up of *Leaving (With Four Half-Turns)*, as four musicians performed semi-independently, each one situated in proximity to one of the four large vertical projections installed throughout the length of the cavernous main gallery. Entirely unscored (without even those indeterminate scores characteristic of Cage), each of the four "simultaneous" soloists was free to create his or her own soundscape or statement as they desired, just as each audience member was free to circumnavigate the space to produce his or her own individuated audiovisual "mix." In looking back to the type of differential

5. Anthony McCall, "Two Statements," in *The Avant-Garde Film: A Reader of Theory and Criticism*, ed. P. Adams Sitney, Anthology Film Archives Series 3 (New York: New York University Press, 1978), 250-251.

acoustical spatialization instituted by *HPSCHD*, the performance went beyond the phenomenological—instigated by viewers' careful investigation of McCall's slowly moving, diaphanous, visual forms—to engage with the historical roots of the observed phenomena, providing not only an aesthetic involvement, but an empirical examination that reignited the intertwined, cross-disciplinary pedigree that lay behind the most celebrated aspect of McCall's oeuvre. In this manner, the Pioneer Works installation and concert series proved uniquely insightful, an experience unlike any within the artist's ever-growing exhibition history.

Anthony McCall and David Grubbs in Conversation

David Grubbs: When you and I first met in 2007, it was in your studio on Jay Street, where we're having the present conversation, and where we regularly came to brainstorm and work on pieces. At that first meeting, I recall you referencing the fact that digital projection—which you had begun using when you returned to making solid light works earlier that decade— is relatively silent, certainly as compared to 16mm projection, and especially compared to works that use multiple 16mm projectors. The use of digital projectors created a problem of sound, a problem that you said you knew that you eventually would have to tackle.

Anthony McCall: That's right. In the 1970s, when I was working in 16mm, the projectors were in the same room as the audience, and my films were silent. The steady mechanical purring of the projector was a distinctive part of the experience, though it was simply part of the background noise of projection and rarely remarked on. But I remember noting that when the film finished, and the projectionist turned the projector off, it left a sudden, almost deafening silence. Fast-forward to the digital era, when I started making films again. Digital projectors make no sound, and I found that I missed the drone-like tone of the film projector, which provided for the spectator a type of acoustic privacy. When I embarked on *Leaving (With Two-Minute Silence)* (2009), I began to consider the possibility of creating a very low-amplitude sound, which could then be removed in order to create a significant silence.

DG After you began working digitally—and prior to *Leaving*, which is the series on which you and I first worked together—you had exhibited solid light works that were silent.

AM All the 1970s solid light works were silent, and then between 2003 and 2007, just before we began talking about *Leaving*, I'd made about ten works, all silent. And I'd begun making vertical pieces, too.

DG Until the *Four Simultaneous Soloists* performance series at Pioneer Works, the only pieces that you and I had worked on together were horizontal pieces. It was quite a shift for me, coming to spend that amount of time in the presence of the vertical works.

AM To begin with, the vertical works were seldom shown, simply because of the rarity of thirty-two-foot tall exhibition spaces.

But once I was looking at them, it was clear how different they were from the horizontals, which still reference cinema quite directly. The verticals seem almost architectural.

DG When we started discussing *Leaving* and the possibility of combining the solid light works with sound, you usually had a pencil in hand, sketching, showing ideas. One of the things that we talked about was the way in which there was a demand, given the context of an exhibition, to produce pieces that work compositionally in loop mode. This was especially apparent to me as I watched you in real time sketching compositional structures. I'd often be struck by the beauty or the aptness of a single, start-to-finish composition, but then we'd also have to address the question of how that or a similar idea could best be realized when installed such that it loops, recognizing the fact that a viewer is likely to amble in at some point other than the beginning of the structure. And so I remember the conversations taking account of that, but also that we began thinking about the possibility of working with sound in a concert or performance where the work could also be experienced as a presentation that doesn't repeat, and one that has a clearly defined start time.

AM For the solid light pieces there are always two format choices: once through to an assembled audience or throughout the day with individual visitors who come and go. I chose the latter in the mid-seventies from *Long Film for Four Projectors* (1974) onward for a number of reasons, and have mostly kept to this. And I use a cyclical structure, which for me is different from a "loop." A loop means that you take whatever you made, with whatever structure it has, and just keep repeating it. Cyclical form, by contrast, would require that the structure took into account the repetition that would follow, and so even the small internal units of the composition anticipate the larger repetition, and the end of one cycle is indistinguishable from the beginning of the next. With our project at Pioneer Works, it was more complicated since the once-through live music performance was to be superimposed onto vertical works which were cyclical.

DG In the first version of *Leaving* that we worked on, going back and forth in conversation and spending time in the recording studio, there were several different runs at it that involved foghorns. After two years, we locked down—although it hasn't been exhibited—a single-channel projection version with five

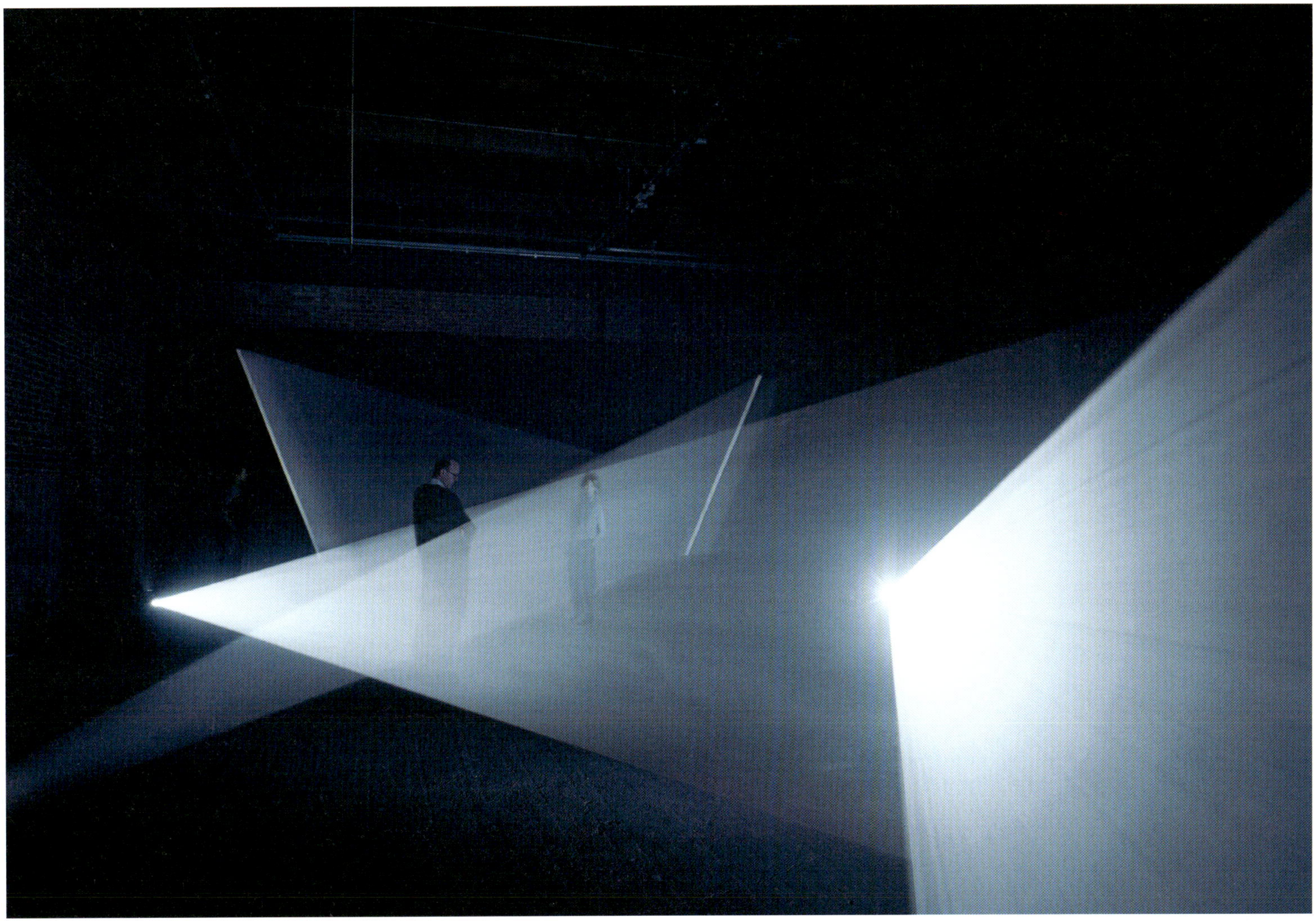

A

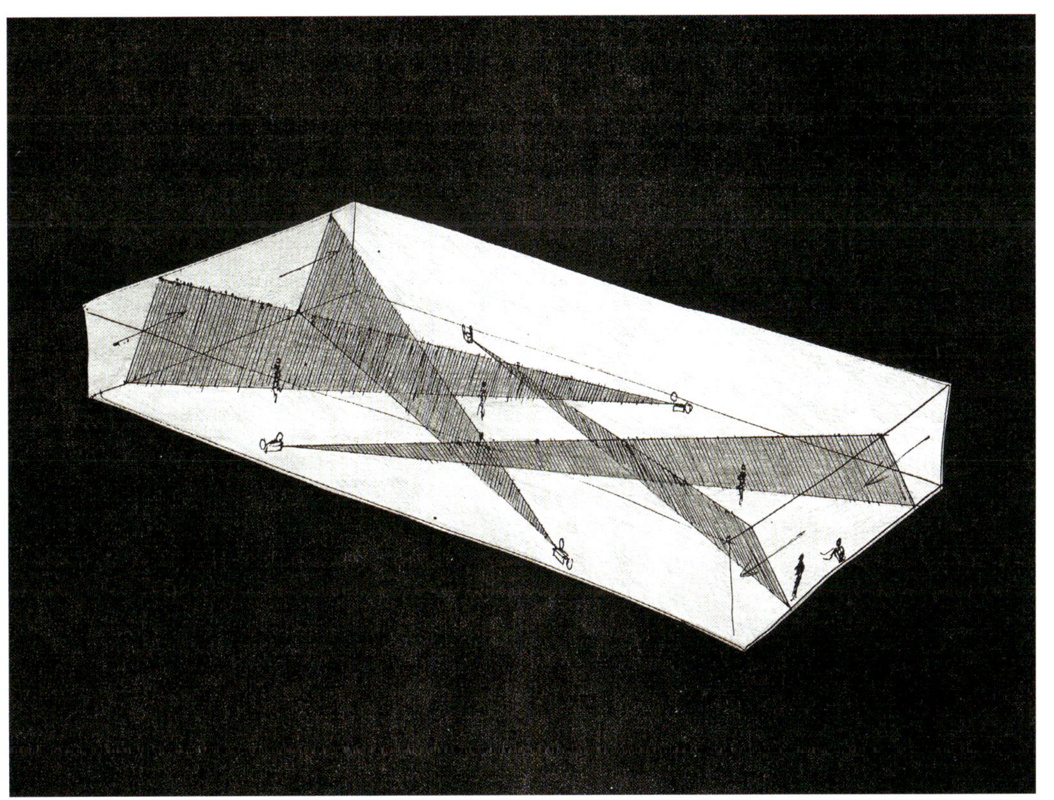

B

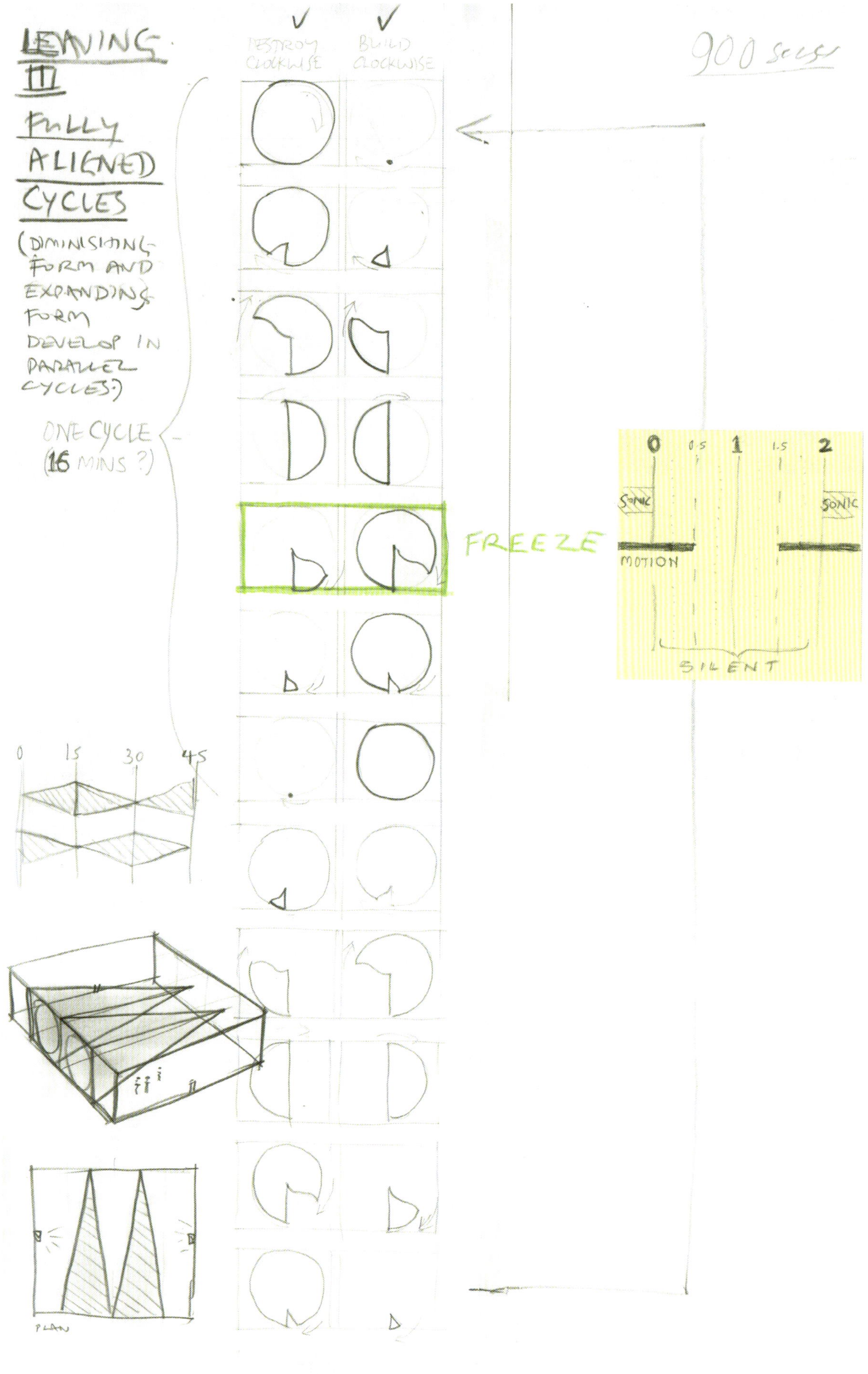

LEAVING
III
FULLY
ALIGNED
CYCLES
(DIMINISHING
FORM AND
EXPANDING
FORM
DEVELOP IN
PARALLEL
CYCLES?)
ONE CYCLE
(16 MINS ?)
DESTROY
CLOCKWISE
BUILD
CLOCKWISE
FREEZE
900 secs
0   0.5   1   1.5   2
SONIC
SONIC
MOTION
SILENT
0   15   30   45
PLAN

tracks of audio and five speakers, each dedicated to a distinct foghorn, so that each loudspeaker conveys one and only one sounding body. The foghorns are composites in which electronic sound meshes with recordings of actual foghorns, but they consist primarily of electronic sound. In this version, the disappearance of the solid light form—it leaves—occurs in counterpoint to the sound, is counterbalanced by the sound, which over the course of the work steadily grows in volume and intensity in a single arc. There's a suggestion that one replaces the other, one compensates for the loss of the other, and that sound eventually supplants image. But in the end you and I agreed that the experience of the audio component was too much that of listening to a musical composition, no matter how spare. Even with just the five pitches, at a certain point it sounded like an organ concert.

> AM Yes. I had assumed that the exchange between visual and sonic space would remain legible. I wasn't ready for the foghorns to redefine themselves as music.

DG After we locked down that version, we set it aside. The visual component of the subsequent piece is a dual projection in the cyclical mode that you've described, and this is *Leaving (With Two-Minute Silence)*.

> AM *Leaving (With Two-Minute Silence)* is a two-projector work, with the two forms projected side-by-side across a thirty-foot space. Two things happen. The first of the two forms starts as a projected conical object that begins whole, but by the end of the piece—some thirty-two minutes later—it has vanished; it's gone; it's been reduced to nothing. The second form moves in the opposite direction. As the companion form gradually disappears, this second form gradually grows. At the precise moment when one has gone, the other becomes complete and whole.

DG The two-minute silence—there are actually two of them within the piece's thirty-two minute cycle—is at the heart of the sound composition, which creates the possibility of thresholds into and out of silence, something like the fantastic, arresting silence that you've mentioned when a projector is shut off.

> AM And in order to create the silences we had to set about making two tracks of ambient sound.

DG Yes, the audio for the piece consists of two separate mono tracks. The first was built from the quieter kinds of non-sounds, non-events, sonically, of New York Harbor—the plashing sound of water against the side of the boat and buoys with bells in the harbor—but also really an experience of the sonic vista of distance on the harbor, of sound across the water. For the other channel, you and I made a recording on the street in Manhattan near the entrance to the Holland Tunnel, recording at a time of comparatively little traffic so that the cars were flowing freely. You had the concept of having the two sounds—harbor and street—quiet enough that one doesn't have an all-over sound perspective when entering the space. There's no privileged place where you can stand and take it all in. The visitor has to choose to walk toward one of the two speakers that were approximately thirty-five feet away from one another.

> AM They were on opposite sides of the room.

DG Yes, and the speakers were installed so that they were flush with the wall. At a low volume both collections of sounds, even though the source recordings were so different from one another, were likely to suggest white noise until you actively walked toward one or the other and brought it into focus.

> AM And when you walked into the room, you didn't necessarily notice the sound, not at first. Though you might. It depends on the moment in the recording.

DG My experience of the sound in *Leaving (With Two-Minute Silence)* is that in some points in the room, and at some points in time, the two sounds begin to mix, but the more memorable aspect is the way in which in much of the room they remain distinct from one another. The viewer or the listener needs to explore the space in its entirety to really experience the sound components. I remember an early conversation that we had about the tempo or rate of change being very important in the solid light compositions; you said something along the lines of "If the image moves faster than the viewer it's cinema, but if the viewer moves faster than the image it's sculpture." I thought that sound composition for *Leaving (With Two-Minute Silence)* responded to this dictate. Nothing about the sound composition would leave the listener rooted to the spot. In fact, they need to root around the space.

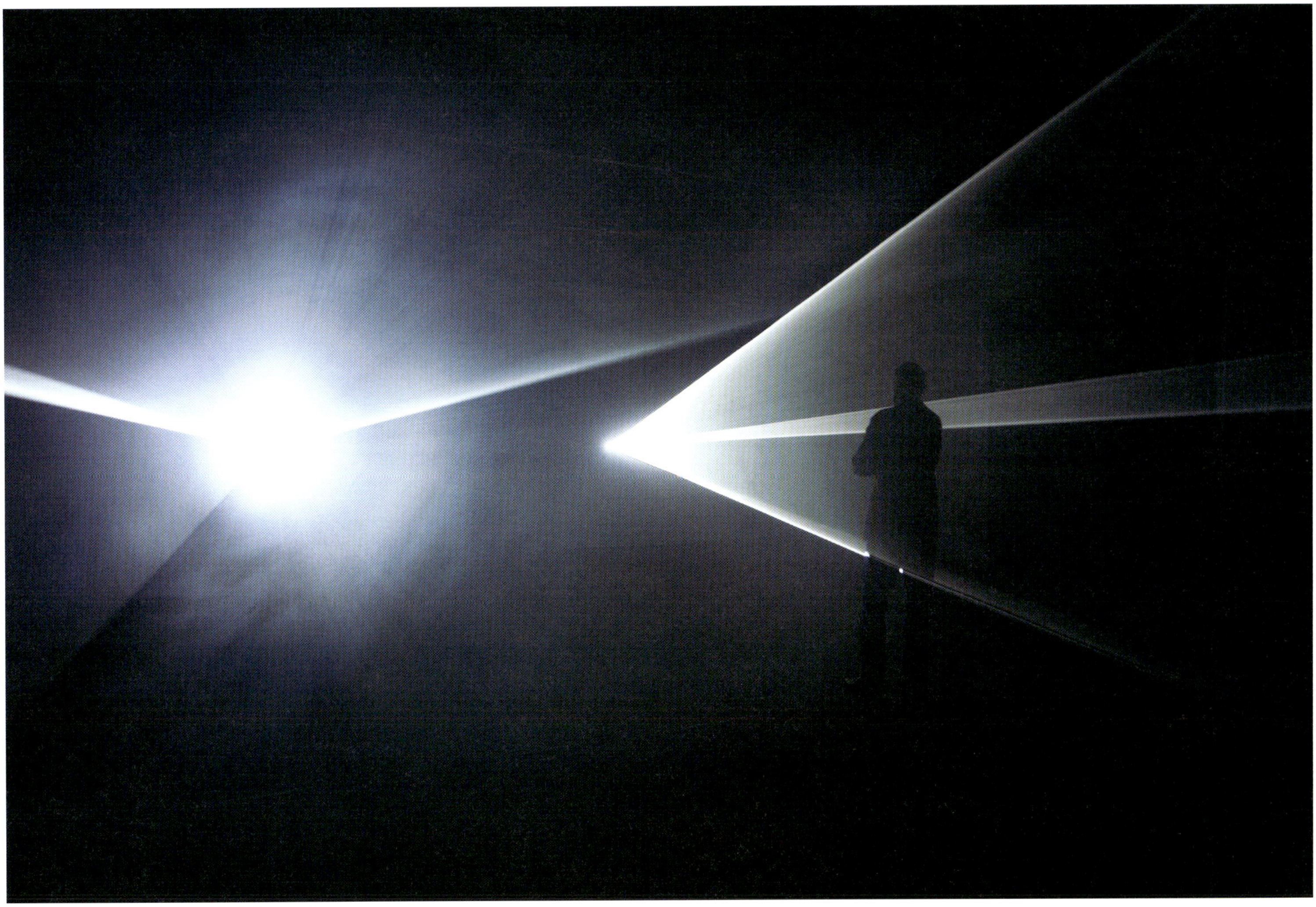

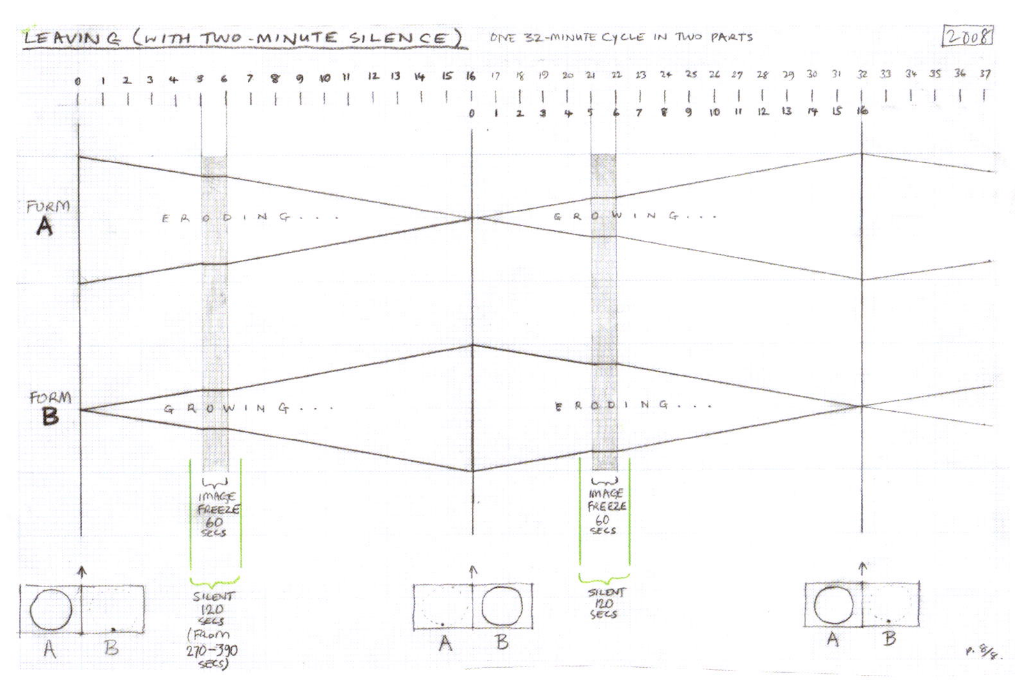

LEAVING (WITH TWO-MINUTE SILENCE)   ONE 32-MINUTE CYCLE IN TWO PARTS   2008
0 1 2 3 4 5 6 7 8 9 10 11 12 13 14 15 16 17 18 19 20 21 22 23 24 25 26 27 28 29 30 31 32 33 34 35 36 37
0 1 2 3 4 5 6 7 8 9 10 11 12 13 14 15 16
FORM A
ERODING . . .
GROWING . . .
FORM B
GROWING . . .
ERODING . . .
IMAGE FREEZE 60 SECS
IMAGE FREEZE 60 SECS
SILENT 120 SECS (FROM 270-390 SECS)
SILENT 120 SECS
A   B
A   B
A   B
P. 3/4

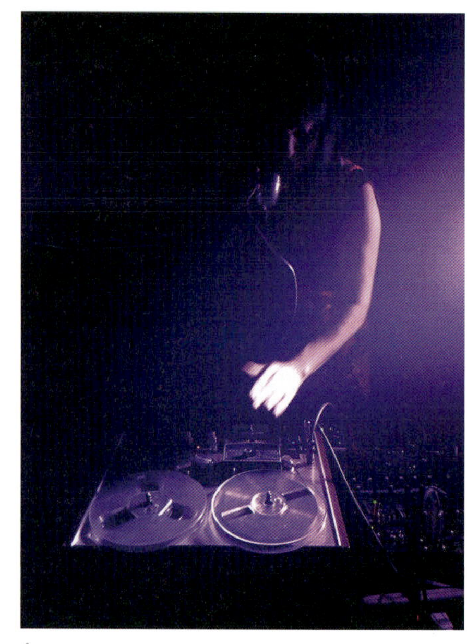

A

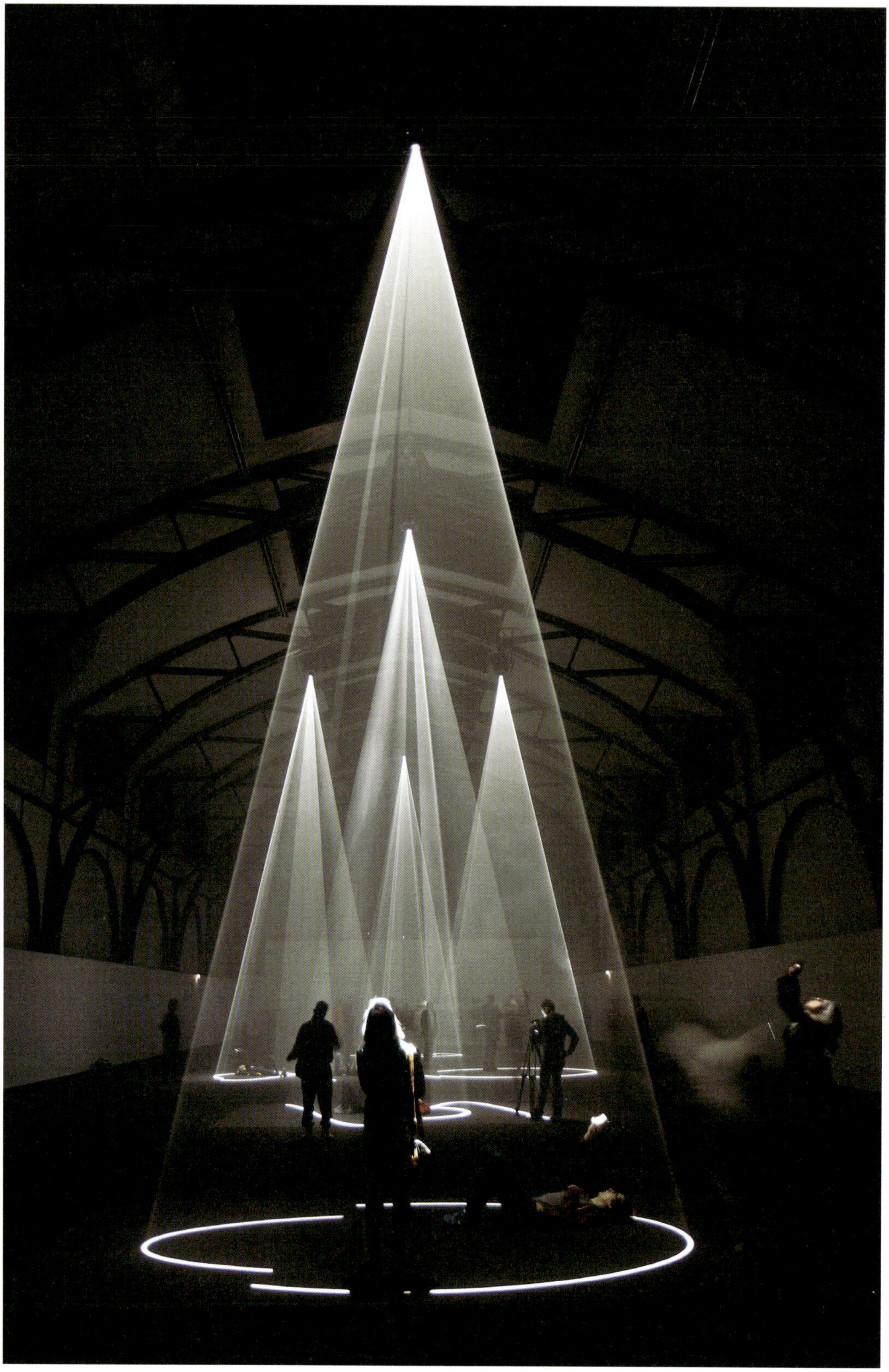

34

B

AM The listener must find the sounds, much as the visual forms must be approached. There is no single place from which to secure an overview, whether you are looking or listening. When you are incorporated, say, inside the form that is being cut away, you cannot also be inside the form next door to it that is growing. When you are near the audio speaker that produces the traffic sound you are as far as you can possibly be from the other speaker across the space. When you walk into the room, your first impression isn't of a room full of sound. If anything you see the visual first, and then it gradually dawns on you that the whole installation is shrouded in sound.

DG The first time that *Leaving (With Two-Minute Silence)* was exhibited was in 2009-10 at the Sean Kelly Gallery in Manhattan—where if its westernmost wall were to disappear, what you would hear are the sounds of the Hudson River.

AM It was a sort of conceptual sleight of hand, because you could assume that you were just hearing the traffic outside the gallery, in the distance.

DG I think that there were plenty of people who heard nothing. It's a bit like not hearing the projector, perhaps even more subtle than that.

AM The two-minute silence occurs every sixteen minutes. It intrudes abruptly and noticeably. In spite of the volume of the ambient tracks being low, the silence is emphatic.

DG The two-minute silence is like stepping off a curb—and thankfully at precisely that moment the traffic vanishes. But the image also at two points in the cycle has a similar sort of interruption. Thirty seconds after the sound cuts out—after thirty seconds of watching the images silently move—the images stop.

AM They freeze.

DG It's a chilling moment as the image holds for a minute…and then resumes its movement. Presumably anyone who has been paying attention is holding their breath—and thirty seconds later the sound returns.

AM Yeah, you get a complete shutdown for one minute, in fact, between the sound and the image.

DG Apart from this being such an arresting, unexpected

interruption, the freeze is interesting because it's a rare acknowledgment within your work of sound and image existing in an isomorphic, even somehow distantly causal relationship.

> AM   Right.

DG   When we installed it at the Hamburger Bahnhof in Berlin, as part of an exhibition of your solid light work, there were hanging speakers.

> AM   They floated above our heads.

DG   The hanging speakers were necessary, given the scale of the exhibition space. There weren't walls close enough to enclose the individual solid light works, and so we used highly directional speakers pointed downward at the area contained within each cone of light.

> AM   The sound was sufficiently contained without bleeding into the adjacent, silent works.

DG   The next iteration of *Leaving* was a performance piece that's been presented twice, *Leaving (With Four Half-Turns)* (2011).

> AM   Right, where you play live.

DG   The sound element consists of an extremely simple set of materials for solo electric guitar. Just as the projections contained three graphic elements—a circle, a straight line, and a traveling sine wave—I had a repeated note, an open string, and a small ornament, like a turnaround.

> AM   And then you had a feedback process that increased during the thirty minutes. Am I right?

DG   There was distortion toward the end of it, a tremendous thickening of the sound at one point.

> AM   And those performances were quite unlike *Leaving (With Two-Minute Silence)*, in that there was an audience there sharing the real time of the once-through composition, and once-through music.

DG   *Leaving (With Four Half-Turns)* is not so different from the experience of the *Four Simultaneous Soloists* performances at Pioneer Works.

> AM   Go on.

A.   Anthony McCall with Sachiko M at Kill Your Timid Notion festival, Dundee, Scotland, 2004.
B.   Anthony McCall. "Sachiko M and *Line Describing a Cone*," Kill Your Timid Notion festival, Dundee, Scotland, 2004. Notebook study, 2004.
C.   Anthony McCall and David Grubbs. *Leaving (With Four Half-Turns)*, 2010. Performance view, Sprüth Magers Gallery, Berlin, April 18, 2012.

A

PERFORMANCE SEQUENCE

0'00" : First film starts
5'00" : Sachiko first tone starts
15'00" : Second film starts
20'00" : Sachiko secon tone starts
30'00" : First film ends
35'00" : Sachiko third tone starts
45'00" : Second film ends
46'00" : Flapping of film reel ends
47'00" : Hazers turned off
50'00" : Sachiko tones end

"KILL YOUR TIMID NOTION" FESTIVAL,
DUNDEE . DEC 12, 2004

18 BIT STEREO REALTIME SAMPLER
TWO BELL & HOWELL 'TQM' PROJECTORS
(WITH HALOGEN LAMPS). 30MM LENS FROM
30-60MM ZOOM . IMAGE SIZE 10'6" X 14'

73'
48'
IN/OUT
FILM 2
FILM 1
SACHIKO
AT TABLE

SACHIKO M
AND
"LINE DESCRIBING
A CONE"

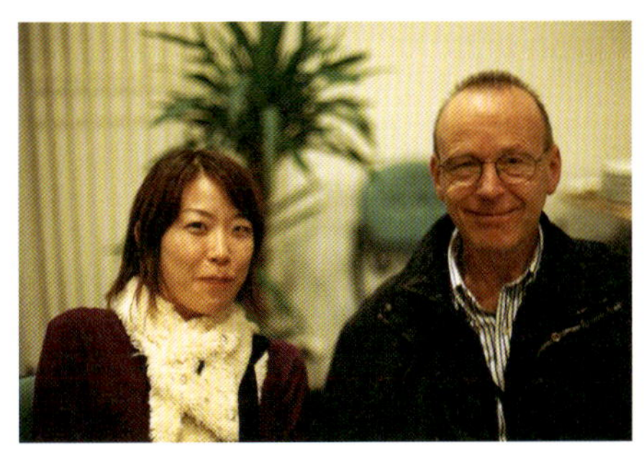

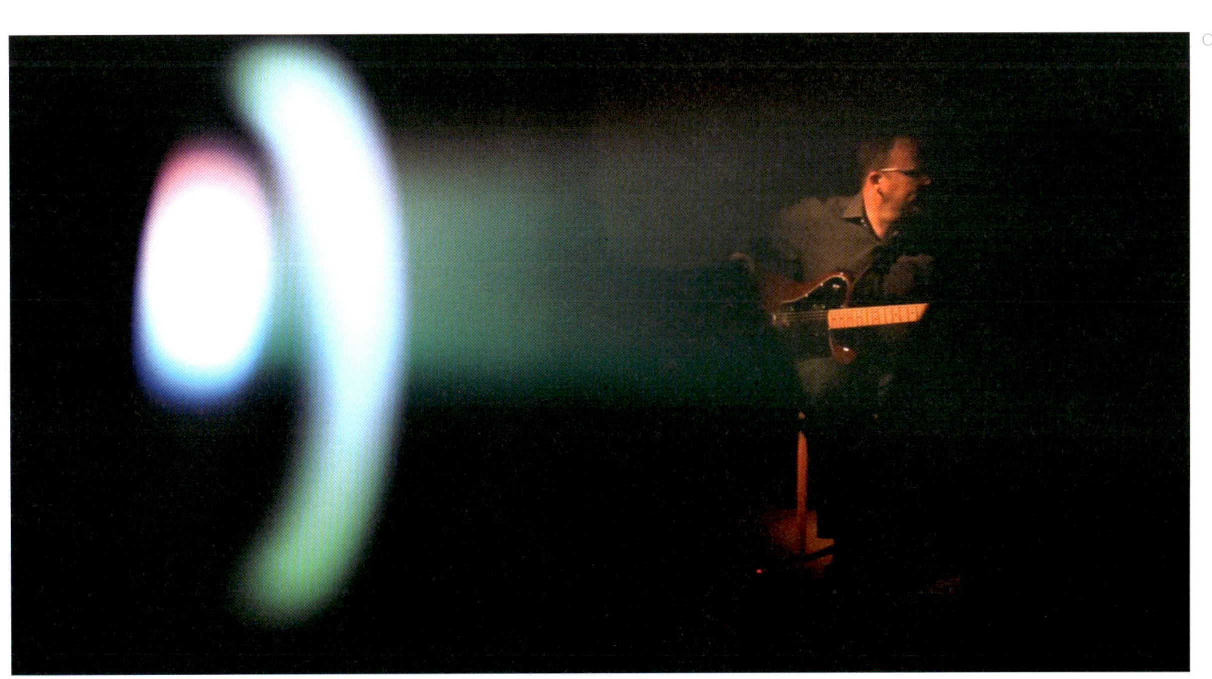

B

DG In both cases a crowd gathers for a single, start-to-finish musical performance within the context of your solid light work. There's a starting time, and it definitively concludes.

AM With the difference that, as you once put it, the four vertical works were the pre-existing condition, which were there before the music started and there continuing after the music had finished, whereas with the *Leaving* piece, the composition and the music were one and the same structure.

DG That's correct. With *Four Simultaneous Soloists,* you have the cyclical structure on display of the four vertical works, and a single, start-to-finish, sixty- or seventy-minute musical performance. Here's a backstory question that I'm not sure that I've ever asked you: with the exception of *Four Simultaneous Soloists*, on what occasions previously have there been musical performances during the exhibition or screening of your works?

AM Just one, I think. That was my collaboration with Sachiko M. The performance took place in 2004 at Kill Your Timid Notion, a festival in Dundee, Scotland devoted to works in which projected image and music were paired. The festival invited Sachiko M and myself to make a work together. She was interested in *Line Describing a Cone* (1973), which she had seen before, and stated her interest in the sound produced by a projector. I proposed that we should project not one but two prints of the thirty-minute *Line Describing a Cone*, on two different projectors, arranged side by side, but facing opposite directions. One projector would run fifteen minutes ahead of the other. In effect, there were three fifteen-minute events: Line Describing a Cone I, Line Describing a Cone I plus Line Describing a Cone II, and, finally, Line Describing a Cone II. So there were two beginnings and two endings. Sachiko M responded to the structure by not playing in the first movement, then when the second movement began she introduced a pitch from her empty—

DG The sampler without memory.

AM That's right.

DG Very Philip K. Dick instrument. Beautiful.

AM So it was a single high pitch.

DG The sampler evidently comes with several test tones.

AM It was crowded, with an audience of about 150. People were walking around watching the overlapping films and experiencing the different sounds. And then at the very end, I'd arranged for the second projector to just go on projecting until the film ran through the projector. This makes a distinctive clatter, and then it goes flap, flap, flap, flap, flap, flap. And then the second projector was turned off, and then the two haze machines were turned off. The room was dark now, and there was nothing to see; but we could hear the three tones. At this point, everyone turned around to see what Sachiko was doing. During the double projection she'd been sitting at a small table with her sampler, at the center of the room. There was a little work light on the table. One by one she turned off the three tones. Then after a long pause, in silence, she leaned over and switched off the light. That was the end of the performance. I thought this simple collaboration between film and music was very well balanced, and I have always viewed the event as a success. One of my criticisms of some music and projection work is that, more often than not, one of the mediums is dominant. So typically you get a musician or music group doing an energetic improvisation with the music, while the visuals act simply as wallpaper. Or you have the opposite of that, which is—

DG An excessively polite musician.

AM Exactly. Finding the conceptual key that holds the two in a productive tension is quite difficult.

DG In the first go-round of solid light works in the 1970s, you didn't have people coming to you and saying that the following musical performance is exactly what this work needs?

AM Early on, no. You must remember the atmosphere of un-pleasure around rigorous conceptual work!

DG Yes, right. 2018 must feel so different.

AM I did occasionally have choreographers making proposals, and still do. And I'm a little resistant. Probably not as resistant as I was, but my resistance to it has to do with the fact that if the choreographer makes the projected work their field of activity, their field of action, then it usually means that the audience is back on the seats watching the performance, when they need to move freely in and around the pieces. Since then, I have come up with ways in which it could work

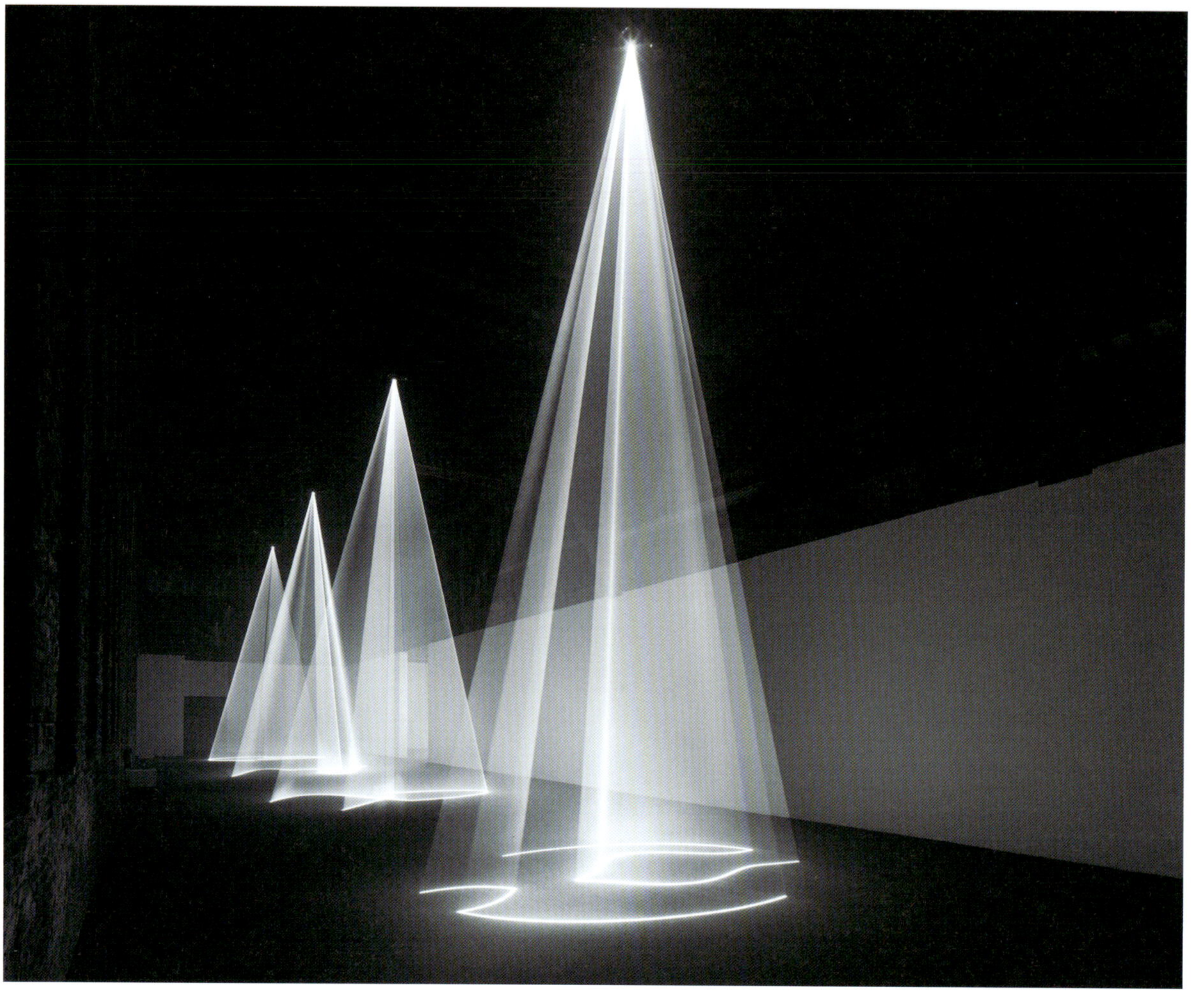

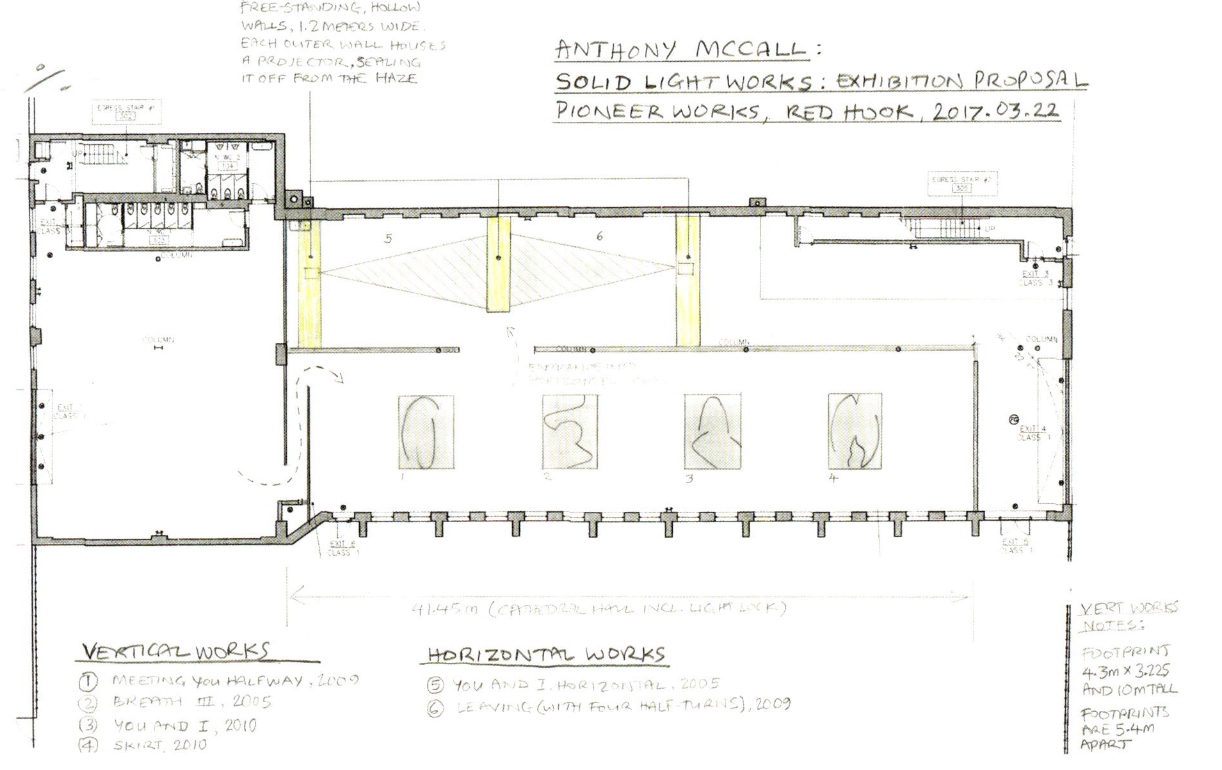
B

FREE-STANDING, HOLLOW
WALLS, 1.2 METERS WIDE.
EACH OUTER WALL HOUSES
A PROJECTOR, SEALING
IT OFF FROM THE HAZE

ANTHONY MCCALL:
SOLID LIGHT WORKS: EXHIBITION PROPOSAL
PIONEER WORKS, RED HOOK, 2017.03.22

41.45m (CATHEDRAL HALL INCL. LIGHT LOCK)

VERTICAL WORKS
1 MEETING YOU HALFWAY, 2009
2 BREATH III, 2005
3 YOU AND I, 2010
4 SKIRT, 2010

HORIZONTAL WORKS
5 YOU AND I, HORIZONTAL, 2005
6 LEAVING (WITH FOUR HALF-TURNS), 2009

VERT WORKS
NOTES:
FOOTPRINT
4.3m X 3.225
AND 10M TALL
FOOTPRINTS
ARE 5.4M
APART

perfectly well, in which you would allow the two—the audience and the dancers—to share the space. It would require a certain special kind of choreography to handle that. But it would be possible. And actually, in 2012, I had the productive collaboration with choreographer Jonah Bokaer, *Eclipse*, shown at BAM Fisher—which you and I worked on together. That project began with my establishing a field of thirty-six hanging light bulbs as the set and a temporal structure which determined an order of lighting and extinguishing. These rules laid out a basis for the choreography.

DG   When you contacted me in advance of the exhibition at Pioneer Works, you sent me a number of images of previous installations of vertical works, such as in the Hangar Bicocca in Milan, and also the floor plan for the exhibition, which was tremendously helpful. The first thing I noticed about the floor plan was that with four vertical works in Pioneer Works' 130-foot main hall we would have the opportunity to place musicians at some distance from one another. Almost instantaneously I had the idea of a zigzagging arrangement of four musicians as far away from one another as possible, illuminated by the four vertical works, but just outside of the individual cones of light. The worst possible idea—almost comically bad, in retrospect—would have been that of four spotlights. I also thought about my experience seeing the vertical works as installed at the Hamburger Bahnhof.

AM   Of course, you were there...

DG   I thought about the way in which the viewer toggles between experiencing a single work and taking a wider view, eventually looking at two, three, or four at a time. One of the first ideas that led to *Four Simultaneous Soloists* was that four musicians performing in the space should be quiet enough that an audience would want to be ambulatory.

AM   You were talking about your Los Angeles concert, where you said that the performance space was so long that the performers at each end could not hear one another.

DG   Yes, that was an improvised trio performance with David Watson and Steve Roden in a parking garage in Los Angeles. It turned out to be a much smaller audience than the ones at Pioneer Works, in a cold parking garage—an unseasonably cold parking garage in Los Angeles. From my perspective, tethered to a guitar amplifier, I could see the audience of a

couple of dozen people come toward me; they'd hang out
for a little bit, and after a while they'd start to migrate away
from me and toward one of the other performers. When David
Watson or Steve Roden weren't playing at their maximum
volumes, I couldn't particularly hear them. But again, it was
not so dissimilar from *Leaving (With Two-Minute Silence)*, in
that we were playing sufficiently quietly, and we were set up
sufficiently far apart, that I don't believe there was a sweet
spot where folks could hang out and hear all three performers
at once. Or if they did, they'd be looking at performers in the
distance. My main recollection of the event is that moment of
seeing the audience walking away, watching their backs as
they trundle off.

> AM My experience of this kind of thing was seeing John Cage's
> *HPSCHD* at the Roundhouse in London in 1972. And it made a
> big impression on me. There were seven instruments, all harp-
> sichords, forming a circle, about a forty-foot diameter circle,
> and each harpsichord had a player. Each player was playing.
> But they were all simultaneously playing different pieces
> of music. And this created a marvelous cacophony. And
> the thing that really stayed with me was this memory of the
> moment when I suddenly grasped it: that my job as a member
> of the audience was to mix. And the pleasure of doing that,
> of moving around the space, finding the place at the center
> of the circle where the cacophony was at maximum, and then
> moving toward or walking past a particular musician, and
> gradually filtering out the various other musicians in varying
> degrees...that really never went away. The idea of there being
> multiple viewpoints and a mobile spectator was an inspiration.
> My first solid light film, *Line Describing a Cone*, came the fol-
> lowing year.

DG For *Four Simultaneous Soloists*, just as we talked about the
fact that the vertical works preexist the musicians entering
the space and performing in their midst, I approached it by
thinking about what kinds of instructions, or what kinds of
coaching or exhortations could be given to a group of musicians whom I admire and want to see work together. I wanted
to find people that hadn't played together. But one of the
things that I said to each of the four groupings of musicians is
that these solid light works are typically presented in silence.
They don't need musical accompaniment—and yet this should
be taken as an opportunity to contribute something.

 The installations went on every day as an exhibition, with visitors coming and going, whereas these would be four special evening performances. They were marked as quite different from the installation during the day, and they involved an assembled audience.

DG When Eli Keszler and I exhibited collaborative work at the MIT List Visual Arts Center in 2014, it was part of *Open Tunings*, a sequential group exhibition for which curator Henrietta Huldisch proposed that a performance open each of the three phases of the exhibition, and that the residue of the performance remain on display for the month following. Eli and I approached it somewhat differently, but one component of our piece was a sound installation, and we also performed on the opening night of the exhibition. We felt that it was important that the sound installation be running as people entered and as people left, before the performance and after the performance.

AM But the musicians were live. They were playing.

DG Yes. There was a sound installation consisting of seven large wall-mounted boxes containing mechanically driven percussion devices. On the first night, the audience assembles, and there's a duo concert of Eli and me, in addition to the sounds that are already present in the space—this mechanical clattering of hidden objects within a visually spare presentation. That was on my mind as well, that the musicians enter the space as guests, and they have to work with the given of what's already taken up residence in the space. With *Four Simultaneous Soloists*, you and I discussed whether there should be a composition, or instead a simple set of rules.

AM It got down to about two or three.

DG Yes, two or three sentences. I performed at the first concert, and was present for the load-in and rehearsal and discussion for the other three. There were several rules of thumb: that the performance should unfold organically as a series of solos, duos, trios, and a quartet, but otherwise not structured in advance. Ideally there should be a sense that the location of the sound—the place of the sound—moves continuously throughout the performance. I suggested that each performer play for approximately half of the time and listen for half of the time. The sounds should be quiet enough that their point source, either from a musician playing acoustically or with amplification placed alongside the musician, should be apparent. The sound shouldn't be bouncing off the walls or filling the entire space. For me as a listener, some of the most striking moments were surreptitious duets between someone in the first position and someone in the fourth position, two people more than a hundred feet away from one another and playing so quietly that it wouldn't necessarily be apparent that they could hear one another, but sensing…

> AM But then you would notice the pitches that are suddenly coming into sync with one another, from a cello and from a siren, say. It's remarkable when you grasp those correspondences. Didn't you say, half-jokingly, that there were only two things that could go wrong?

DG It seemed to me that the only things that could go wrong were if people chose to play too loudly or to play continuously. There was some question early on about the length of the performance, and how to facilitate that, given that musicians weren't able to make eye contact, and I didn't think it a good idea to have timers or any sort of illuminated screens visible. In the end, we agreed upon a series of taps on the shoulders.

> AM There was a fifth person who was doing that—you, in most cases—which was a ten-minute cue toward the end, or something like that?

DG When it was my job to provide the shoulder-tap cues, I felt like the grim reaper—although everyone without exception received the summons. Was cut down in their prime. You and I both felt that the first concert—about seventy-five minutes— was too long.

> AM Yes, by about seven minutes.

DG The strange thing about the first concert was that nearly the entirety of the audience was still there at the sixty-minute mark, but somehow by the seventy- or seventy-five-minute mark, we must have crossed a line where people felt that this could go on forever, and so the crowd thinned out: "this isn't going to end any time soon."

> AM We hadn't really announced it as such. I think probably that was something, if we were doing it again, we might do. It's quite good for people to know what, to pace themselves for something, because the structure of the performance is not particularly evident, because it's being made up as the

musicians go along. So to know how long something lasts is probably a good idea.

DG You were in the UK during one of concerts, but you were present for—

AM For three, yeah.

DG Three of the four performances. What were your senses about commonalities and differences among the three that you attended?

AM I think hearing the last one was very interesting, because it was almost as if that was the result of the musicians having done it three times before and gotten better at it.

DG We should say that for the final concert Jules Gimbrone played amplified objects; Okkyung Lee played cello; Christopher McIntyre, trombone and synthesizer; and Yoshi Wada was on bagpipes and sirens, both electronic sirens and a hand-cranked siren. Yoshi and Okkyung hadn't been to any of the performances. I know that Jules and Chris had, and I'd had conversations with them about the previous concerts.

AM Because there were more moments where you felt a communication going on between one or more musicians. For instance, Okkyung Lee picking up on certain pitches that were coming from Yoshi's instruments.

DG There were 250 tickets sold for each night, and more people than that attended. The door to the exhibition space opened at 7:30 sharp, and as far as the musicians were concerned, the performance began as soon as the first audience members walked in. People wandering in, blinking in the darkness, encountering this incredible vista of the exhibition space, and seeing the four vertical works. I was cognizant of the fact that the concert performance might be the only time that a number of people would visit the exhibition, so I thought that it was important that people experience the works in their natural state, in their natural state of silence before any sound is added. For each concert I asked the person in the fourth position, which was the furthest away from the entrance, to be the first person to create a sound, but only after a number of minutes. In the fourth performance, Yoshi Wada decided to begin with bagpipes, and had asked me to open the sliding section of wall at the far end of the exhibition space five minutes after the performance begins, so that he

could come marching in with the bagpipes. When I slid the
section of wall back, there was no Yoshi Wada there, and I
was terrified that he had gotten lost, as had happened earlier
in the day, because backstage at Pioneer Works is a labyrinth.
Poor Yoshi! I was starting to freak out. I looked for him in the
green room. I looked for him back in the space. Bagpipes
make noise as you're getting them—

AM Pumped up.

DG Exactly. It turned out that he was in a storage closet getting
his instrument ready, wanting to be as quiet as possible, and
to my great relief someone eventually found him.

AM I found him.

DG Thank god. I hadn't been able to do so and was totally flum-
moxed. How do you lose the bagpipes-and-sirens guy? When
Yoshi appeared and entered the space, almost immediately
his bagpipe drone was matched by Okkyung Lee, who was
in the second position, so she was approximately a hundred
feet from him, playing a pitch that was several cents flat of
the lowest drone note from Yoshi's bagpipes. In that way she
extended and modified the texture of the bagpipes, rather
than choosing a different pitch to add to the chord of the bagpipes. Amazing.

AM It created a dimensionality if you were the listener, because
now it was coming from two places, apparently, or something
complex was going on. So I remember that stuck out for me,
and then also Maria Chavez's turntable in the first performance was interesting, because it wasn't clear if she was
picking up on the sounds that were being generated at that
moment, but it was almost as if she was. And there was something going on between her and the other musicians because
of that.

DG I thought that Maria's contributions were fantastic. Prior to
the first concert, she corrected me as regards her instrument:
she performs on turntable, rather than turntables.

AM And I asked her, what sort of sounds do you make? What is
your project? She said, "I ruin other people's music."

DG Unlike most turntablists, she's an improviser who responds by
means of the needle and the pickup on the turntable; she's
not bringing a catalogued, prepared series of records from

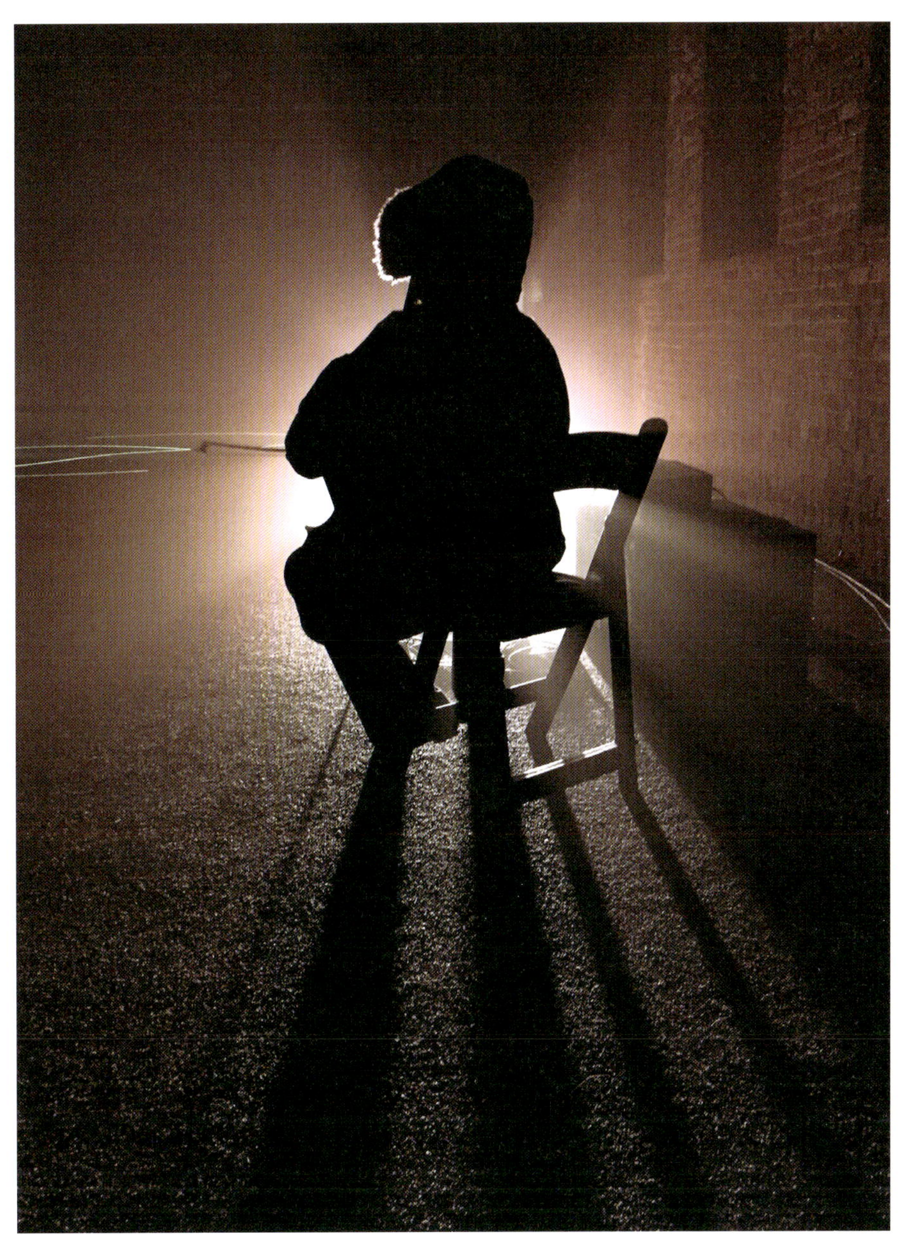

C

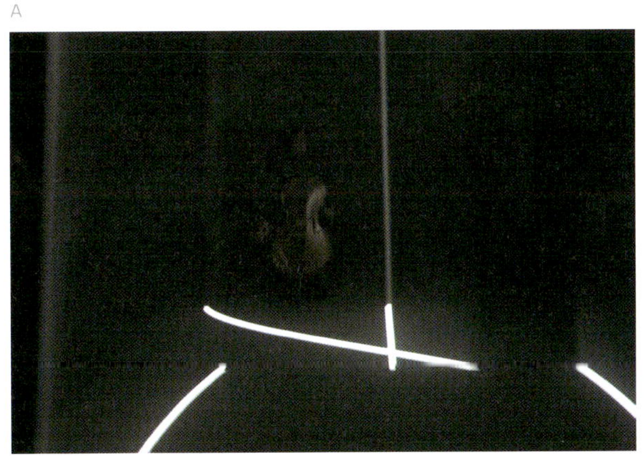

A

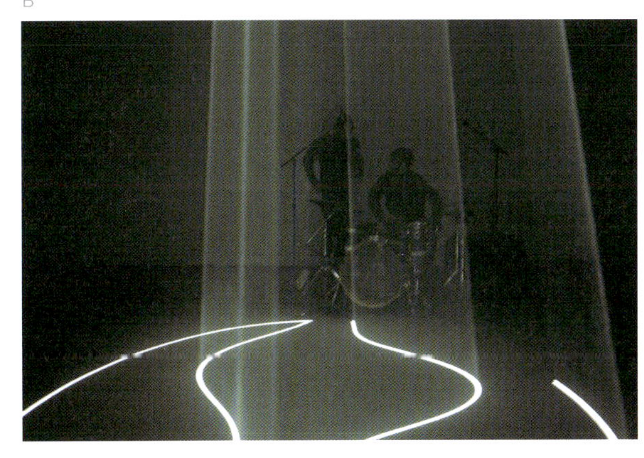

B

which she knows precisely what they'll provide. In that first
concert, I played electric guitar; Maria played turntable; Sarah
Hennies, vibraphone, tremendously subtle, in the fourth position, playing very, very quietly.

> AM The vibraphone was something you had to go and find. And
> you would sometimes hear it just enough that you'd be drawn
> to it. But she played almost under the sound radar, spatially
> speaking.

DG And C. Spencer Yeh performed with violin and voice. I remember long sections of him making snoring noises. With the
first performance, I would say that if you had asked me to
diagram what happened in those seventy minutes, I could
do so. I could say Sarah Hennies began, followed by a duo
with Spencer Yeh, and it seemed that every five to ten minutes there was a shift to a different section, and that it had
the feeling of a composed work with clear and occasionally
dramatic transitions. The other performances structurally
had more of an all-over quality, in which activity occurred in
shorter bursts. Someone might play for fifteen seconds and
be silent for thirty seconds, and play again briefly, which created a continuous sense of movement, of sounds restlessly
traversing the entirety of Pioneer Works' long hall.

> AM In the last performance, I noticed that Okkyung shut down
> for like five or six or seven minutes at a time, and became like
> a sphinx, just immobile, and that was quite helpful, because
> it signaled you could walk away. I found myself anticipat-
> ing when she might play again and going toward her. And
> sometimes I was right, and sometimes I was wrong. But then
> something else would happen. So I thought that from a point
> of view of walking around the space and finding sounds and
> staying mobile, that rather suited those moments when you
> definitely knew someone was playing or was not. On the other
> hand, we should mention something that happened in almost
> all of them, I think, which is, from about halfway through, or
> maybe two-thirds of the way through, members of the audi-
> ence, who previously had acted as mobile visitors to an art
> installation, began to occupy and settle down inside some
> of the cones of light, forming great big audience banks. And
> they looked like travelers in tents.

DG Bedding down for the night.

> AM Branden Joseph mentioned that this was quite usual in music

performances. People would cluster and sit on the floor. I
suppose we should say there were three hundred people in
the room. It became difficult to actually engage the solid light
works so you could decipher their structure. So perhaps what
you could say happened is that at a certain point the sculptural event ceded to the musical, and the visitors decided
they'd try sitting down in one place.

DG I think it's hard to see the vertical works when there are three
hundred people in the space. That was also my experience
of the opening, when there were several times that number
of people and the horizontal works at a certain point were
almost incomprehensible. They were just projected on people's chests and backs.

AM Yes, they were sometimes so densely packed…more solid
people than solid light.

DG After the opening, I suggested to a number of people that
they see the exhibition when there are not very many people
present—be there when it opens at noon. The drawing component of the vertical works—the two-dimensional elements
that are visible on the floor—are complex and more than
reward the time spent with them. In the *Leaving* series, the
title more or less describes what happens, gives the plot
away: it's the disappearance of the cone of light. Drawing
hadn't even necessarily been an operative category for me
with the horizontal works. I always thought of sculpture and
cinema, and the element of drawing in the vertical works is
tremendous. Even having spent hours and hours at Pioneer
Works looking at the two-dimensional projections on the
ground, I'm not sure that I could adequately describe what
happens. I couldn't narrate them after the fact in the way that
I feel that I can with most of the horizontal works.

AM I would agree that the verticals have more difficulties associ-
ated with them than when you're looking at the horizontals.
For one thing, with the horizontals you've got the comfort-
ing relationship to cinema. Cinema is still in there somehow.
You've got the projector and the image, and it's very clear.
You can turn around in two directions. You can see the
volume, or you can see the drawing. And you're comfortable.
You'll just rotate your head or your body.

DG I experience the horizontal works as more visceral.

AM   It comes straight at you.

DG   It comes straight at you and also, as you're walking up the cone toward the projector, you might be staring into a bright light at a distance of just a few feet. Unless you bring your ladder with you, you're not getting hit between the eyes with the light in the vertical pieces.

AM   Well, the vertical works, first of all, instead of nodding to cinema, they seem to nod more toward architecture. They are exactly the same scale as the horizontals, but they tower above your head. And unlike the horizontals, where you just have to rotate your head or your body, here you have to do two things that are quite difficult. You have to crane your head back to look upward, or you have to turn it down to look at your feet, essentially. And those aren't particularly comfortable positions. They're extreme positions for our heads. And it's harder to put things together. Then if there are six people standing on top of the drawing, you're losing that information, which might otherwise have guided the way you're looking. So they are harder to look at anyway, and particularly with three hundred people in the room. That's too many, really.

DG   I also regard the vertical works as more ambivalent and more complex, particularly as to how they might relate to musical performance. I find them to be more gentle or environmental in that I think more about the *curtain* of light, rather than the *projection*.

AM   I think these four evenings were really successful. But I found it very interesting, these different moments where the last third belongs to the music, perhaps the whole second half. And the first half, there is a sort of equality in a way, because people were trying to figure it out.

DG   Yes, that's very interesting. I recognize that when people collapse onto the floor thirty or forty minutes into it, the music largely takes over.

AM   People are accepting the fact, without necessarily being conscious of it, they've made a decision they're going to listen from here, from this vantage point, and they're not going to move around anymore. They accept that there's an ambient sound, that what they hear is what they'll hear, and they've made a decision.

DG   They did tend to look exhausted when they threw themselves

in those piles, as if they'd been walking for hours. I think it
largely has to do with the expectations of attending a concert,
that people aren't used to wandering around for that length of
time during a performance, and maybe it did feel like hours.

> AM Perhaps we should mention one thing, too, which I'd like to
> ask you about, actually, which is that for my own reasons,
> visual reasons, I always carpet a space. It removes reflection.
> It's acoustically more pleasant an environment. The rever-
> beration is damped down. And it's also comfortable, because
> people stay a long time in my installations. But I received
> comments from a lot of musicians who've played in Pioneer
> Works before. It has a poured concrete floor. You've got brick
> walls, sheet rock walls, and a wooden ceiling. Contrasted with
> my installation, where you had the brick wall, the sheet rock,
> and the wooden ceiling, but you had a carpeted floor. Many
> of the musicians who played in Pioneer Works before said
> that they found that with the added element of the carpet, the
> acoustics were almost perfect. Apparently in that space the
> reverberation can be quite extreme.

DG With hard exposed surfaces and a several-story atrium, it can
be a nightmare for certain kinds of music, and it can be glori-
ous for other kinds.

> AM Did you find that the acoustics were sympathetic?

DG They were so much better than I anticipated. The carpet
together with the exposed brick walls brought to mind a
recording studio that combines hard exposed surfaces—short
reflections—with those that dampen. The sound was also
helped by the fact that everyone played at modest volumes
and that the four sound sources were spatially distinct.

> AM Yeah, everything sounded crystal clear. I was surprised how
> much I could hear from the other end.

DG The reverberation time is reduced. When musicians play in
intensely reverberant spaces, unquestionably it affects the
ways in which they play.

> AM It means your overlaps get muddied, right?

DG Yes.

> AM Because it goes on reverberating, and then it gets caught up
> with the next sound.

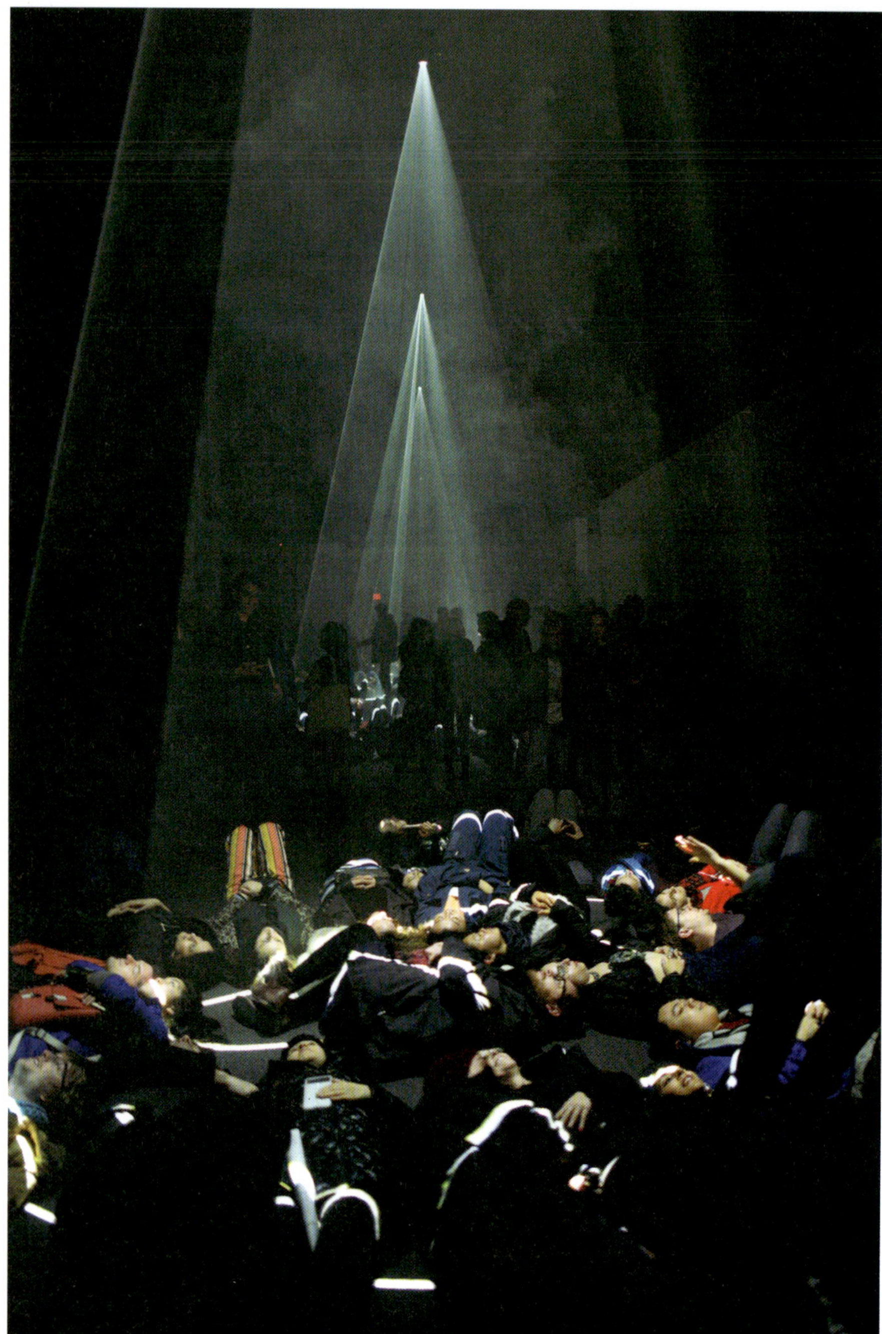

A

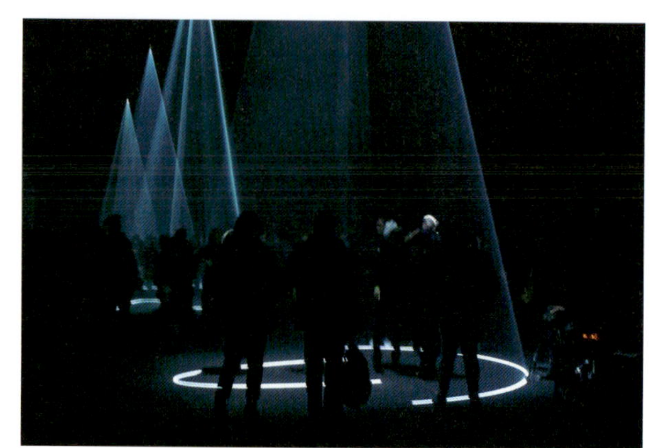

B

DG Exactly. If there had been no carpeting, I think that it would have been more common to hear things like single notes ringing out so you hear those gorgeous tails as they echo throughout the space. My sense is that a lot of musicians are sympathetic to playing in gallery spaces or exhibition spaces because there tends to be a kind of conversation from the ground up. Everything is open to negotiation as far as how the space will be used.

AM Because it's an open, empty space.

DG Yes, and curators are used to those kinds of conversations with visual artists, so they tend to approach them with musicians in the same way. But the problem is that acoustically those spaces can be tremendously limiting.

AM I think your title *Four Simultaneous Soloists* is conceptually really suggestive. What sort of comments have you had from the musicians about the relationship between the title, the space, the audience, and their actions as musicians?

DG First of all, most everyone asked me how literally they should take the title; should they approach the performance with this sense of autonomous playing—that they're strictly not listening to the others—or are they welcome to engage in a more sympathetic kind of improvisation? The title tends toward the programmatic, perhaps misleadingly so, and I did find myself clarifying that people should listen and respond, and that "soloist" was by no means intended as a strict conceit. What resulted was a series of solo, duo, trio, and quartet performances, even if part of the joy of listening was an opportunity to hear multiple soloistic centers of gravity. Sixteen musicians took part in this series, and they tended to see the proposition of bringing sound into the space as something that needed to be wrestled with. There were numerous conversations among musicians about the ways in which setting up and playing for a half an hour in the afternoon when no one was there, and when they could look at the two-dimensional drawing elements on the floor as a kind of prompt or score, how those kinds of weirdly pristine, dreamlike performance situations differed from when the doors opened, and three hundred people suddenly came pouring in. Sometimes people on cell phones, sometimes people very close to the musicians, sometimes literally people standing with their backs to the musicians. For me, the first performance felt a bit, you know, draft version, very hypothetical, as in, "we'll see how

this first one goes and adjust accordingly"—although that's
me speaking more as a curator or organizer than as a performer. When we played for a half an hour in the afternoon
before the first concert, it was a dream. It was fantastic,
maybe the high point of one's year. It was great, loved it, tell
your grandchildren about it. And then the actual performance
at times felt messy, chaotic, borderline-overwhelming—the
experience of people wandering around in the dark while you
wait for someone to trip over your equipment.

> AM   Are they moving away because of indifference, or because
> they're going to...you were saying about when you see—

DG The backs of the audience? It's a weird thing to watch. When
one finishes playing, inevitably people that you know come up
and ask "Did you enjoy that?" or "Were you happy with that?"
After a relaxed rehearsal in the afternoon, I would have said
that it was a heavenly experience. With the evening performance, it took a few days for me to make sense of it.

> AM   To assimilate.

DG Yes. That's how unfamiliar of an experience it was. When you
took part in the public discussion at Pioneer Works during the
exhibition, and almost all of the photo documentation that
was shown during the discussion consisted of these incredible images of the works installed with not a person in sight,
I found myself reminded of the experience of playing within
the exhibition space in the afternoon with no one around. I
had all the time in the world to meditate on the works, and on
the relative flawlessness of the installation. Those images are
in stark contrast to the photos that Melissa Ragona showed
during the discussion, namely images of dense groupings
of folks sprawled on the ground that were taken during the
concerts.

> AM   Those pristine photographs were from Pioneer Works' official
> installation photo session, which they did late at night, after
> the place was closed.

DG They look almost like computer simulations. In the two photos
that Melissa brought from the performances, it's the audience
members that are primarily illuminated. Musicians are largely
in shadow, because they're outside of the cone of light. As
far as photographic compositions, they're fantastically messy
images.

   Yes, spontaneous smartphone images.

DG   And also like history paintings, dense with narrative. They
made me think of the series of photographs that Chris Marker
did relatively late in his life during protests in the suburbs of
Paris that are terrific character studies, studies of individual
faces within crowds. I'm excited to see more of those photos
of the performances.

AM   Yeah, me too. They're like the hidden truth. Here you have
people with a vengeance. Anne Wagner wrote an essay once
about Dan Flavin, and the essay was about the fact that he
was militant about keeping people out of the photographs
of this work. It occurred to me that this was probably true of
Judd and Andre and many of the other minimal artists.

DG   Not so keen on photos of people touching the Judd boxes,
stretching out on top of them.

AM   Yet photographs of my installations are hard to understand
without people in them. They are taken in the dark, where
without a person or two there are no clues left about scale:
no walls, windows, ceiling tiles, floorboards, etc. Another
problem is that almost everyone's memory of being in my
installations is connected to the almost tactile engagement
with the membranes of light, and also of negotiating the
space with other people. So I hope that there will emerge a
body of smartphone pictures that will act as a counterbalance
to the formal installation views.

DG   Those first two photos that I saw from the performances
reminded me of images of concerts where the audience has
invaded the stage, hardcore punk shows where people are
lining up to stage dive or shout backing vocals, although I
have to say that in these images the audience looks a good
bit more relaxed. Soothed.

AM   But to come back to the difference for a musician between
one and the other, in the end was it bewildering, or was it elat-
ing, the experience for the musicians? Or your experience as
a musician playing with that many people and trying to, as it
were, hold it down?

DG   It tended more toward bewildering.

AM   Yeah, because you didn't have the full attention of anybody.
That's the thing, isn't it?

^{DG} Exactly. For better or worse, musicians are used to having an audience paying attention. But in its very design, this is a performance where that's not demanded of the audience.

> ^{AM} But neither is it background music, because the audience is there to hear the sounds.

^{DG} Yes. It's an unfamiliar situation for a musician, to have an audience grant you their attention and then to walk away. Or to be talking amongst themselves. Or lying on their backs staring up at a projector. The energy of the crowd, even these large crowds, was above all diffuse. It was in my experience a unique situation in which the mode of attention differed with each individual and deviated from the way in which an audience frequently is a kind of uniform mass, oriented in the same direction and paying attention.

> ^{AM} Very interesting. Maybe we should talk a little bit about the afterlife. Some very careful recordings were made, I believe, with each musician having a fixed microphone.

^{DG} Yes. There was a close microphone on each musician, as well as two different locations in which stereo microphones were set up. It's good that we have the close recordings, because some evenings were louder than others in terms of the audience.

> ^{AM} And it's only done with one timecode, right?

^{DG} Yes. They're multitrack recordings, so they're synchronized.

> ^{AM} So it makes possibilities for a mix. Have you had any thought about this? It's clearly quite an interesting, completely unique situation, in fact.

^{DG} Several days after the first concert, Pioneer Works sent me a link to a rough mix of it. The bewilderment was still present—I was still trying to make sense of what had happened—and I didn't want to go down the path of listening to the recording, of entering into the distinct world that is the recording, because I wanted to think about the sound in relation to the image and the presence of the audience members, and I didn't want to start thinking about the concerts in the series simply in terms of musical content. Eventually I'll have the desire to go back and listen closely. Right now, I'm still luxuriating in the memory of those concerts. But that leads me to mention that the musical performances were made not

A

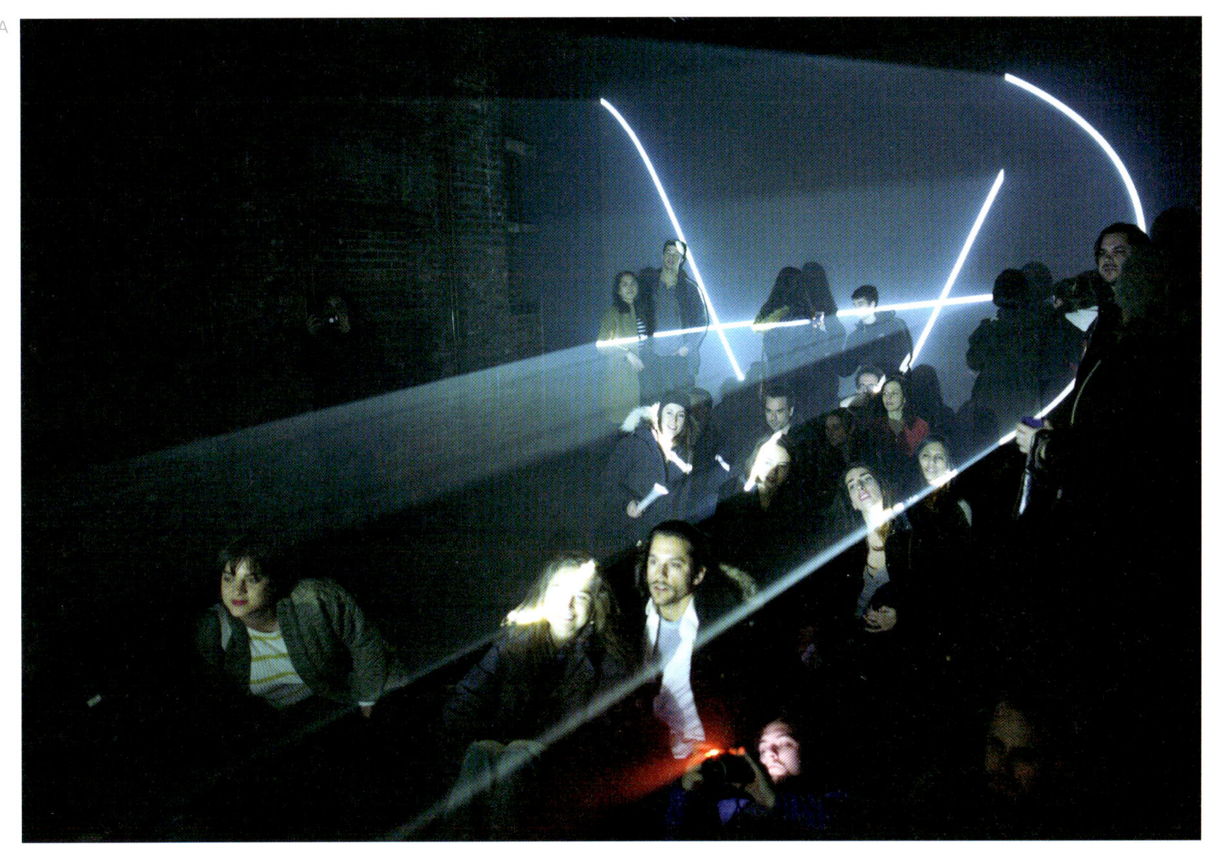

B

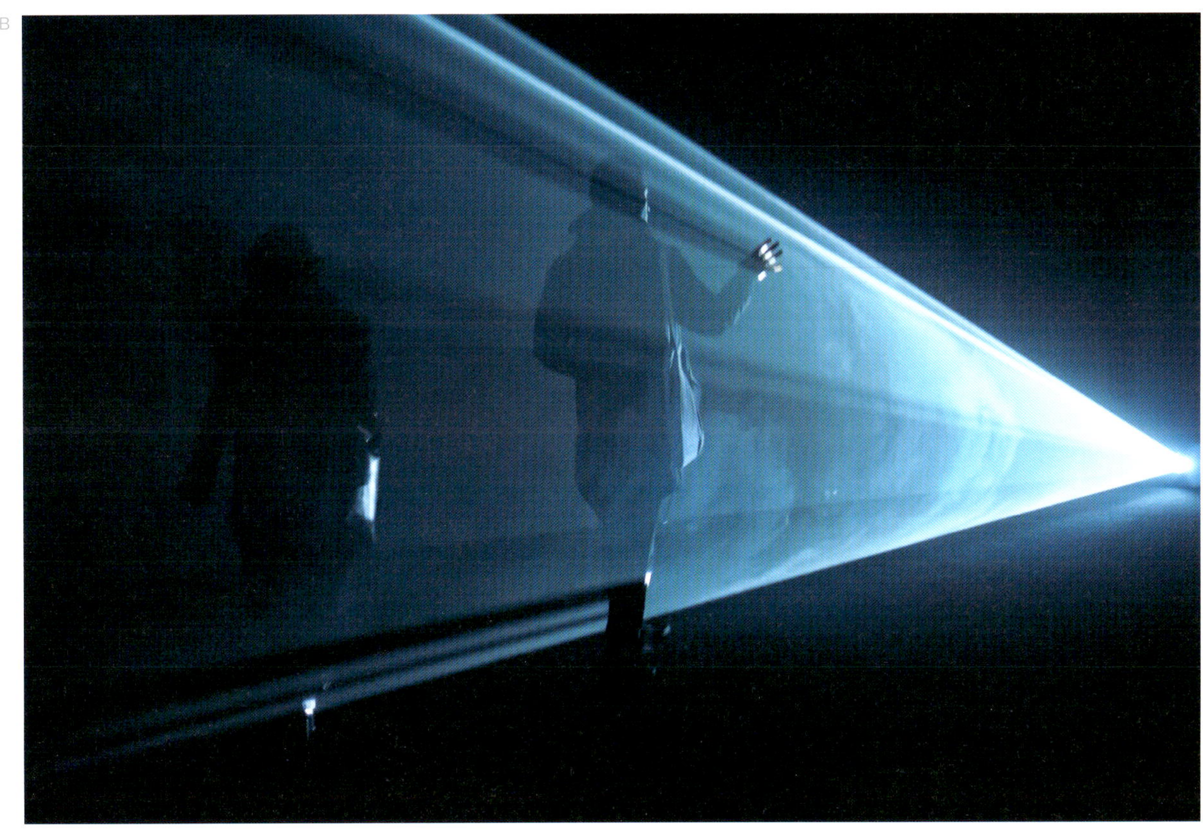

simply in view of what was happening with the audience, but also in view of and in response to the works being exhibited. It's an appealing, difficult question of how best to frame the presentation of the recordings, because as exclusively aural documents they can be misleading—or maybe the best way to describe it is to say that they are especially distinct from the experience of the performances. The tempo of the unfolding of these performances seemed to me to have everything to do with all of these elements, and not simply the musical considerations. The best way ultimately to do it would be to make it so that people can access the recordings in a very low-key, unfussy way, and not to present them unproblematically as performances undertaken with an end goal of commercial release. I think it might be preferable as well that the recordings not be presented in terms of a final mix, but rather to have an interface through which the listener can explore the space virtually and mix the sounds of the four musicians in that way. You want to convey to the future listener that these are offered so that they can access the sound content of the performances—they can hear these first-time groupings of all of these marvelous players—and yet please understand that this isn't the experience of the event at all. Sometimes a low-fidelity recording is a better indicator of its being a document once-removed from a live event because it reduces the illusion—that there's no mistaking this for the experience of being present at a given performance.

> AM It might be incomprehensible because of the missing solid light works, nonetheless you could imagine a large space with just four carefully separated speakers with one evening's sounds on it.

DG Right, or a room with sixteen speakers.

> AM A room with sixteen speakers. Now you're talking.

DG Yes—as if we wanted to present the recordings in the space of the installation, but we could only get this one evening, so we decided to play all four concerts simultaneously: *Four Simultaneous Soloists Simultaneously*.

> AM Fantastic! [laughs] But there are performances that I'd like to go back and listen to again, just to see if what I thought I heard, I heard.

DG There were exceptional performances, but I think that future

listeners would really be missing something essential, just
stripping out the audio only, coming to it exclusively as musical performance. Ideally these layers can't be stripped out
like this, and the players' contributions are not exclusively
musical contributions—they are at the same time dialogical
engagements with the work and with the live event. I think
that as a musician, some of my being initially ill at ease had
to do with the exceptional spareness of the musical performance. I mean, musicians are supposed to be attuned to a
restless audience, and either you burrow deeper or you do
something to assuage that restlessness. At no point in these
four concerts did I sense the musicians struggling with that.
The audience is restless; they're moving around because they
have multiple centers of focus.

    AM Yes, which they're not used to, mostly.

DG They're not used to it either. It was really unfamiliar, I think,
from the musicians' and from the audience's perspective. My
slight bewilderment—I don't want to overstate it—in performing on the first concert, was a bit of the sense that, wow, this
is a profoundly restless audience, and here we are making
very quiet sounds separated by long silences. And so when
you were asking about people's responses to it, I expected
to have more responses along the lines of "Okkyung Lee is
an incredible musician, and she was just sitting there for five
minutes at a time fully silent." I thought that music fans might
come at it with this misunderstanding that, well, you had all of
this musicianly firepower, and what did you do with it? Almost
nothing. But again, it seemed that people understand that the
works within the exhibition typically function within silence,
and that the musical performance is a contribution to an
already-existing environment.

    AM This sounds familiar. In the early seventies, when I was doing
outdoor performances such as *Landscape for Fire III* (1972),
I came across a similar restlessness. I became aware that my
audience, which was only fifteen or twenty people, seemed
puzzled or even disappointed. It turned out that a misunderstanding had crept in: some of the spectators thought that
they were coming to see something dramatic like a firework
display.

DG That was some of my concern as a performer on this first concert, that the restlessness of the audience bespeaks a certain
kind of disappointment: we were expecting music.

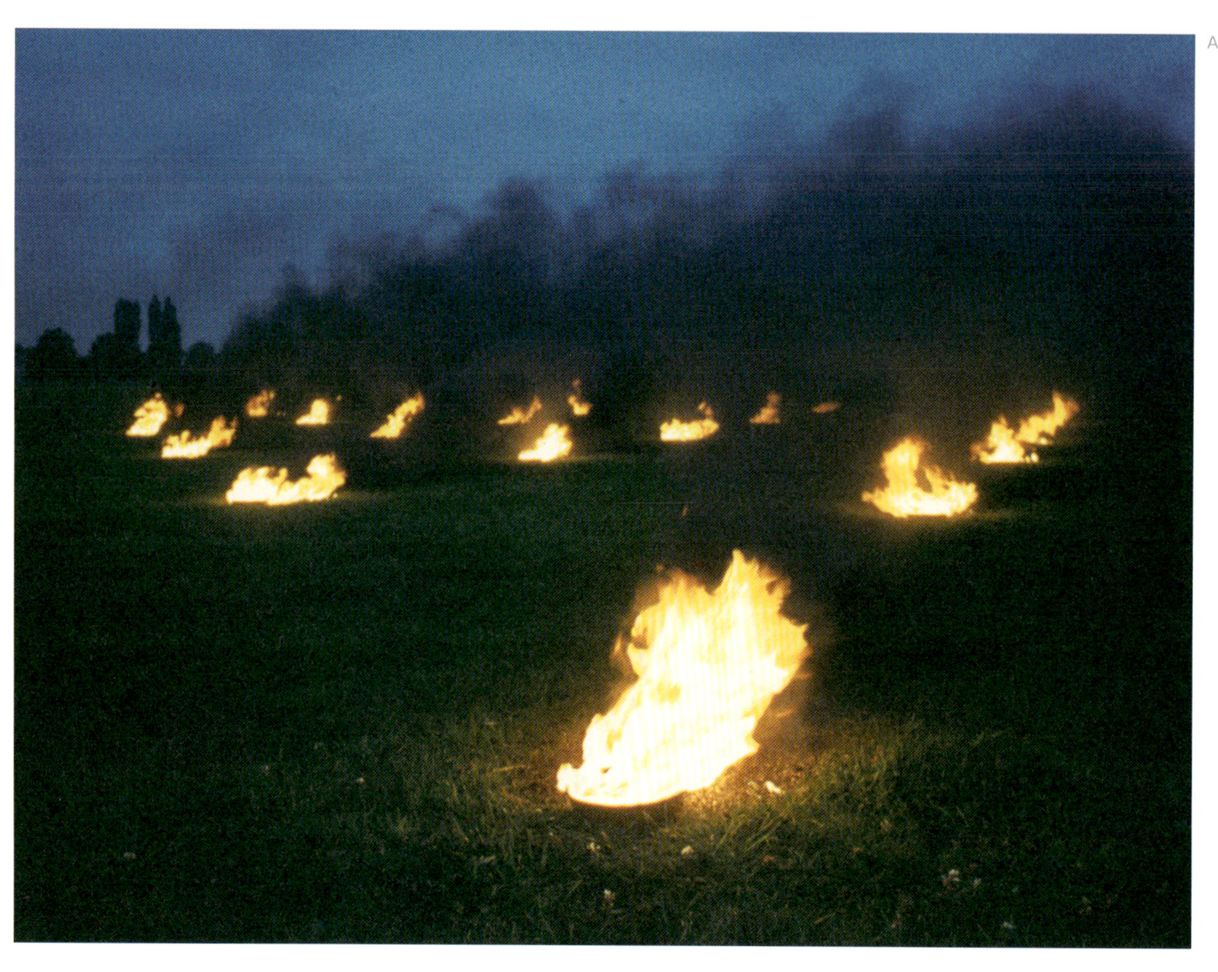

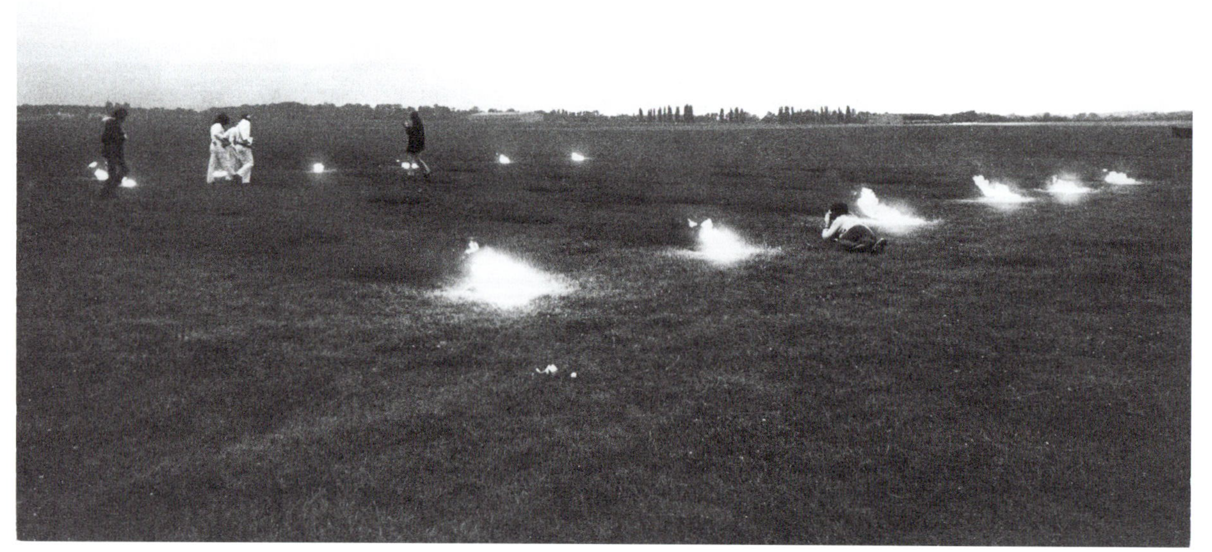

AM   I puzzled about this until I realized that I had not sufficiently defined what I expected from the spectators. I had seen them not as a group to be entertained, but as individual witnesses to a sculptural event that would unfold very gradually over time. But individual witnesses are different from audiences that arrive together for a shared experience. I decided that the problem was the *assembled* audience. My solution was to identify it as a problem of duration, and to make things last much, much longer. So instead of an assembled audience, I had independent visitors who came and went as individuals at various different times during the unfolding of the piece. They could come for five minutes, or they could come for an hour, but they each took on the responsibility of how to look, and for how long. That is how I began working with cyclical structure in subsequent fire pieces, like *Fire Cycle I* (1973), and indeed in my next solid light works such as *Long Film for Four Projectors*. From that point on, each was conceived as an all-day, continuous event.

Anthony McCall's Solid Light Works and the Afterlives of Spectatorship[1]

Swagato Chakravorty

1. Although McCall's solid light artworks have historically been understood as "films"—by critics and scholars as well as the artist himself—this essay is primarily concerned with his experiments with solid light in the last two decades. In this context, McCall has made it clear that he has come to prefer the term "works," which conveys "some idea of an installation, while remaining usefully vague about the actual medium" (Anthony McCall, correspondence with the author, July 2019). The terms are used accordingly throughout this essay, not least because it argues for distinctive shifts in McCall's solid light practices between the 1970s and in recent years.

2. Hal Foster, "Light Play," in *Anthony McCall: Breath* (Milan: Hangar Bicocca, 2009), 9.

3. Michelle Menzies, "On Cinema as Media: Archeology, Experience, Digital Aesthetics" (unpublished Ph.D. diss., University of Chicago, 2016), 6-7. I thank Dan Morgan of the University of Chicago's Department of Cinema and Media Studies for introducing me to Menzies' work.

4. Anthony McCall, "*Line Describing a Cone* and Related Films," *October* 103 (Winter 2003): 46.

5. It must be admitted that McCall's own statements regarding the film at the time likely facilitated such a reception. In 1974, for instance, he commented that *Line Describing a Cone* "refers to nothing beyond…real time. It contains no illusion. It is a primary experience, not secondary; i.e., the space is real, not referential; the time is real, not referential" (quoted in McCall, "*Line Describing a Cone* and Related Films," 43).

6. Ibid.

7. Although Greenberg's thesis of artistic modernism is more nuanced than is ordinarily supposed, generally speaking it rests on a clear delineation of medium-specific ontologies. This is most cogently outlined in the essay "Modernist Painting" (1965), reprinted in Francis Frascina and Charles Harrison, eds., *Modern Art and Modernism: A Critical Anthology* (London and New York: Harper and Row, 1982), 5-10.

Scrolling through the Instagram archive of visitor photographs from Anthony McCall's 2018 exhibition at Brooklyn's Pioneer Works (hashtag #solidlightworks), one conclusion appears inescapable: everyone wants to touch the art (fig. 64.A). But, of course, there is nothing "there" to grasp. For nearly half a century, the paradoxes that constitute the sensuous appeals of McCall's "solid light" artworks have driven critics to seek refuge in ambiguity. Hal Foster, for instance, wrote of 1973's *Line Describing a Cone* that "you cannot help but touch the light as though it were a solid and investigate the cone as if it were a sculpture…"[2] More recently, Michelle Menzies has identified the "volumetric character" and "counterintuitive permeability" of McCall's late-career vertical light works as crucial elements that compel haptical responses.[3] By the very nature of such paradoxes, it has long been held that one simply must be physically present to experience these works in their phenomenological plenitude. The afterlives of the Pioneer Works exhibition, however, unfolding across the Instagram archive as well as the present volume—conceived as an artist's book rather than an exhibition catalogue—call this conventional wisdom into question.

McCall has been quite clear about the fact that "the body is the important measure" in his creative praxis.[4] His assertions notwithstanding, early critical responses to his work followed rather different lines of thought. The radical austerity of *Line Describing a Cone*—a moving-image work by a British artist who had been operating within the orbit of the London Film-makers Co-operative and the Structural approaches with which its various members were concerned—proved irresistible to contemporary criticism, which embraced the artwork as a modernist distillation of the bare ontology of cinema: light, space, and duration.[5] Understood thus as a materialist deconstruction of cinema that dislodged the hegemony of narrativity by privileging, instead, cinema's material assemblage (whirring projector, the "projected light beam itself," and, of course, the architectural space of projection),[6] McCall's thirty-minute moving-image work proved attractive to all who, enthralled by Clement Greenberg's influential formulation of modernism in the arts, were vexed by cinema's uncertain position within that scheme.[7] Here, it seemed (at the time), was the definitive modernist exposé of the literal machinations of cinema (figs. 64.B–C).

Looking back, it's easy to see why such deconstructive readings of the solid light films—McCall made a series of similarly austere, geometrical artworks through the early 1970s before interrupting his artistic career for some twenty

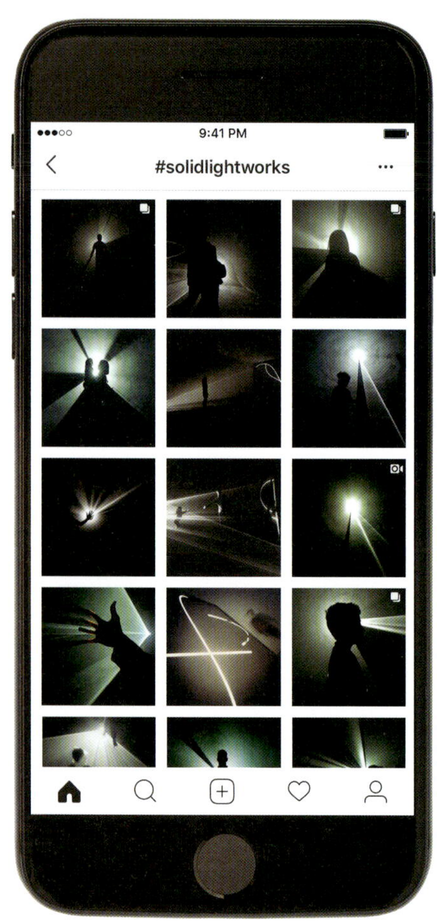

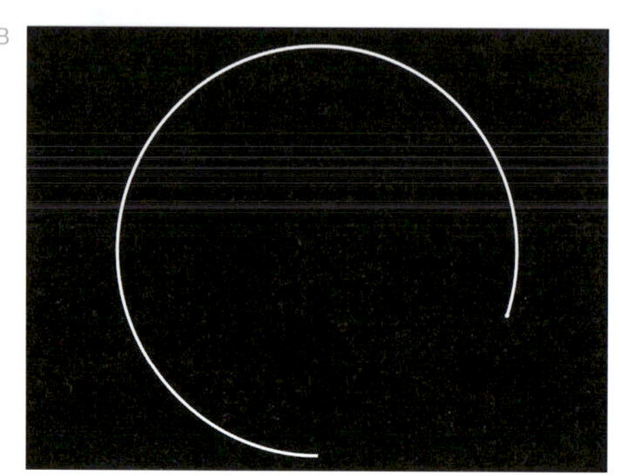

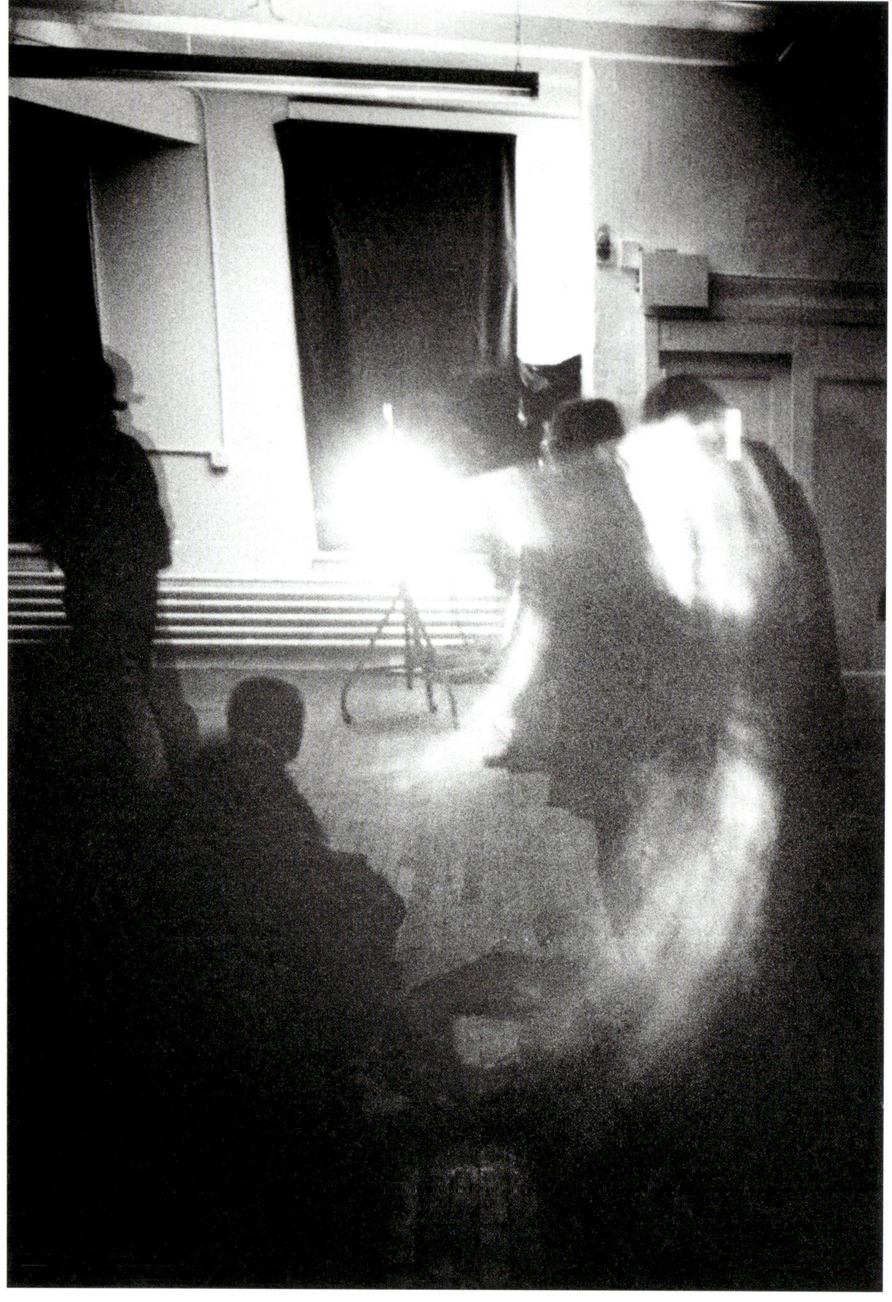

64

8. It is striking to note the prevalence of geometric considerations in McCall's work of this period. This is evident in the titles of the works: *Partial Cone*, *Conical Solid*, *Cone of Variable Volume* (all 1974). And, of course, there is the previous year's *Line Describing a Cone*.

9. McCall had explored continuous-installation formats in the mid-1970s. But it was only in 2001, when Whitney Museum of American Art curator Chrissie Iles included *Line Describing a Cone* as part of the groundbreaking exhibition *Into the Light: The Projected Image in American Art, 1964–1977*, that an early solid light film was finally exhibited as a continually looped moving-image installation.

10. These works are *Long Film for Four Projectors* (1974), *Four Projected Movements* (1975), and *Long Film for Ambient Light* (1975). McCall groups them together with the early solid light films in "*Line Describing a Cone* and Related Films," 56.

11. Foster, "Light Play," 12.

12. The vertical projections, in particular, invite rereading the solid light films as more concerned with embodied spectatorship. The Pioneer Works installation, which presented four of these works alongside two horizontal projections (though not including *Line Describing a Cone*), is especially conducive to comparative readings.

13. McCall has on several occasions offered detailed accounts of how the solid light works, both horizontal (and analog) and vertical (and digital) began life in the form of hand drawings prior to being either photographed one frame at a time or else digitally animated according to a precise "score" that determines the progression of the piece. See "*Line Describing a Cone* and Related Films"; Jonathan Walley and Anthony McCall, "An Interview with Anthony McCall," *The Velvet Light Trap* 54:1 (2004): 65-75; and *Anthony McCall: Elements for a Retrospective, 1972–1979/2003–*, ed. Olivier Michelon (Musée de Rochechouart and Serpentine Gallery, 2007).

14. McCall, "*Line Describing a Cone* and Related Films," 50.

A. Selection of images posted to Instagram during *Anthony McCall: Solid Light Works*, Pioneer Works, New York, 2018.

B. Anthony McCall. *Line Describing a Cone*, 1973. Frame from the twenty-fourth minute.

C. Peter Moore. *Anthony McCall's Line Describing a Cone*, 1973. Installation view, Artists Space, New York, 1974.

years—remained dominant until quite recently.[8] These films, when exhibited, were shown under theatrical conditions of display, i.e., as singular events of definite duration.[9] Three later solid light films, identified by McCall as constituting part of a "series of seven" that began with *Line Describing a Cone*, experimented variously with film-less projection (using ambient light instead) and duration (stretching "screening" time, for one piece, to a full twenty-four hours).[10] But it was the early solid light films' mathematical precision, made palpable in the geometry of their projection—both the figures traced on-screen and the volumes described by the projected light beams—that captured the critical imagination, facilitating their popularization as rigorous critiques of cinematic illusion.

And yet, the body. Perceptive critics noted, contra the above, that McCall's solid light films were not so much about the "essence of film" as about acknowledging that "mediums are…a matrix of conventions and conditions that are not only subject to technological transformation, but largely defined in differential relation to other arts."[11] It is precisely this horizon that is opened up by the solid light artworks—a horizon even more clearly perceptible with the vertical light works, which simultaneously evoke McCall's earliest films and yet remain clearly distinct. Not only does this invite critical reassessments of the McCall oeuvre, but also a rethinking of the relation of the physical body, the spectatorial self, to these projections. Specifically, when considered in the larger scheme of McCall's concerns prior even to *Line Describing a Cone* and those suggested by his recent vertical installations, the solid light works constitute a sustained investigation of the embodied performance of spectatorship.[12]

Begin, if you will, by considering how McCall has titled his creations, these projections of "solid" light that invite, yet elude, our touch. The horizontality of the early 1970s projections (another sense, aside from the defined temporality of their screenings, in which they are justifiably "cinematic") does not immediately disclose the fact that, as McCall has consistently asserted, "the body is the important measure" in their conceptualization. Their titles—*Conical Solid* (1974), *Partial Cone* (1974), and so on—recall their origins in techniques of line drawing.[13] McCall's comments on these films, too, evoke abstract explorations of the properties of geometrical figures. He has described *Cone of Variable Volume* (1974), for example, as "a conical form, which expanded and contracted in volume…" Or take *Conical Solid*: "a flat blade of light rotating from a fixed central axis."[14] Despite these and other formal aspects of his early practice that have been recycled to the point of canonized wisdom over the intervening decades, McCall has remained attuned to the ways in which even the early films intervene within the field of spectatorial relations. Discussing the horizontal films, for instance, he has remarked on how the almost-solidity of the projected volume appears to vary in direct proportion to the number of assembled spectators, as well as noting that the aleatory spatial configurations of spectators that accompany each projection event (continuous or temporally-defined) reorient the screenings as "a type of participatory performance."[15]

It is this latter aspect, namely the affinities between the solid light artworks and the history of performance and live art in Western modernism, that is now being rediscovered. Reviewing *Anthony McCall: Solid Light Works* (Pioneer Works, NY, 2018), I noted that the exemplary architecture of installation and near-unprecedented accompaniment of what had historically been silent (that is, aside from projector noise) events by musical performances forcefully repositioned these moving-image works within a genealogy of artistic modernism that owes most strongly to the work of John Cage.[16] It seems McCall himself has been thinking not just about his continuing creative output, but more specifically the ways in which his unique contributions to art—intersecting as they do histories of sculpture, cinema, drawing, and performance—are being historicized. Witness the shift marked by the titles of his solid light creations since the turn of the millennium. At Pioneer Works, visitors experienced the vertical projections *Breath (III)* (2005), *Meeting You Halfway* (2009), *You and I* (2010), *Skirt (III)* (2010), as well as two horizontal pieces: *You and I (Horizontal)* (2005) and *Doubling Back* (2003) (fig. 67.C).

Gone is the insistence on abstract geometric configurations; by their very titles, these and other recent works are far more thoroughly immersed in corporeal subjectivity. Interested in recent years in what he calls a "traveling wave,"[17] McCall has created monumental (the vertical works are each ten meters tall) projections, the movements traced by which are "fluid and continuous," possessing "distinctly figural [qualities]," and thus "reminiscent of the movement of the body, especially slow movement..."[18] The dramatically increased complexity of these waveforms contrasts with the relatively simple geometry of the horizontal films of the 1970s. Most visitors can guess at the eventual culmination of *Line Describing a Cone*—if the title doesn't immediately give the game away—well before the projection concludes. But such extrapolations are rarely possible with the vertical works, the minutely shifting orientations of which

15. Ibid., 44-45.

16. Swagato Chakravorty, "'The Primary Event was the Performance': Anthony McCall's Play with Light," *The Brooklyn Rail* (March 2018), https://brooklynrail.org/2018/03/film/The-Primary-Event-was-the-Performance-Anthony-McCalls-Play-with-Light. In my review, I argue that McCall's interests in problems of "notation, spatial volume, and the body," which were central to his practice prior to the solid light works, place him closer to performance art than to histories of cinema. He has, in almost every recorded interview, at some point referred to his early performance work, which shared a great deal with the experiments then being undertaken in the United States by Carolee Schneemann, Allan Kaprow, Simone Forti, Yvonne Rainer, Merce Cunningham, John Cage, and the larger Judson Dance Theater collective. Until recently, however, the early performance pieces and McCall's affinities with Cagean modernism have rarely been discussed in relation to his later moving-image works.

17. McCall defines this as "a form...somewhere between the circle and the straight line... essentially a curved line that repeatedly reverses its curve along a straight axis." Translated into three-dimensional space, variations in amplitude produce "an undulating triangular plane...a 'traveling wave'" (Walley and McCall, "An Interview with Anthony McCall," 71).

18. Ibid.

A. Anthony McCall. *Breath (III)*, 2005. Footprint sequence, 2012.

B. Anthony McCall. *Breath (III)*, 2005. Installation drawing, 2015. Pencil on paper.

C. Anthony McCall. From front to back: *Meeting You Halfway*, 2009, *Breath (III)*, 2005, *You and I (II)*, 2010, *Skirt (III)*, 2010. Installation view, Pioneer Works, New York, 2018.

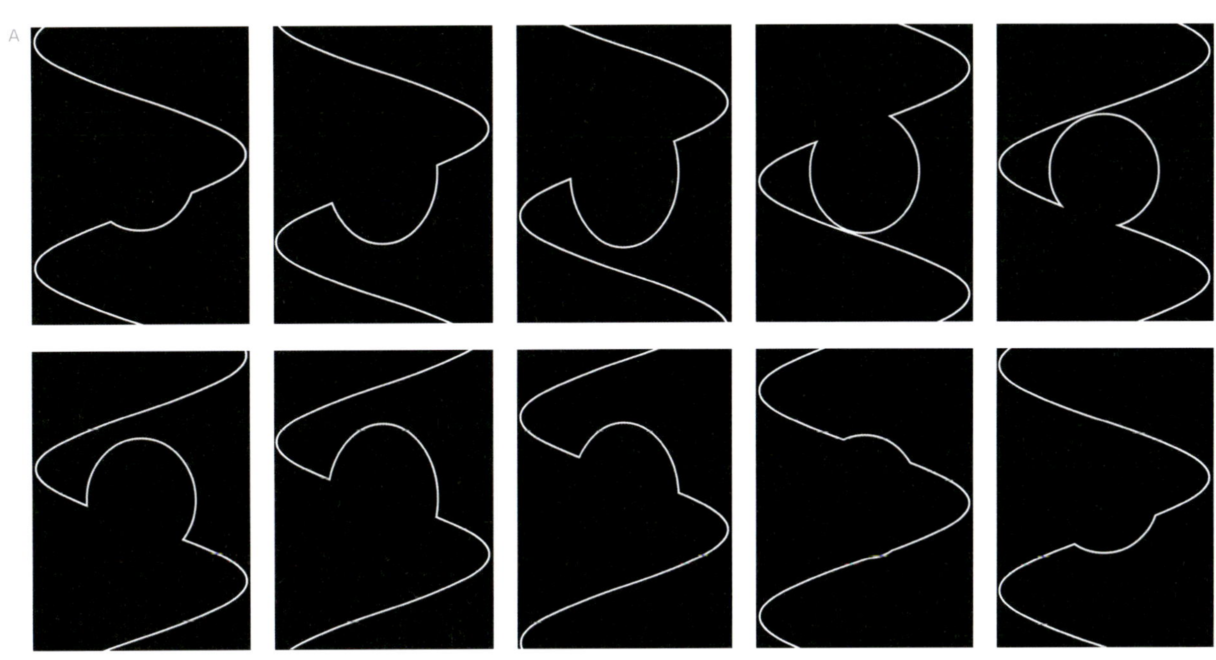

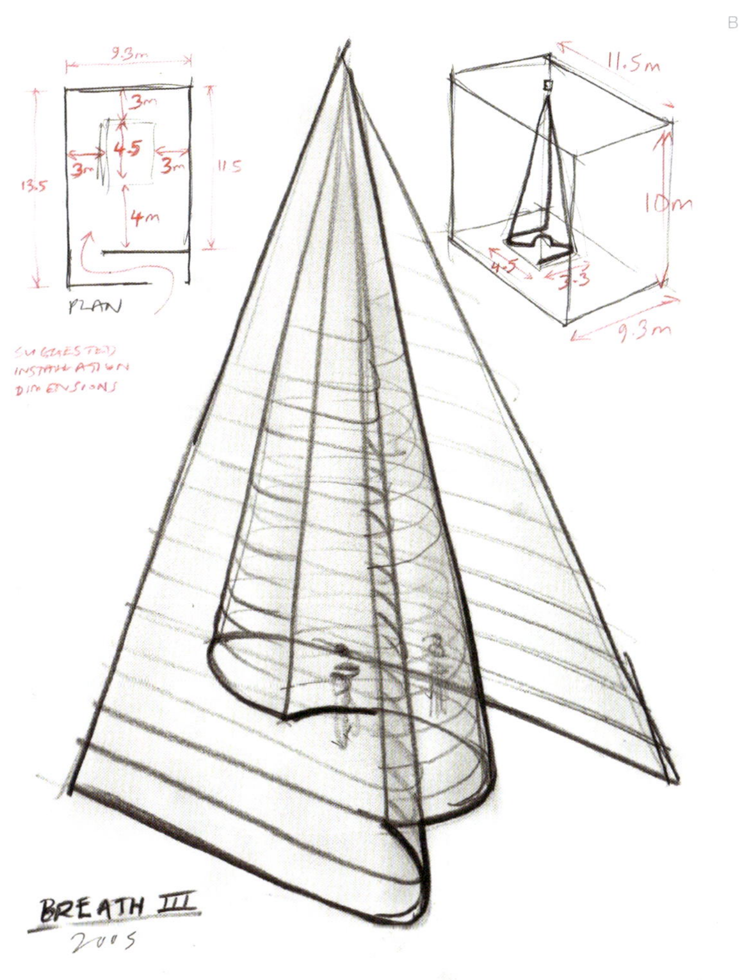

9.3m
3m
4.5
3m
3m
13.5
11.5
4m
PLAN
SUGGESTED INSTALLATION DIMENSIONS
11.5m
10m
4.5
3.3
9.3m
BREATH III
2005

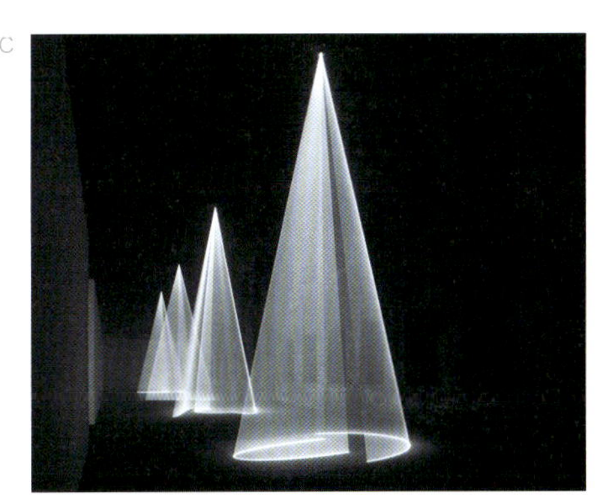

tend to confound attempts at anticipating their progression. And they all begin life conceptualized as cyclical structures,[19] where "permutation rather than narrative" enables the projection to create what McCall calls an "extended present tense."[20] As McCall remarks in his conversation with David Grubbs in the present volume, the objective here is that "the end of one cycle is indistinguishable from the beginning of the next."[21] In other words, rather than simply beginning, ending, and beginning again, the solid light works since 2003 seem to morph without end, transitioning continuously.

The use of digital projection for these recent works marks another crucial move away from the exhibition contexts of the 1970s. In fact, this shift has had an unexpected consequence. Unlike the analog projectors that powered the early solid light films, digital projectors are almost silent. Partly in order to compensate for this, McCall experimented—in an early version of *Leaving*—with a foghorn-driven three-dimensional sonic field that gradually asserted its presence as the projected visuals faded into nothingness. Experiments with sonic accompaniment and acoustical fields aren't entirely new in McCall's career. An untitled stereo piece from 1972, which was never installed, comprised two sine tones originating at points on the auditory spectrum outside of human hearing range. As one tone ascended in pitch, the other descended, the two tones crossing over at the center of their frequency range. Another sound work, begun in 1972, started out as *White Noise Installation*. Here, McCall set in motion a mass of white noise, which moved slowly and repeatedly down a long exhibition space (figs. 69.A–B). The original tape for this got lost at some point, and the work would not see the light of day until it was remade—this time using five tracks and five speakers—in 2013. It has since been exhibited as *Traveling Wave* (1972/2013).[22]

Borne by the strains of sound, then, and aided by the architectural scale of the vertical projections, the sensing body that was always at the core of Anthony McCall's practice is emphasized as never before. The *Four Simultaneous Soloists* performances that accompanied—and I would argue *structured*—the Pioneer Works show marked one of the few occasions any sort of musical performance has aired during the exhibition of a solid light work (fig. 70.A).[23] Elsewhere in this book, McCall and Grubbs treat the organization of *Four Simultaneous Soloists* in fascinating depth, so I shall not rehearse its specifics here. What's crucial is that, as Grubbs notes, these are not works that "need musical accompaniment."[24] So what, precisely, do the solid

19. In correspondence, it's clear that McCall had become fascinated with the idea of cyclical form by the mid-1970s. He mentions Gertrude Stein's notion of the "continuous present," which appears in her 1925-6 essay "Composition as Explanation." It's quite likely that the shift toward cyclical form evident in McCall's solid light works after the first four *Cone* films was motivated, at least in part, by his reading of Stein. McCall's return to solid light works in the last two decades continues to explore cyclical form(s) (Anthony McCall, correspondence with the author, February 2019).
20. Walley and McCall, "An Interview with Anthony McCall," 69.
21. "Anthony McCall and David Grubbs in Conversation," 28.
22. McCall, correspondence with the author. The first exhibition of *Traveling Wave* took place in New Haven at the Yale University School of Art's 32 Edgewood Gallery, January 8–February 6, 2014.
23. See "Anthony McCall and David Grubbs in Conversation," 38.
24. Ibid., 42.
A. Anthony McCall. *White Noise Installation. Surge, in One Direction along One Axis*, 1972. Ink on paper.
B. Anthony McCall. *Traveling Wave*, 1972/2013. Installation view, Yale University 32 Edgewood Gallery, New Haven, 2014.

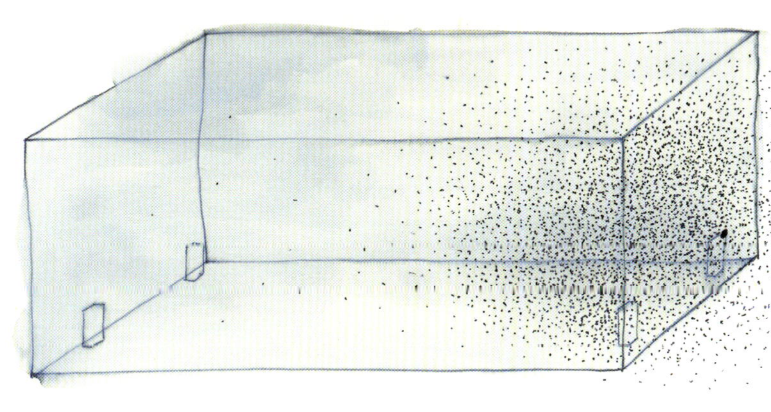

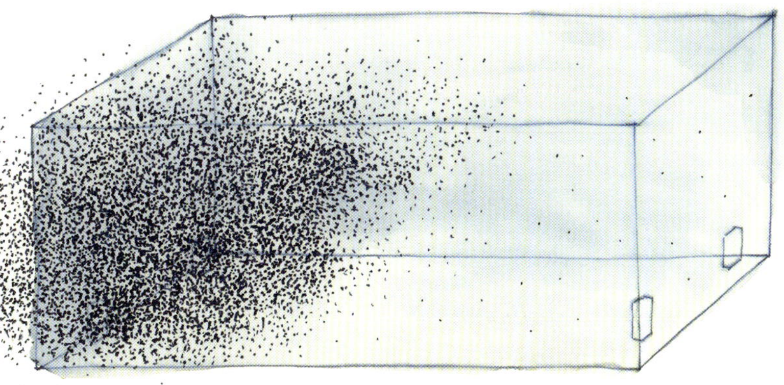

A

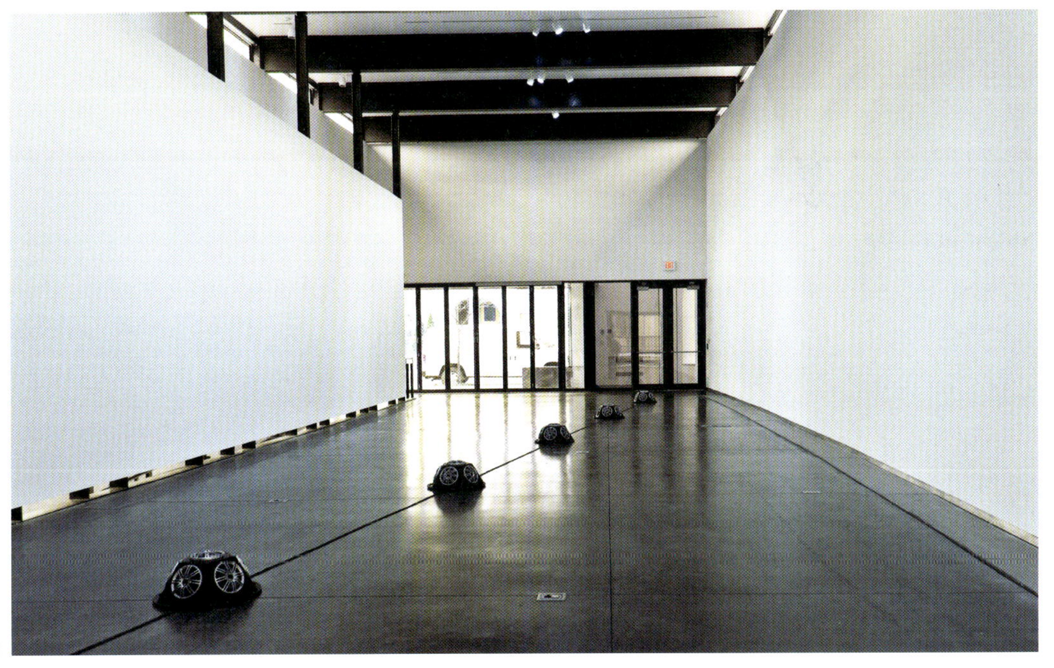

B

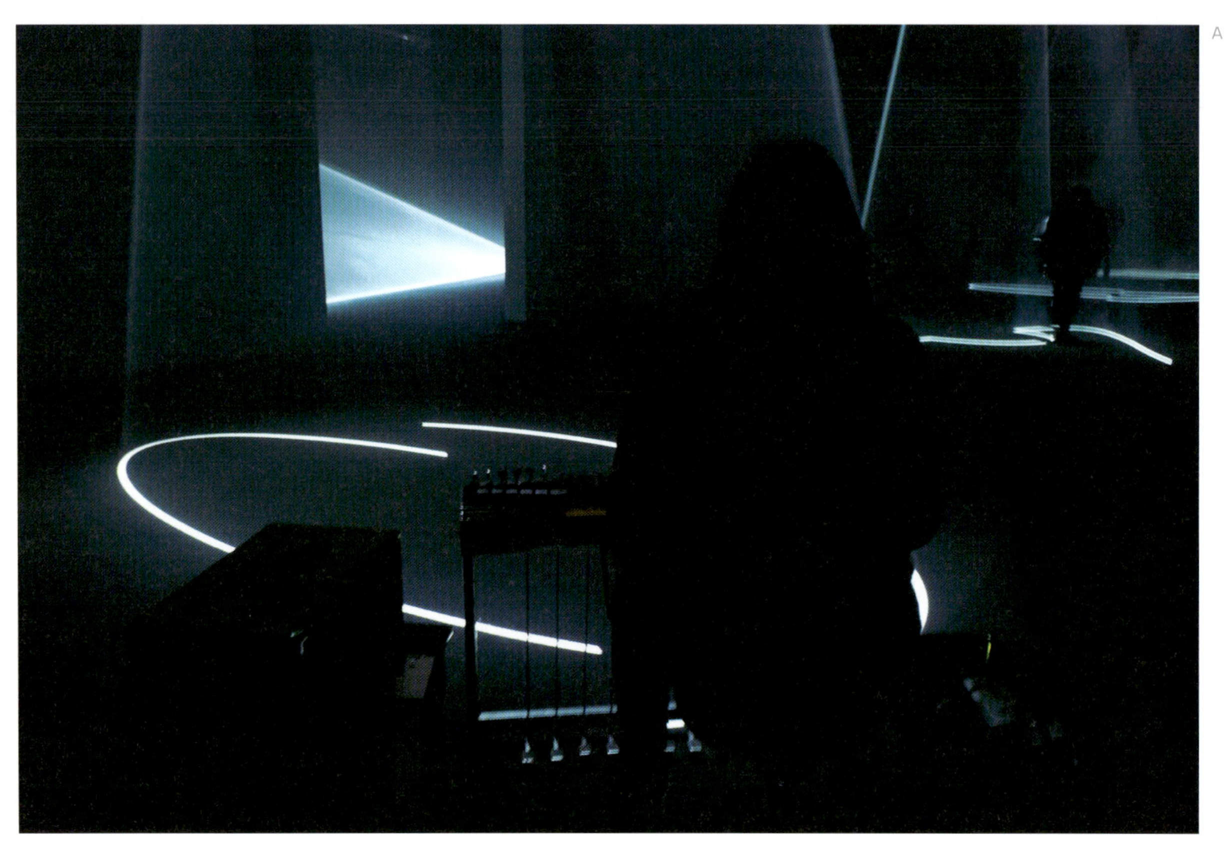

A

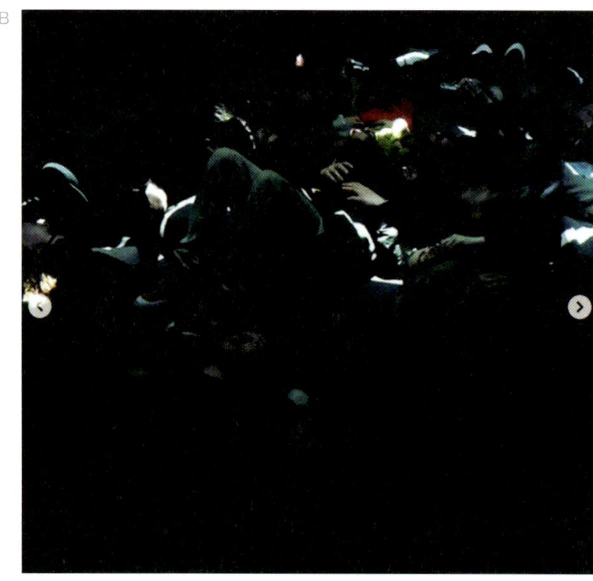

B

25. The work was presented as part of the International Carnival of Experimental Sound (ICES 72) on August 13, 1972.

26. For a more detailed discussion of this crucial work by Cage, see Branden W. Joseph's introduction to this book.

27. McCall, "*Line Describing a Cone* and Related Films," 60.

28. Ibid., 62.

light works gain in such a situation? And how does the expansion of the exhibition, tracked through its documentary afterlives on Instagram, or via this artist's book, affect the conditions of spectatorship and reception that have typically been associated with McCall's projections?

An answer to the first question is perhaps best formulated by recalling McCall's various acknowledgments over the decades of his keen interest in, and the influence exerted upon him by, the multimedia experiments of John Cage and his numerous collaborators. For instance, McCall recalls having attended several of Cage's performances across London and New York throughout the seventies, in particular *HPSCHD* (1967-69; McCall attended a version presented at London's Roundhouse in 1972).[25] In this piece, Cage had arranged seven harpsichords evenly spaced around the perimeter of a circular space approximately sixty feet across. Each instrument was played by a different musician, performing a distinct part. Audience members, free to circulate about the space, in effect constructed their own symphony on the move. Aside from this basic acoustical setup, Cage's staging of *HPSCHD* also included a large number of slide and film projectors, as well as tape recorders.[26] Altogether, it was an immersive multimedia event. McCall remembers "standing at the very center of the circle, finding the place where all the different pieces being played merged into one, rapturous cacophony."[27] I am struck, however, by McCall's precise identification of what might be considered the central ethos motivating much of Cage's work: "integrat[ing] different classes of events, be they images, sounds, music, actions, objects, or language, within a temporal structure based on principles other than those of literary narrative."[28] The lessons McCall adapted from Cage and his circle resonate across his practice, but rarely have they been foregrounded as prominently as in the Pioneer Works exhibition.

Far from merely adding an acoustical dimension to the "extended present" that one experiences when encountering a solid light work, the complexities of sonic interplay that variously negotiated, accompanied, or responded to the unfolding of the luminous projections serve instead to decisively move McCall's work (back) toward a Cagean genealogy of the arts. The powerful *shaping* role played by sound in the Pioneer Works installation is equally evident in the obvious antinomy present in the juxtaposition of "simultaneous" and "soloist(s)." And yet if the opening-onto of the solid light works toward sound makes clearer the affinities between McCall's practice and that of Cage and his circle, the same operation also introduces new challenges that relate to how we document, archive, and circulate the experience of art today.

For some time now, art has had as much to do with its historical networks of production and exhibition as it has to do with what it does—usually, in the form of images—"once [these images] enter circulation in heterogeneous networks."[29] This is one of the key propositions advanced recently by the art historian and critic David Joselit. In *After Art*, for instance, he attempts to "expand the definition of art to embrace heterogeneous configurations of relationships or links,"[30] such that the *circulation* of art following the circumstances of its production may command greater critical attention after the exhaustion of medium and post-medium debates. Crucially, Joselit argues that the "site-specific" framing of art—and the auratic experience intrinsic to this framing—theorized most famously by Walter Benjamin, is no longer adequate to our moment, saturated as it is by technologies, systems, and networks of image circulation.[31] I conclude this essay by taking up these lines of thinking in relation to the ways in which *Anthony McCall: Solid Light Works*, a specific set of artworks exhibited under specific temporal and physical conditions, extends its reach well beyond those settings and complicates the terms of its reception.

Some 42,000 visitors passed through the exhibition at Pioneer Works over the course of eight weeks.[32] Early on, I mentioned that a look through the Instagram archive of visitor photographs and videos suggests a compelling desire on the part of visitors to touch the art. Let me be more specific: a surprising number of these images in fact do not document McCall's projections themselves, so much as the endlessly varying ways in which visitors *interact* with the projections.[33] In this Instagram screenshot (fig. 64.A), we see individuals carefully posing to maximize the silhouette effect: a photograph of a woman holding up a little girl, both sharply silhouetted against the projection; another one of a little girl extending her hand into the beam of light; a photograph of a man reaching out to his child, horizontal projections dramatically framing their bodies....This curious impulse—to document people participating in the projections, rather than attempt to document just the projections, or the musical performances—is something that, I now realize, guided one of my own photographs (fig. 70.B). Spending some hours at Pioneer Works on the final night of the exhibition, I was fascinated by the sight of hundreds of visitors simply sprawled out on the floor of the main hall, bathing in the silvery haze of the vertical projections. Some kept up conversations amongst friends in low tones. Some

29. David Joselit, *After Art* (Princeton and Oxford: Princeton University Press, 2013), xiv.
30. Ibid., 2.
31. Ibid., 13.
32. I thank Vivian Chui, associate curator at Pioneer Works, for providing these numbers.
33. Hal Foster has also noted that part of the enduring appeal of these artworks is that "the experience is sociable," stating that "intimate interaction, which is both private and public, is key to the solid-light films." He relates this to the "benevolent phenomenology" espoused by Maurice Merleau-Ponty. See Foster, "Light Play," 17-20.

stared up into the projections, occasionally (inevitably!) reaching into the beams of the light. Others slept. Still others watched others engage in some or all these activities.

It is precisely this multiplicity of experience that the Instagram archive acknowledges. Put otherwise, you and I do not necessarily share identical encounters with the solid light artworks. A certain randomness is—and has arguably always been—key to these projections, and to the ways in which they are experienced. It is this subjectivity of experience in encounters with the "extended present" of McCall's projections that is reintroduced into their documentary afterlives. Certainly, there is a phenomenological richness to encountering these works in person. And yet that same multi-sensory immersion—in darkness, haze, light, and at least at Pioneer Works, sound—can obscure the sheer variability of this experience. The visitor photographs on Instagram, some of which are reproduced in this volume, remind us that the experience of the solid light artworks is not necessarily circumscribed by the specificity of its installation site(s). They remind us, too, of how varied this experience always is, even if they do not reproduce the precise audiovisual permutations caused by one's physical movements through the exhibition space. In this mass of crowd-sourced visual documentation, we sample not just approximations of the artworks themselves, but also the forms of embodied spectatorial participation they have always invited. And it offers rich testimony to the gift Anthony McCall has given us by returning to, and utterly revising, the work that once transformed how we may think about moving-image art.

Anthony McCall. *Meeting You Halfway*, 2009. Footprint sequence at 100-second intervals, 2011.

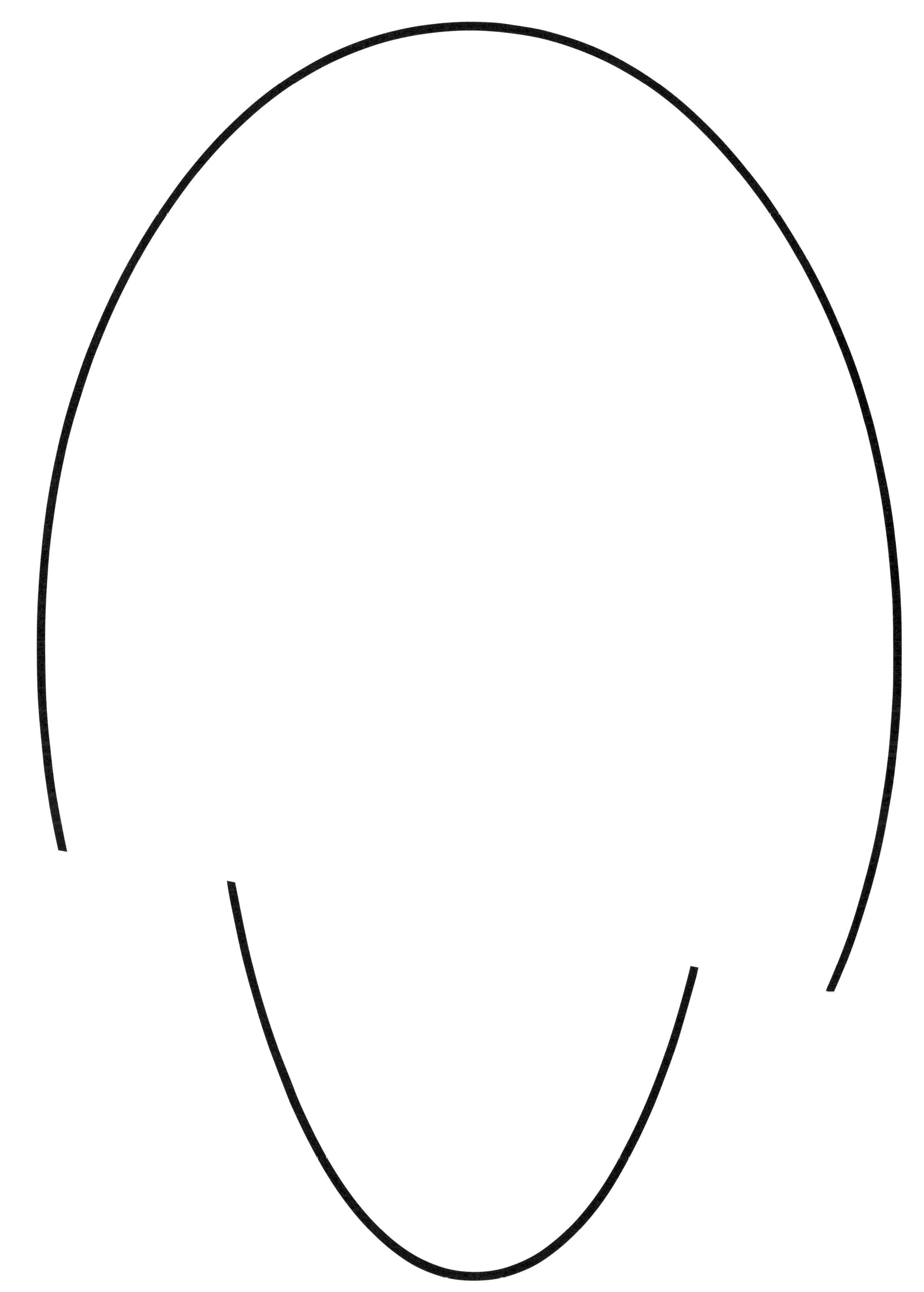

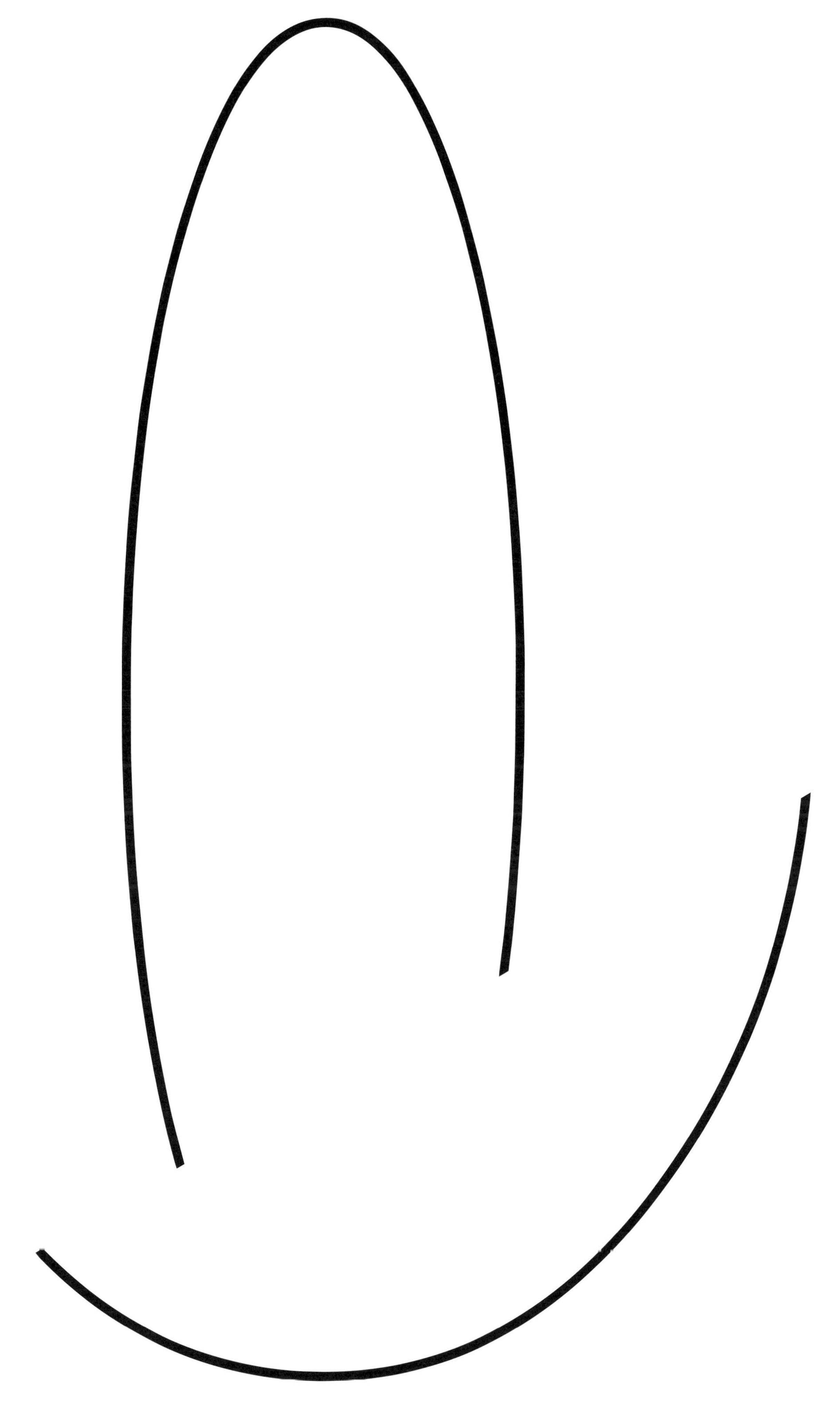

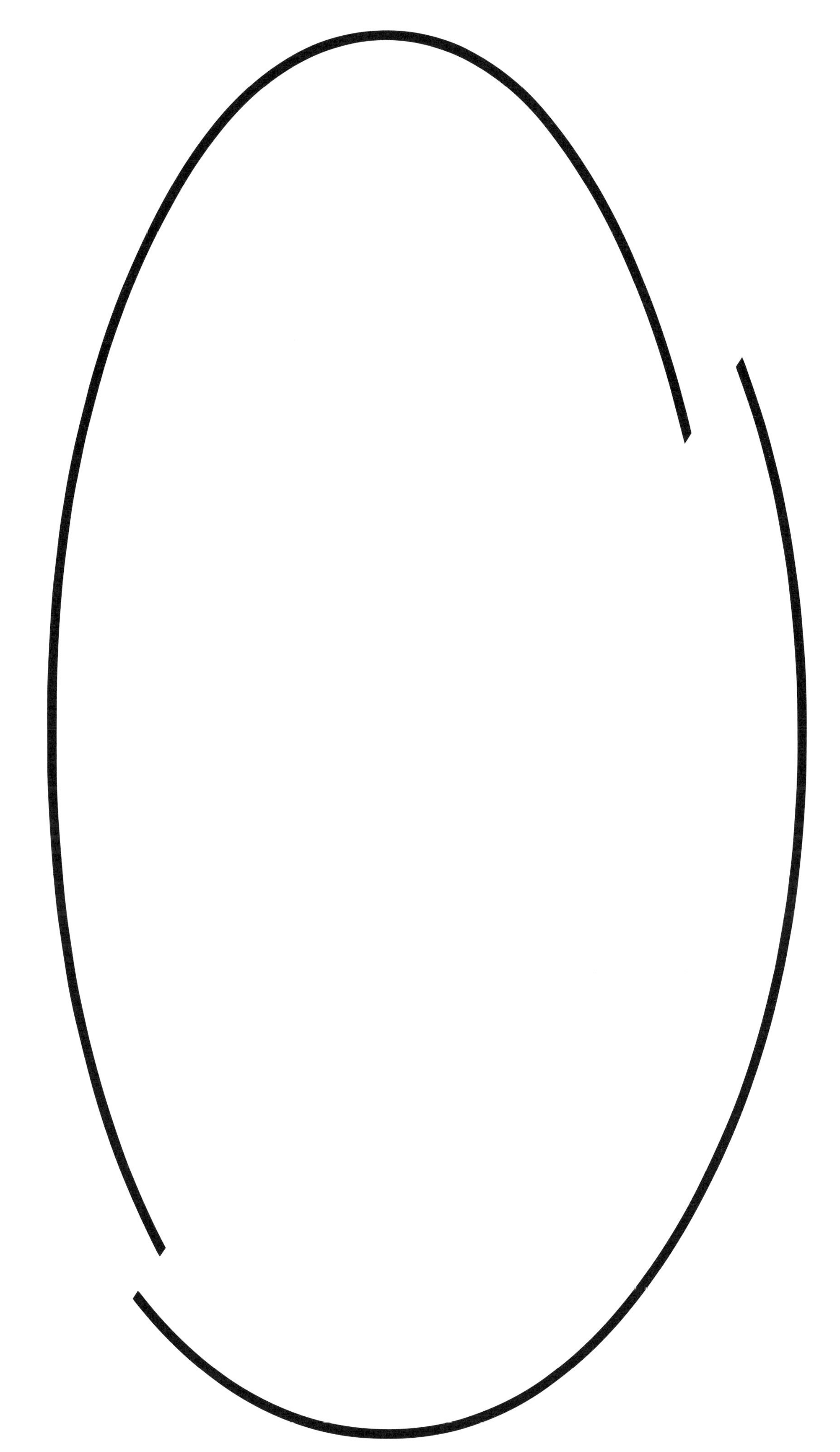

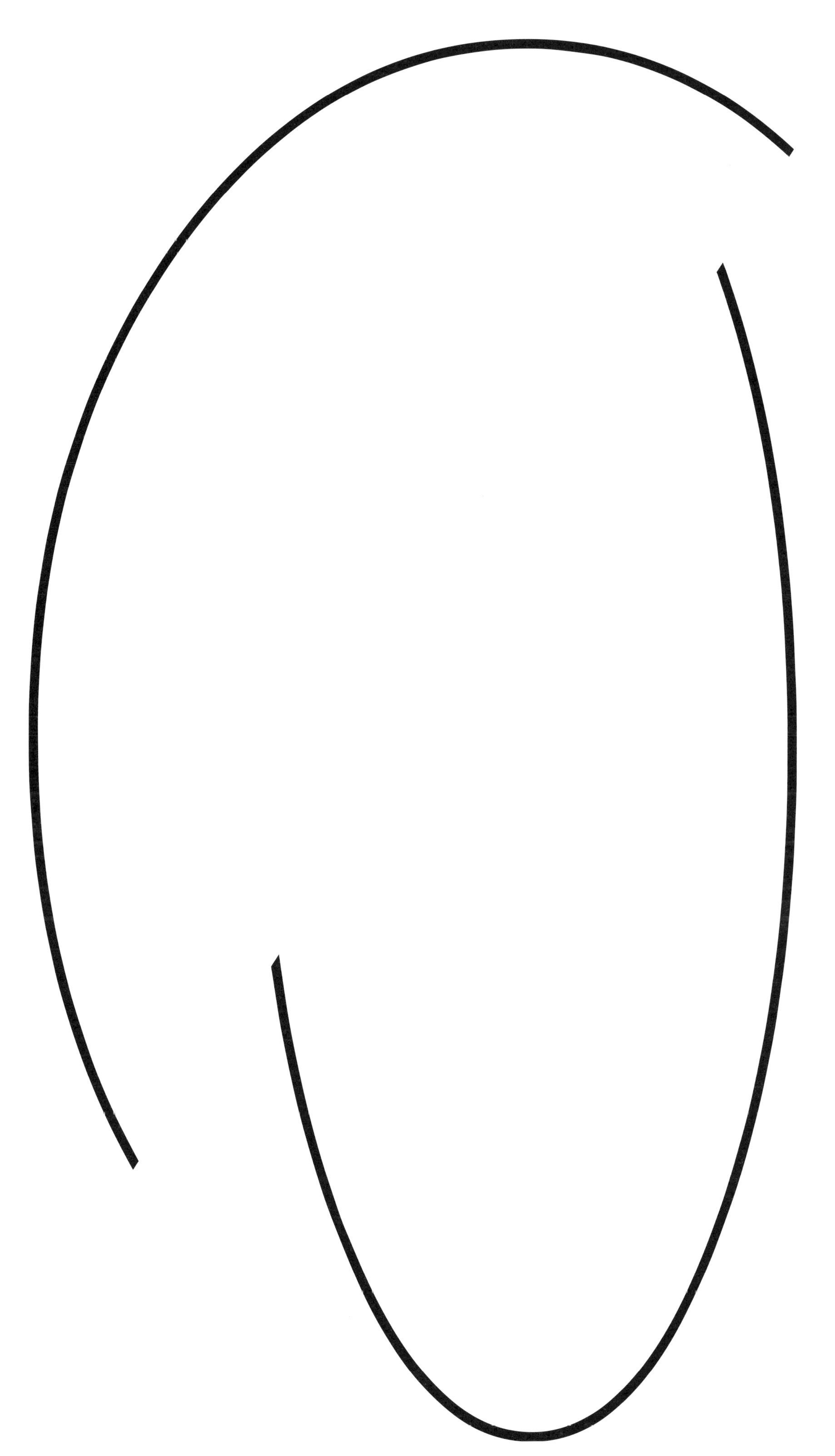

Solid Light Works:
Installation Photographs

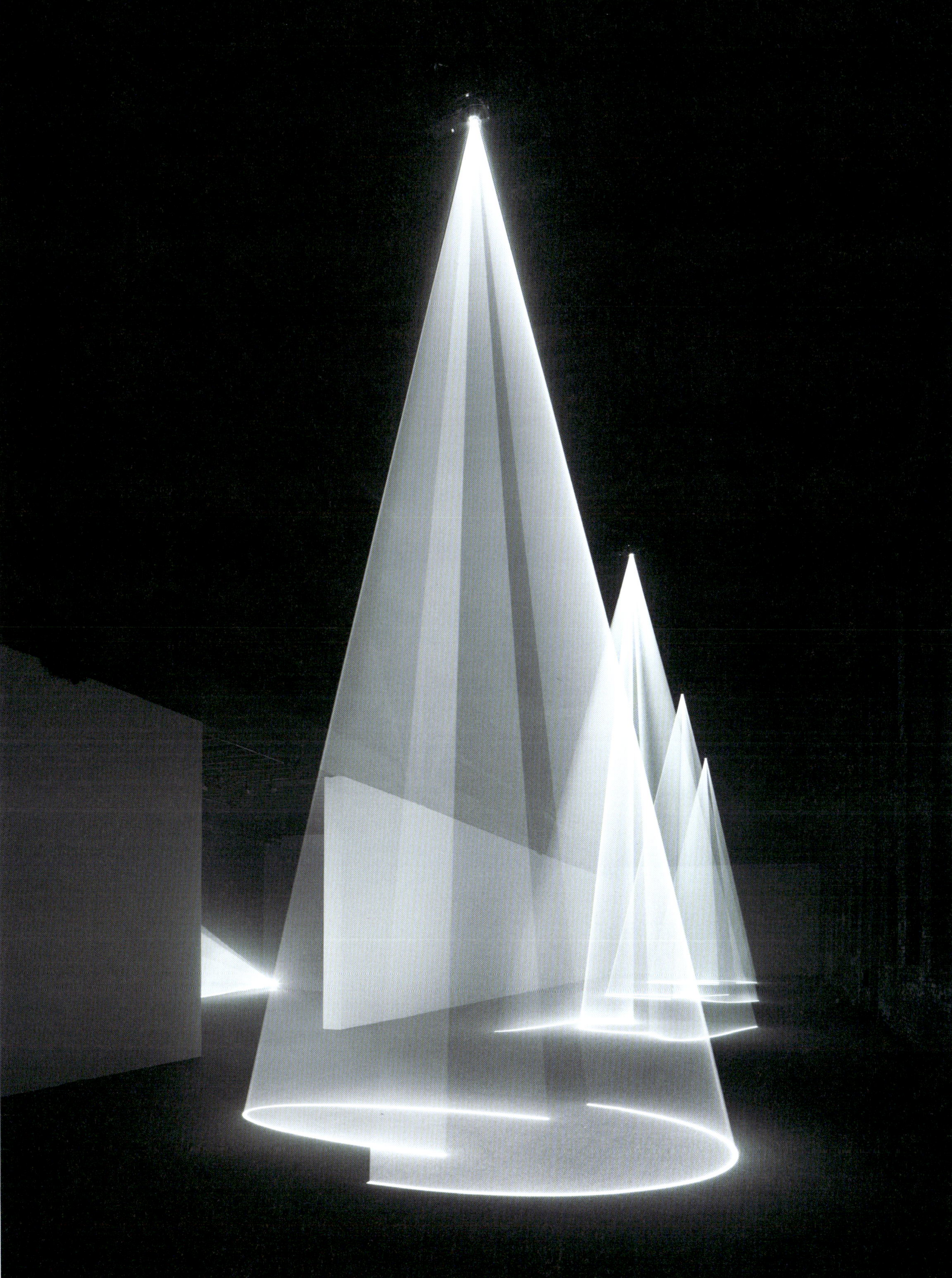

Previous: Anthony McCall.
From front to back: *Meeting
You Halfway*, 2009, *Breath (III)*,
2005, *You and I (II)*, 2010, *Skirt
(III)*, 2010. Installation view,
Pioneer Works, New York, 2018.

Opposite: Anthony McCall.
You and I, Horizontal, 2005.
Installation view, Institut d'Art
Contemporain, Villeurbanne,
France, 2006.

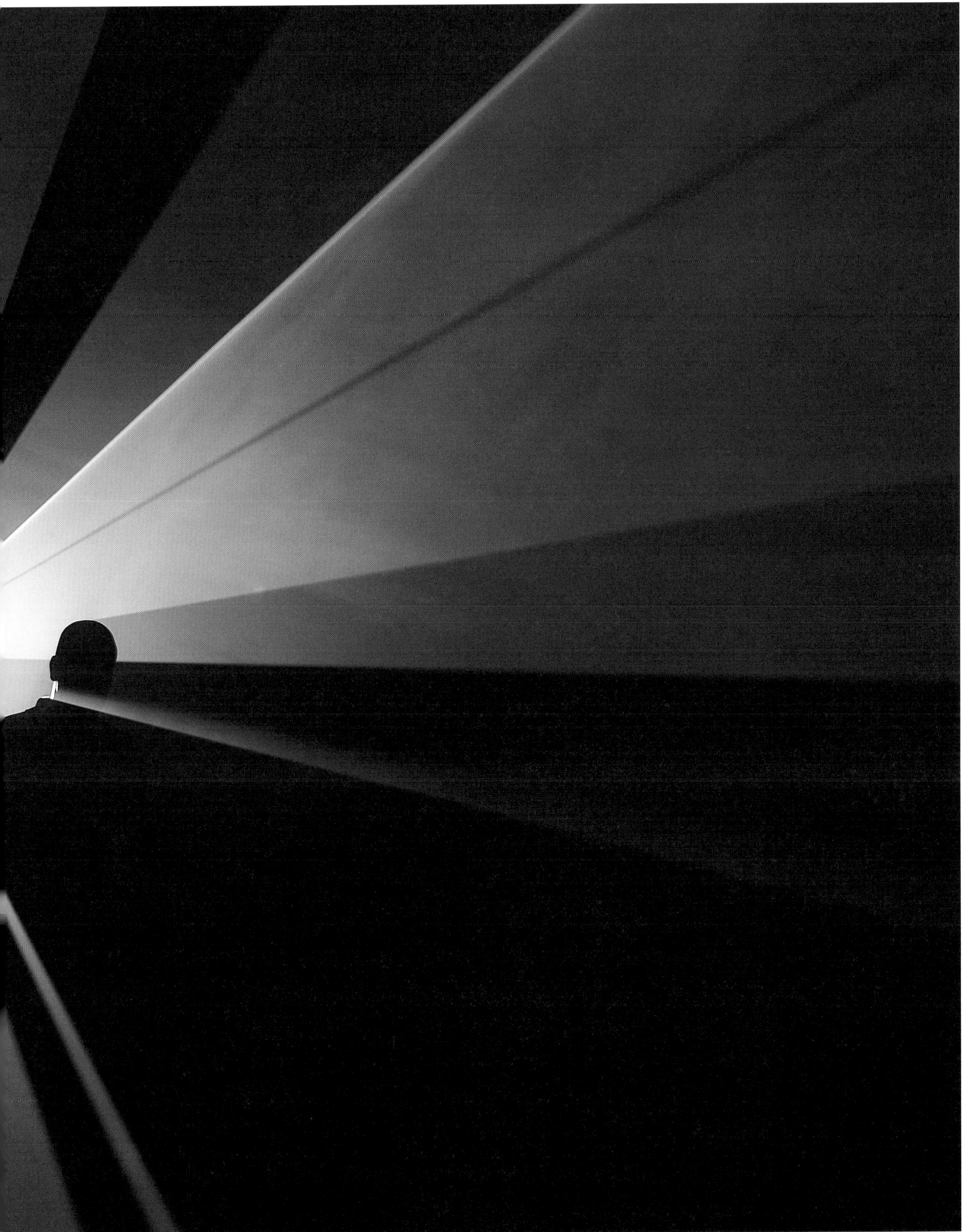

Anthony McCall. From front to back: *Breath (III)*, 2005, *Meeting You Halfway*, 2009; side gallery: *You and I, Horizontal*, 2005. Installation view, Pioneer Works, New York, 2018.

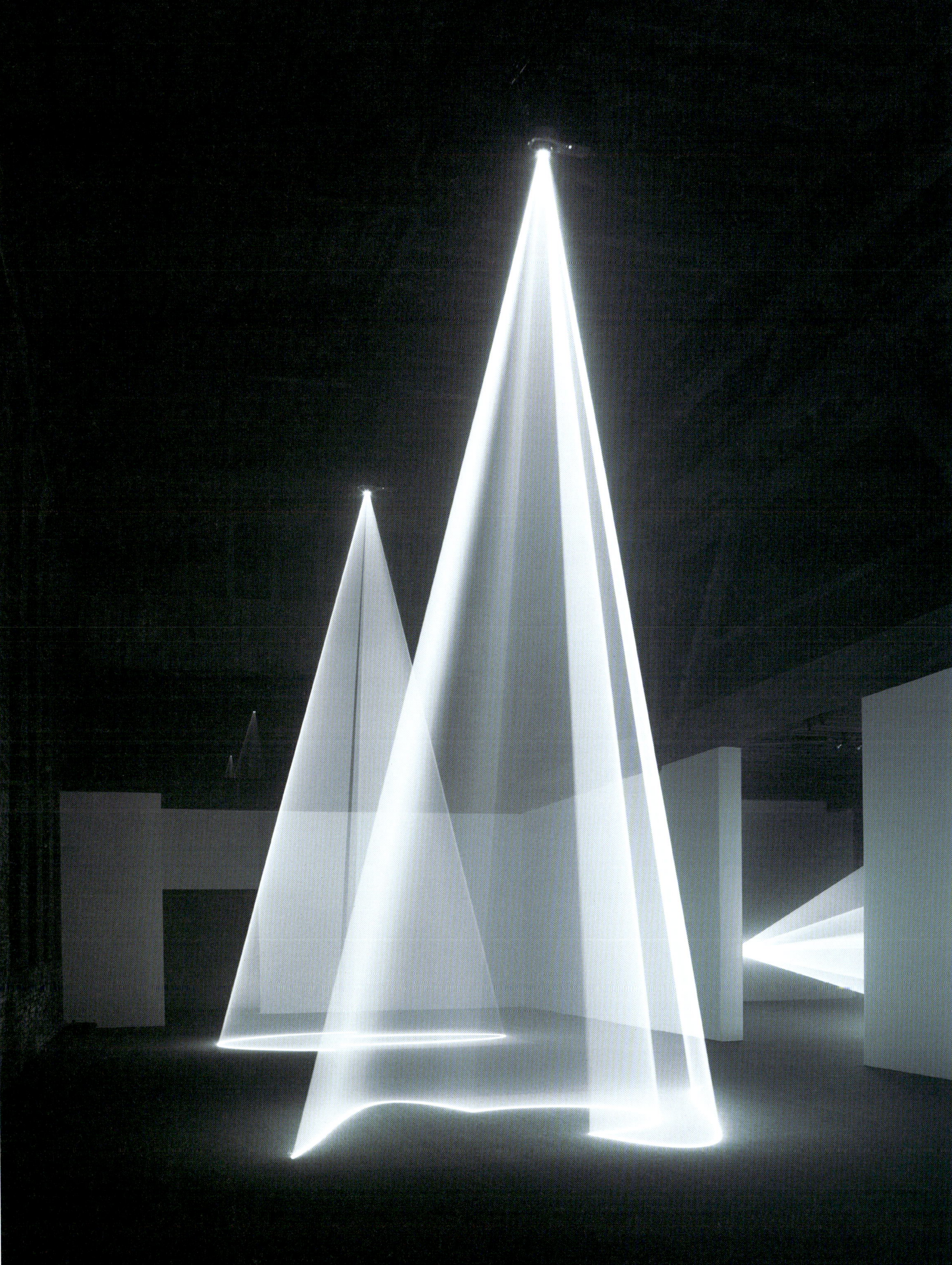

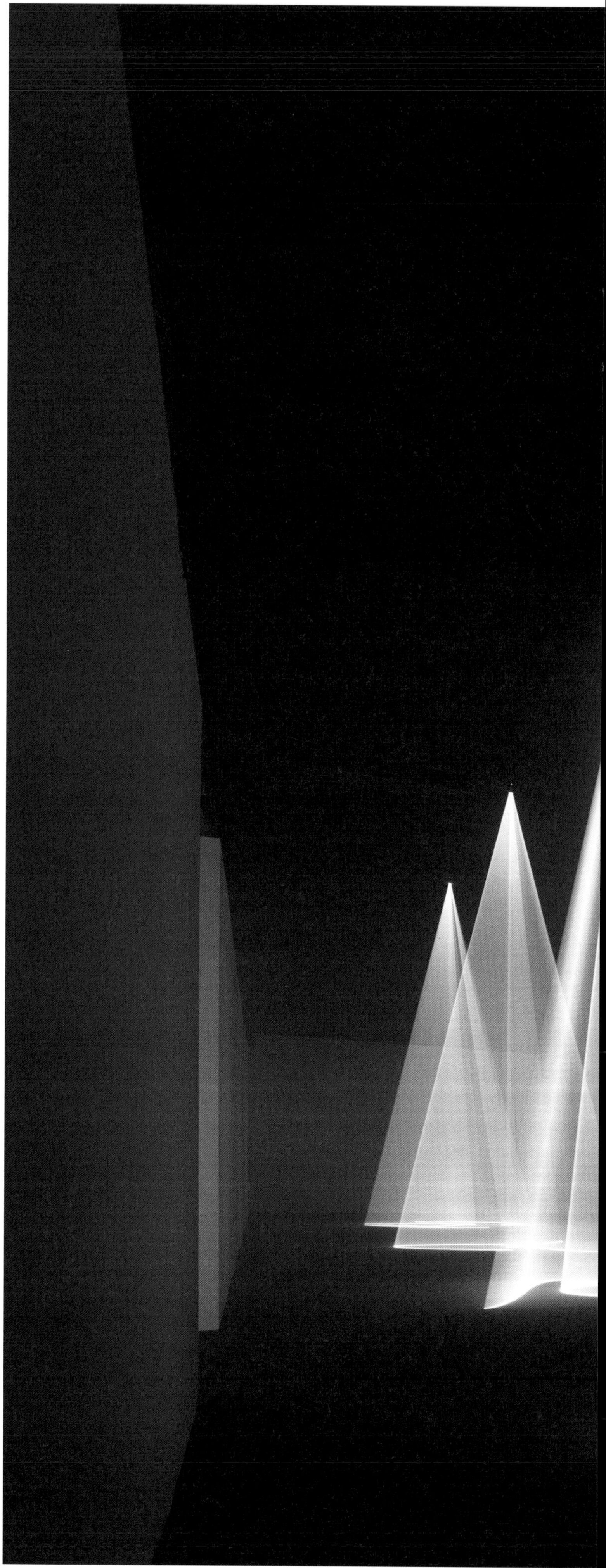

Anthony McCall. From front
to back: *Meeting You Halfway*,
2009, *Breath (III)*, 2005, *You
and I (II)*, 2010, *Skirt (III)*, 2010.
Installation view, Pioneer Works,
New York, 2018.

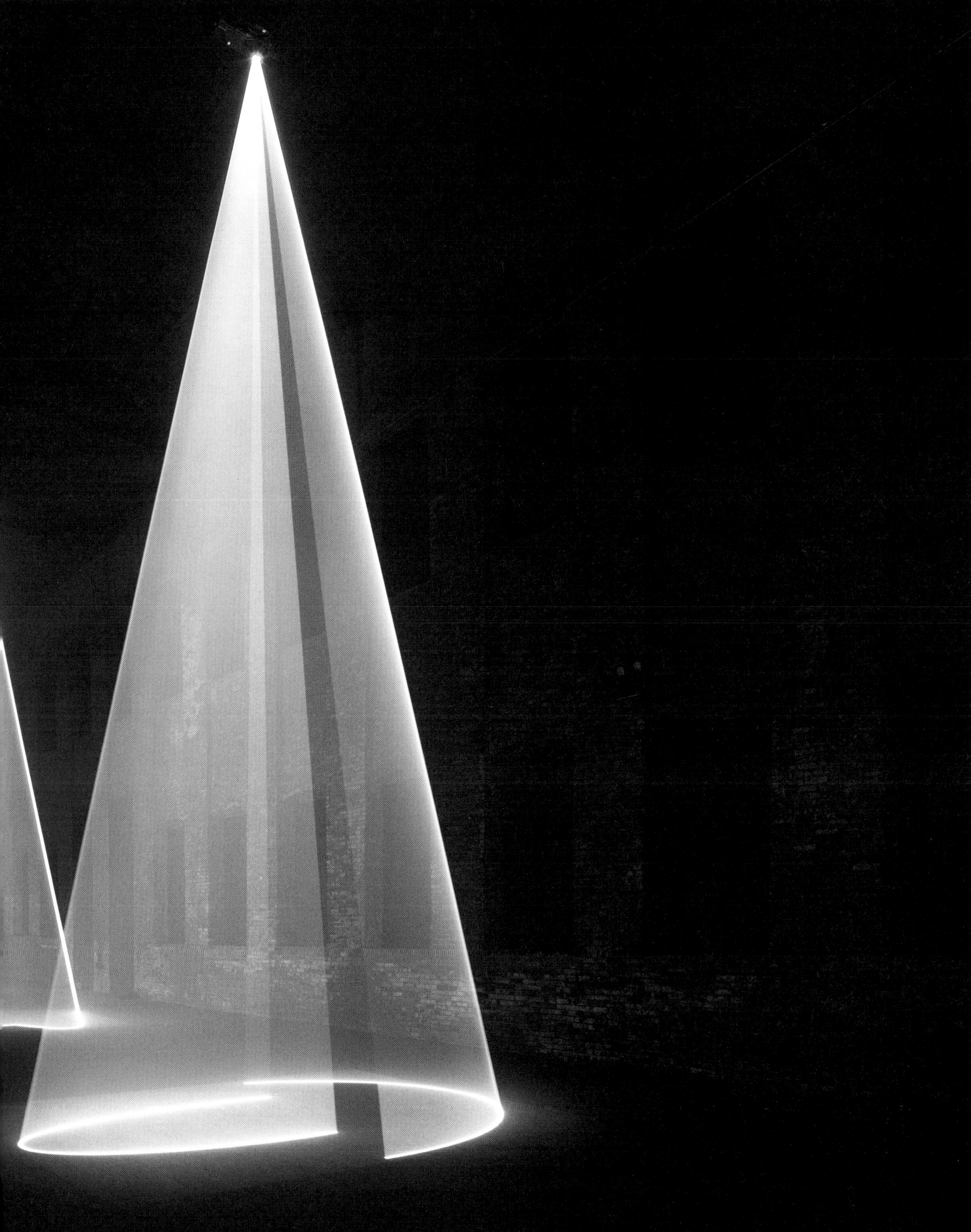

Anthony McCall. *You and I, Horizontal*, 2005. Installation view, Pioneer Works, New York, 2018.

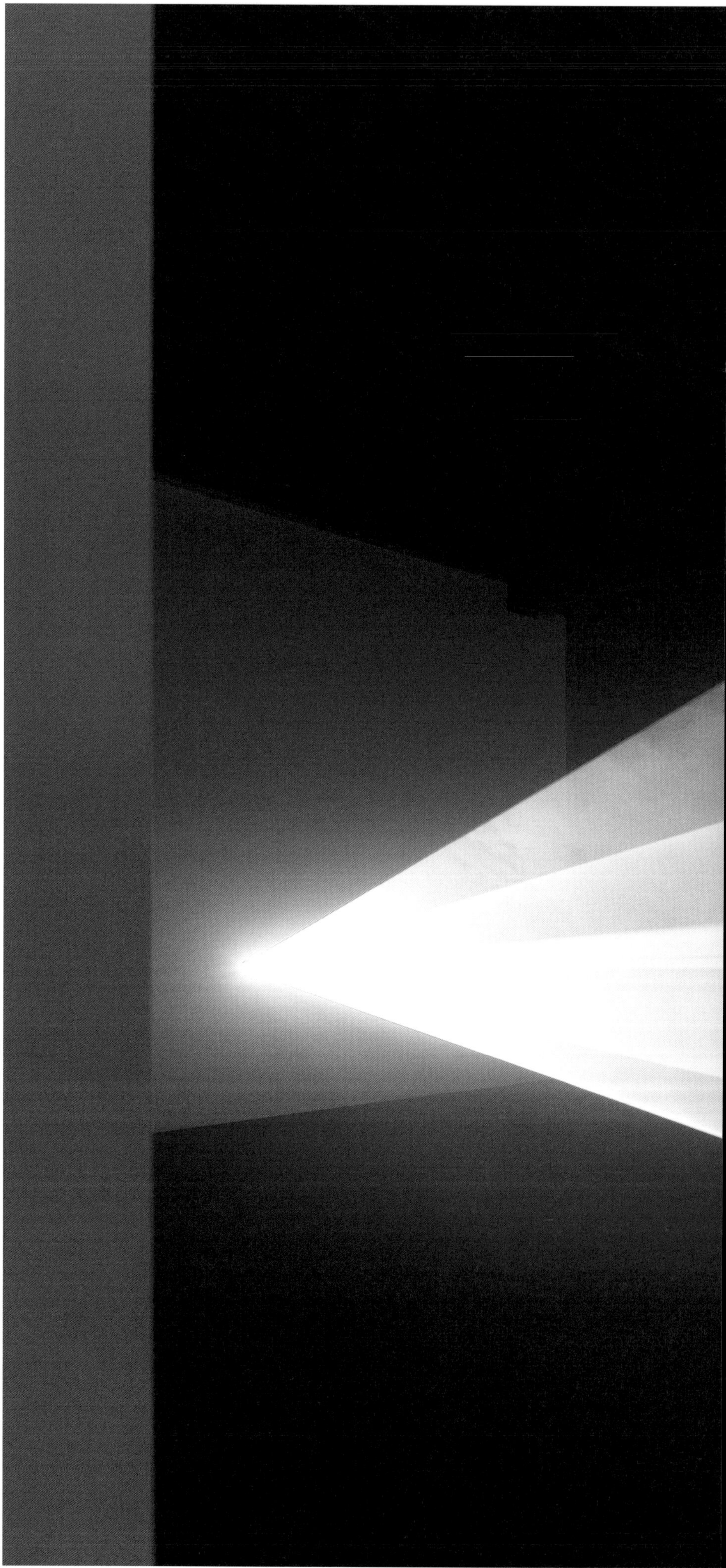

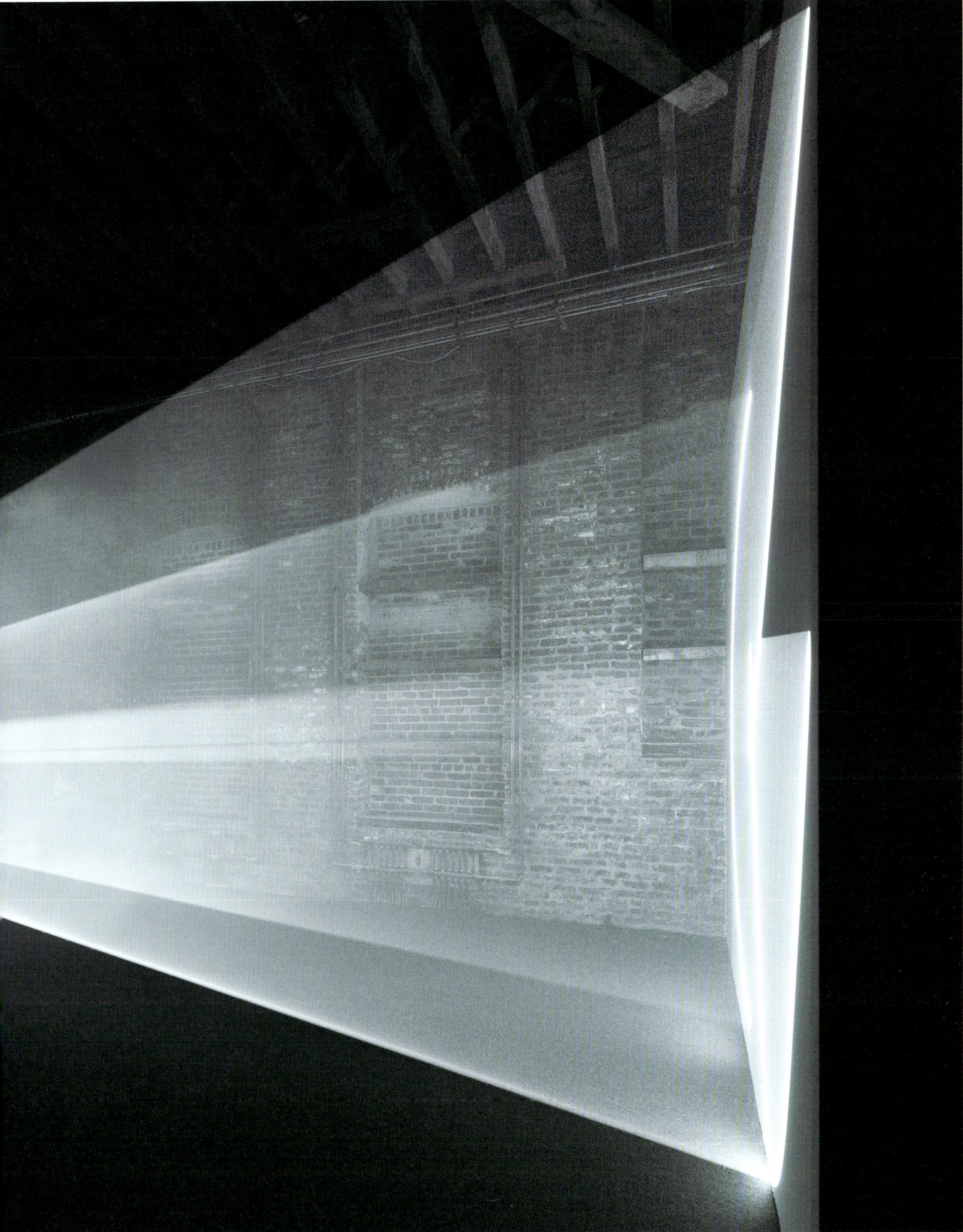

Anthony McCall. *Doubling Back*, 2003. Installation view, LAC Lugano Arte e Cultura, Lugano, Switzerland, 2015.

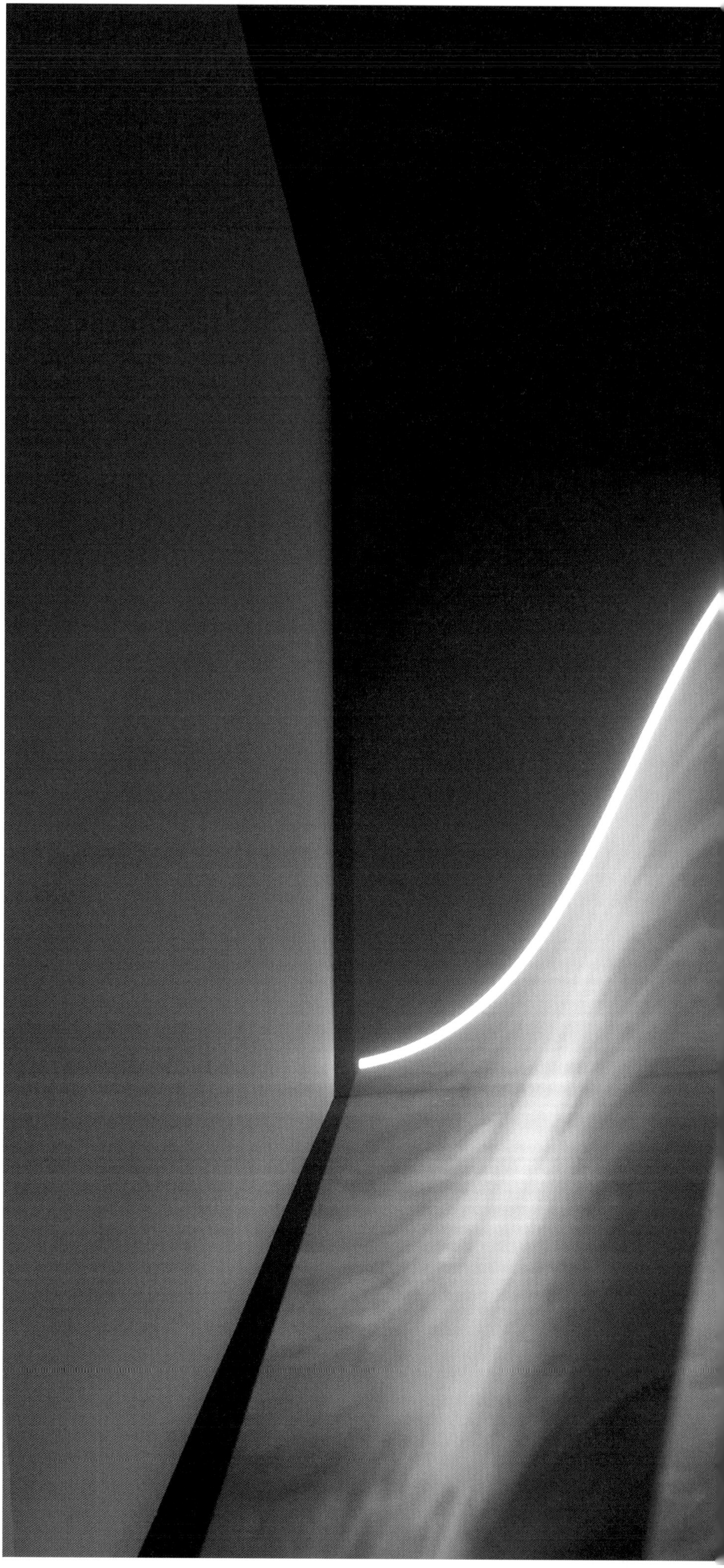

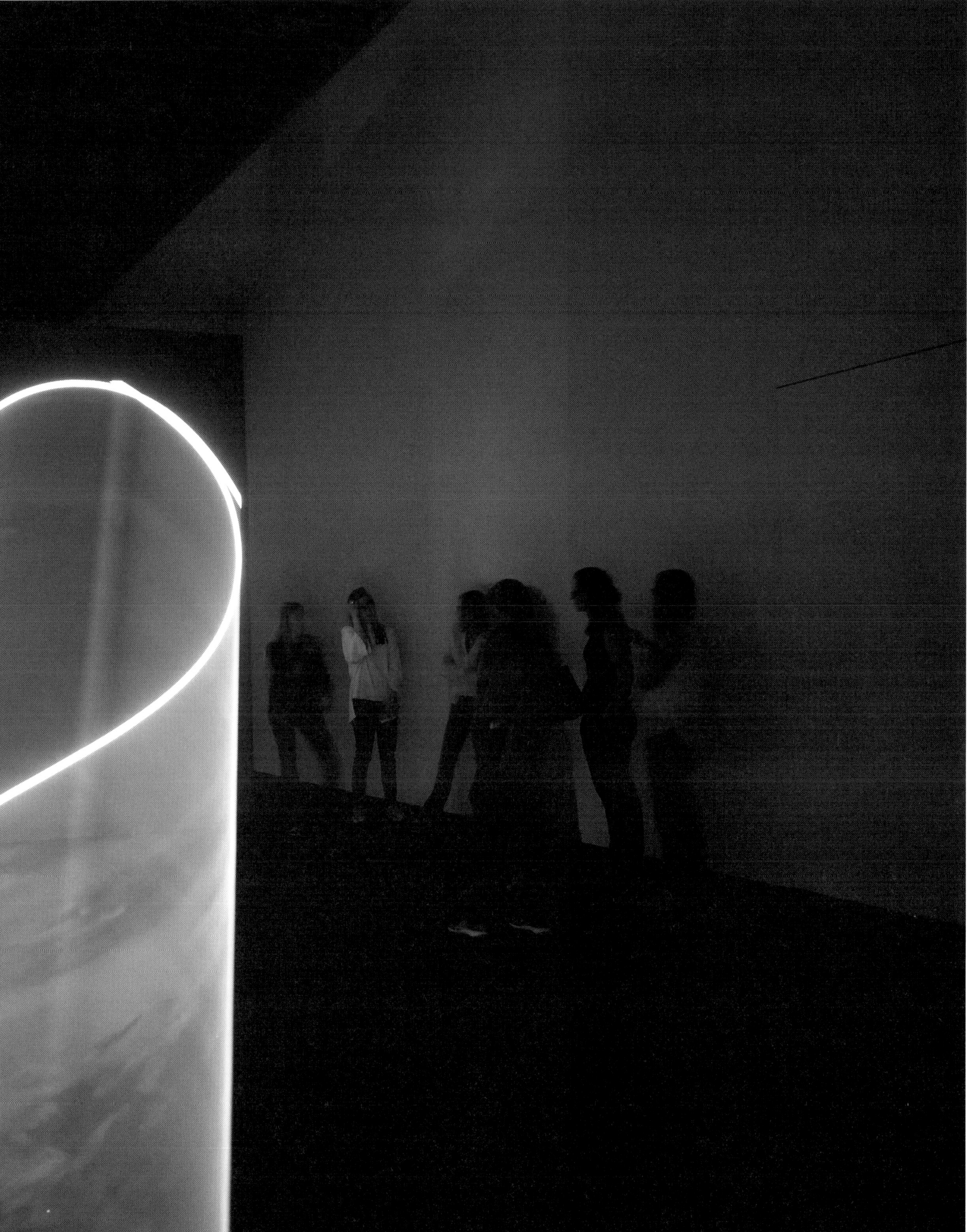

Anthony McCall. *Doubling Back*,
2003; main gallery: *Meeting You
Halfway*, 2009. Installation view,
Pioneer Works, New York, 2018.

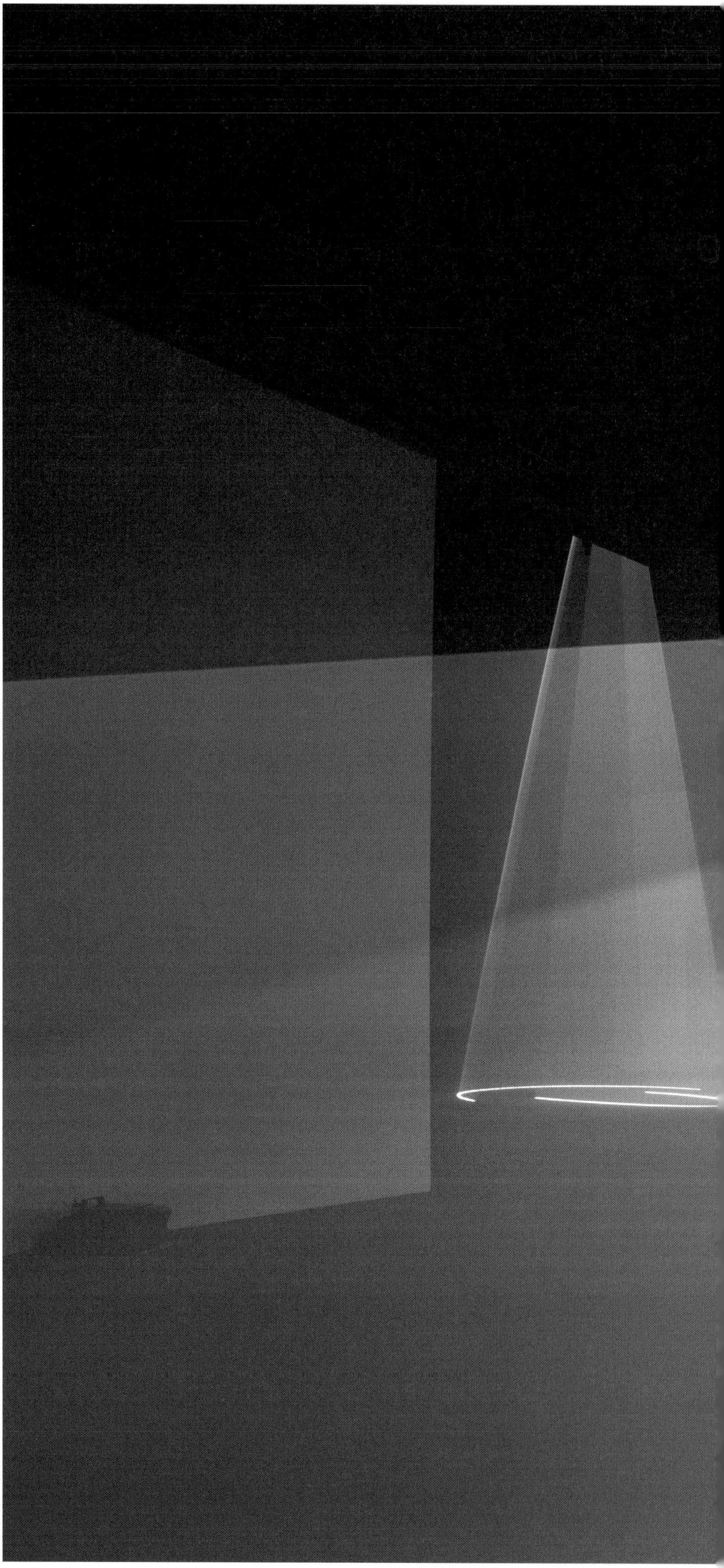

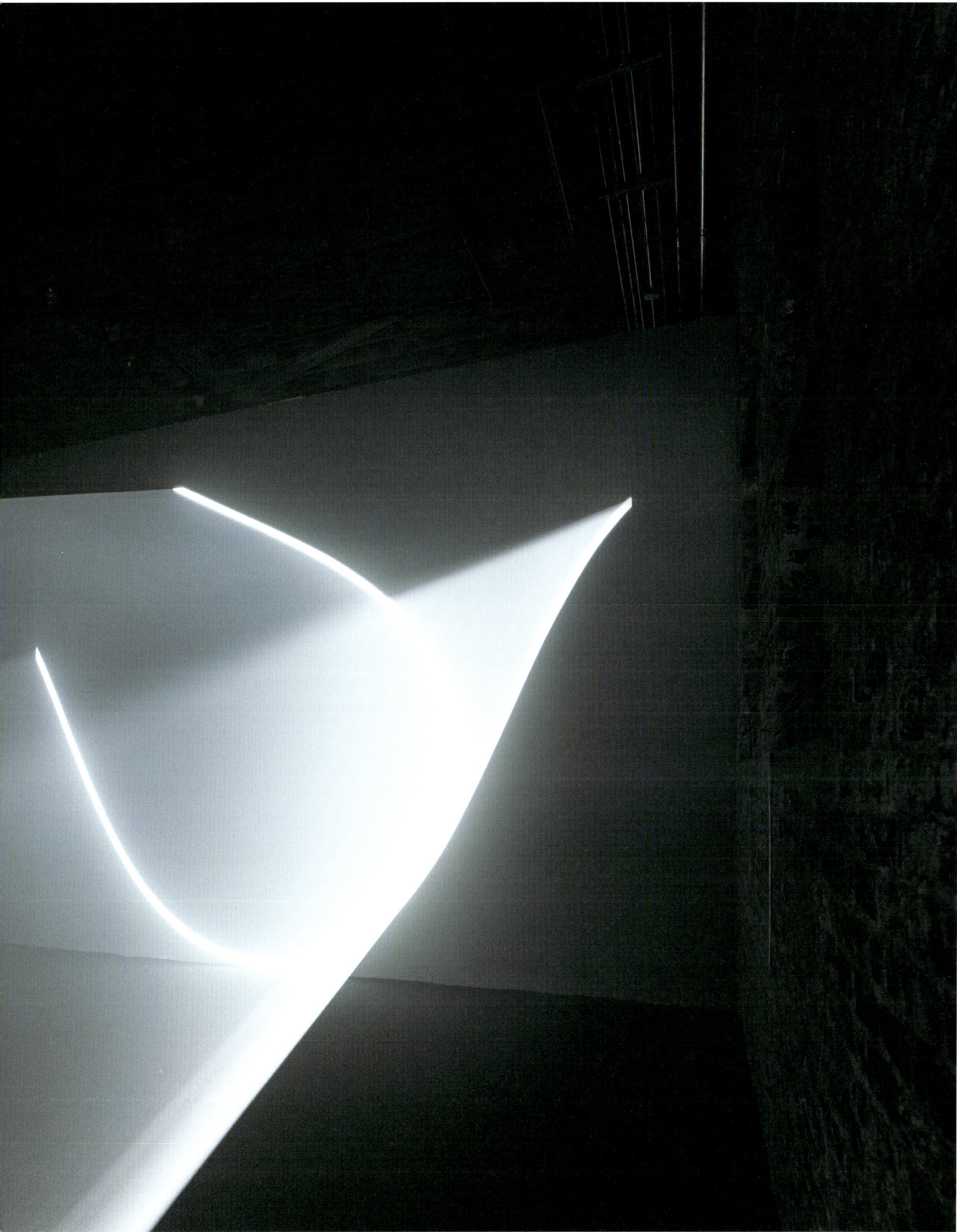

Anthony McCall. From front to back: *Skirt (III)*, 2010, *You and I (II)*, 2010, *Breath (III)*, 2005, *Meeting You Halfway*, 2009. Installation view, Pioneer Works, New York, 2018.

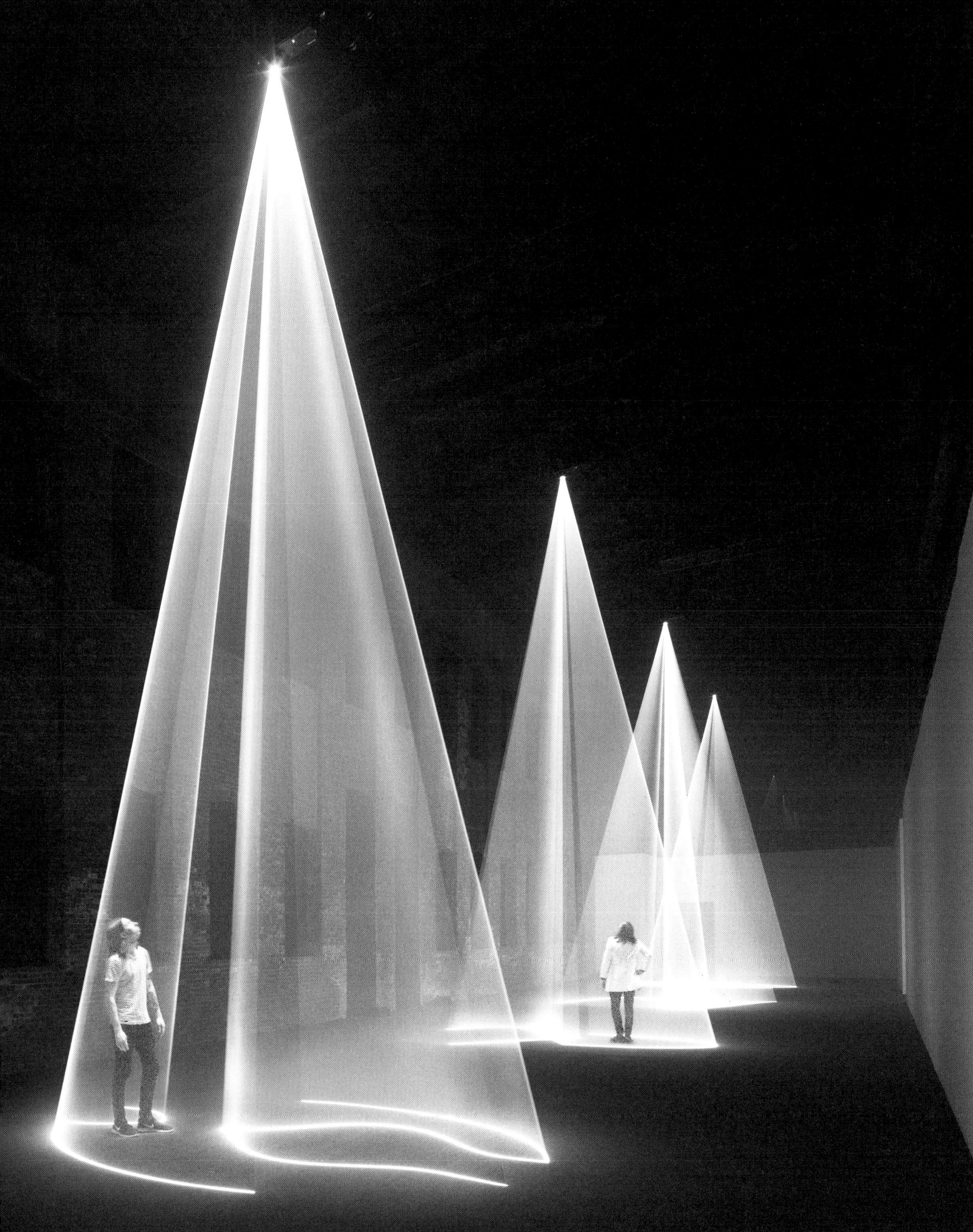

Anthony McCall. *Meeting You Halfway*, 2009. Installation view, Pioneer Works, New York, 2018.

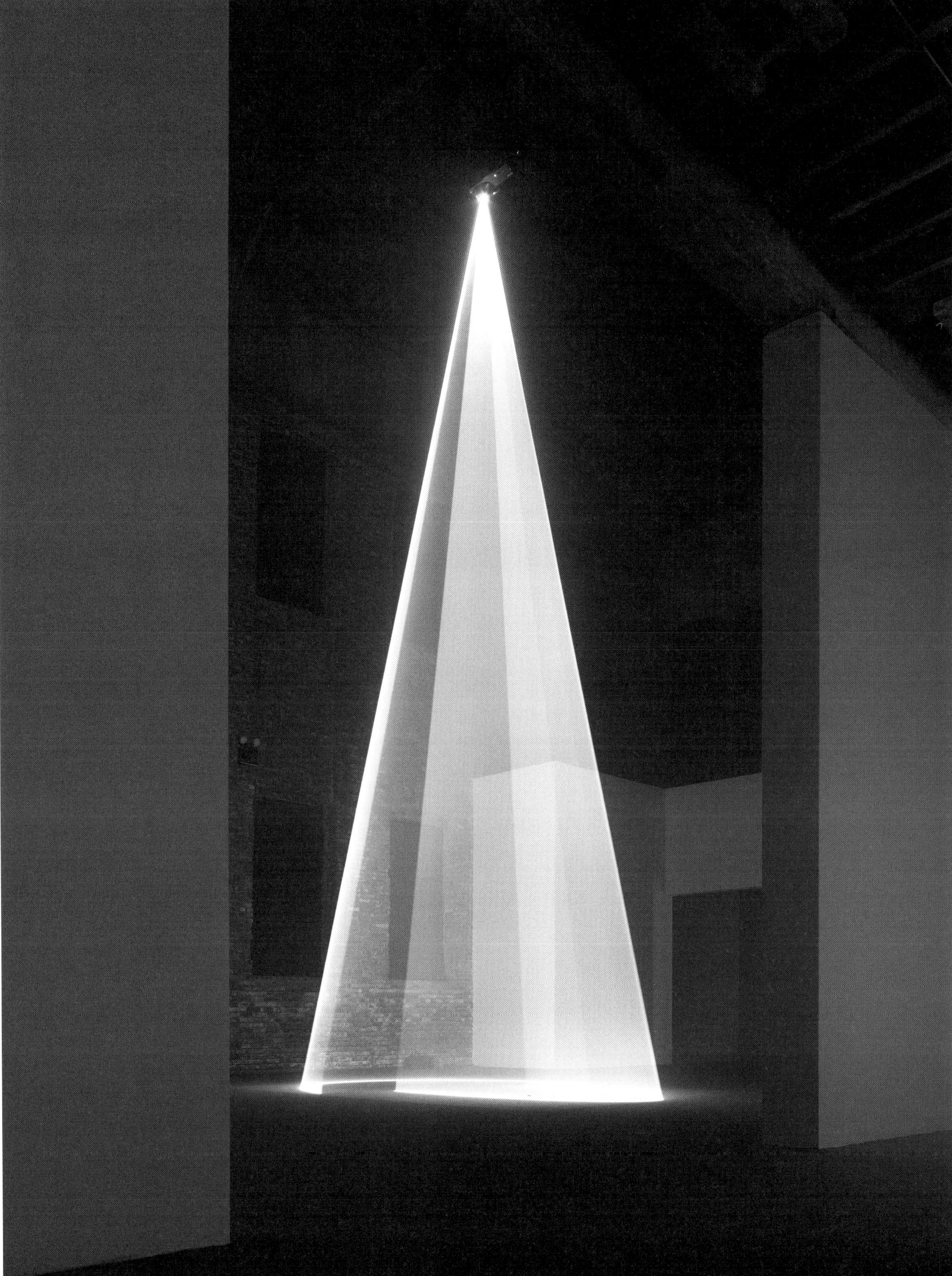

Anthony McCall. From left to right: *You and I, Horizontal*, 2005, *Breath (III)*, 2005. Installation view, Pioneer Works, New York, 2018.

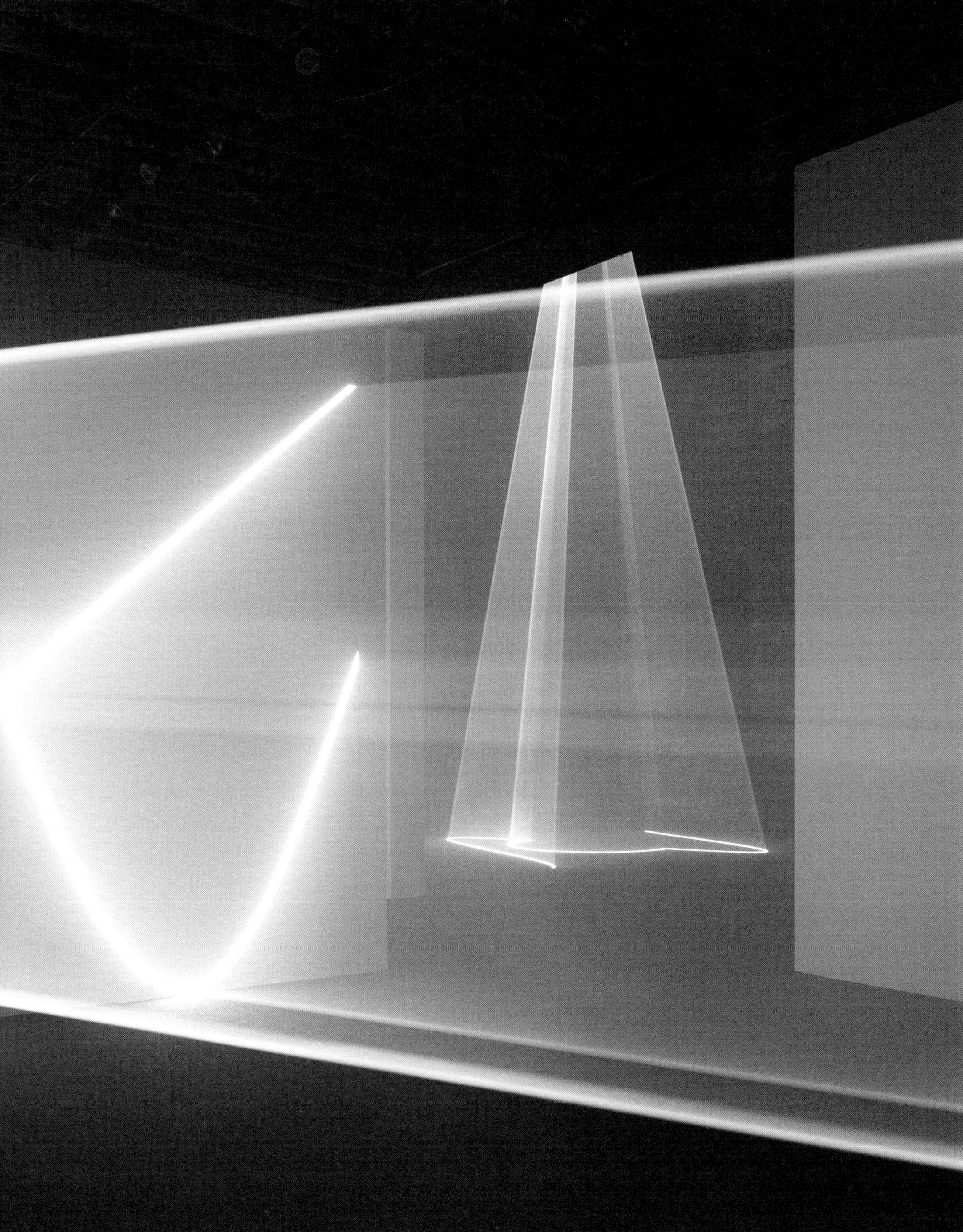

Anthony McCall. From front to back: *Skirt (III)*, 2010, *You and I (II)*, 2010, *Breath (III)*, 2005, *Meeting You Halfway*, 2009. Installation view, Pioneer Works, New York, 2018.

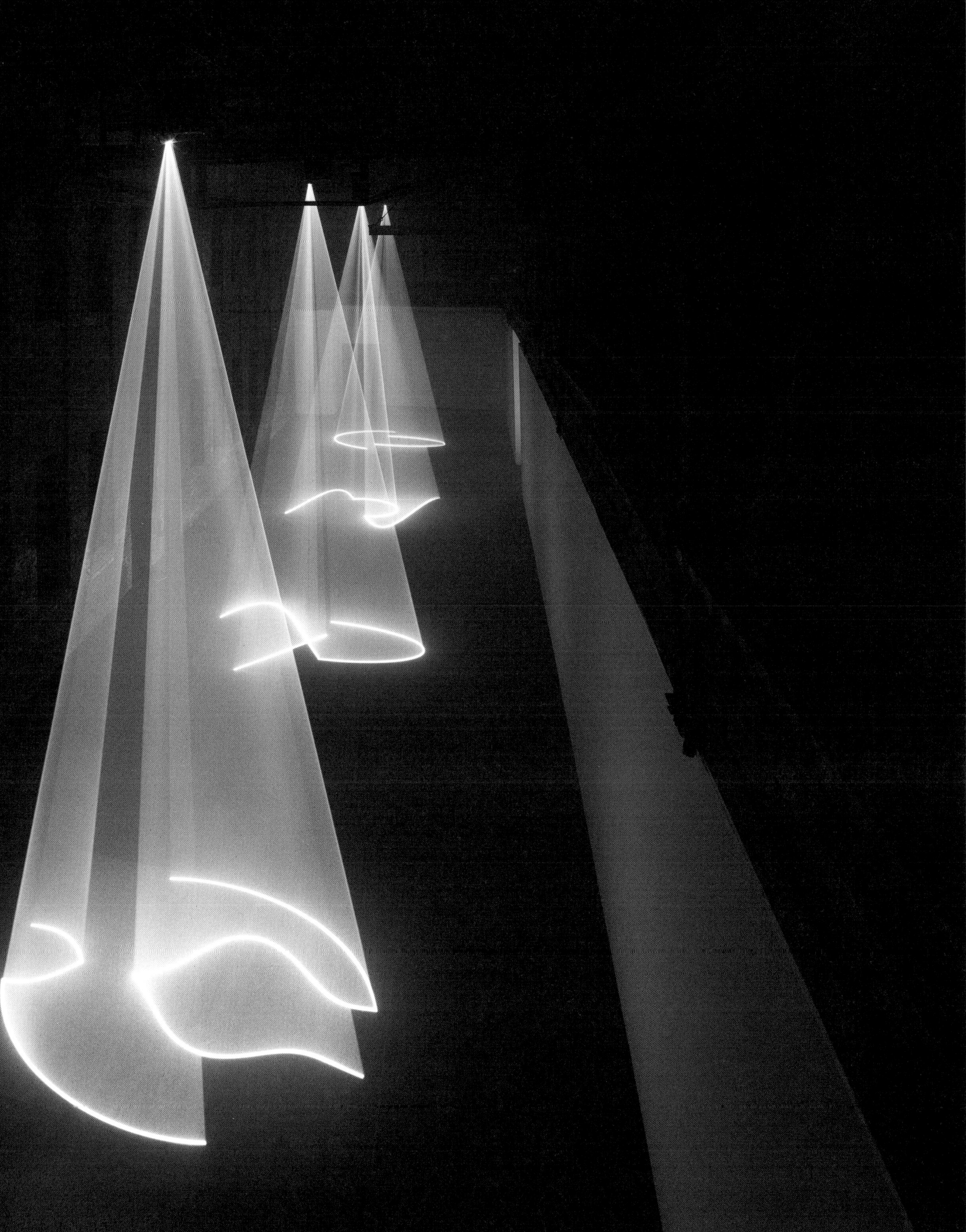

Anthony McCall. *Skirt (III)*, 2010.
Installation view, Pioneer Works,
New York, 2018.

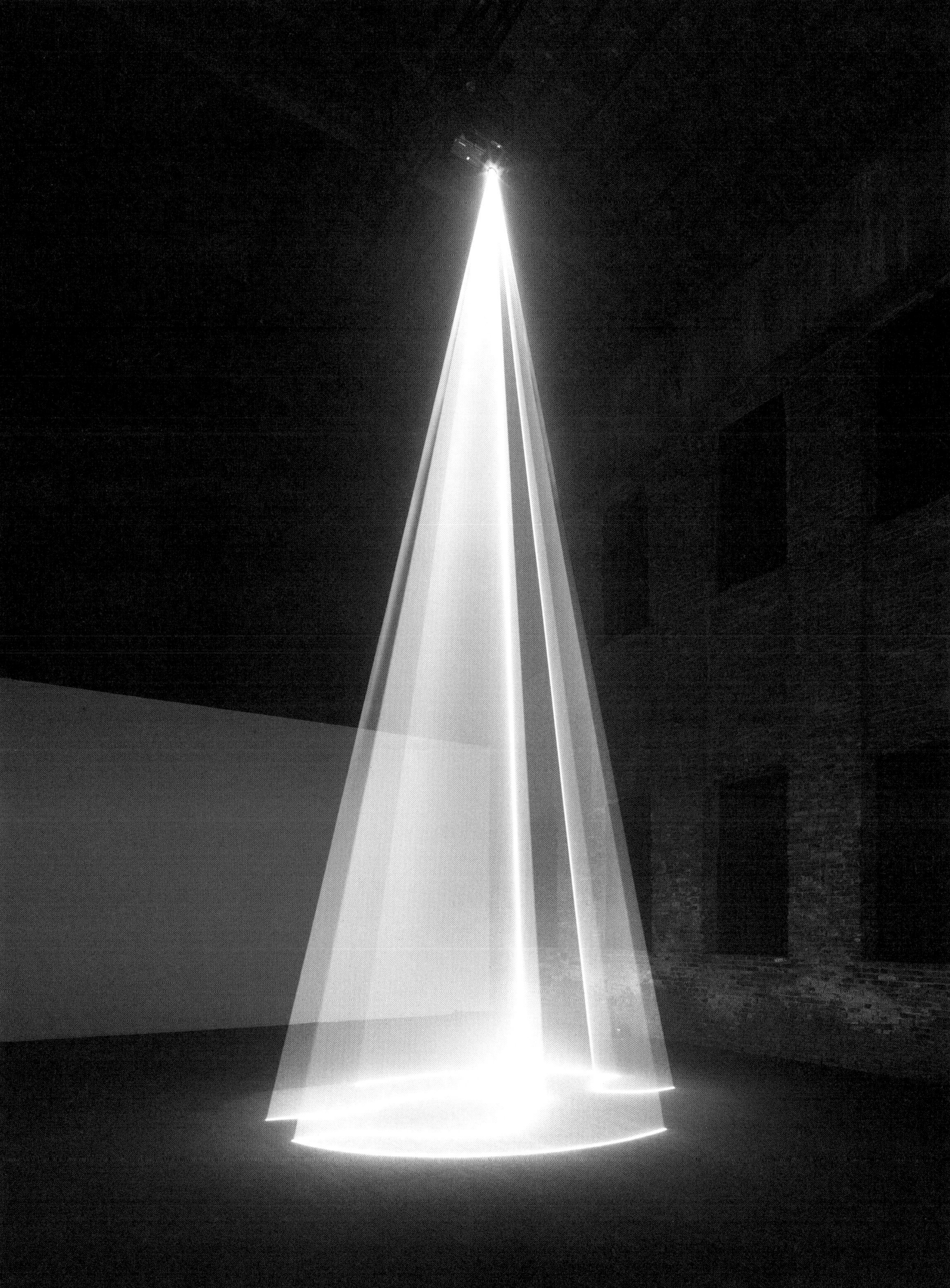

Solid Light Works:
Social Media Images

A.   @xtinaedwards
B.   @akilathebasenji
C.   @arina_curly

A

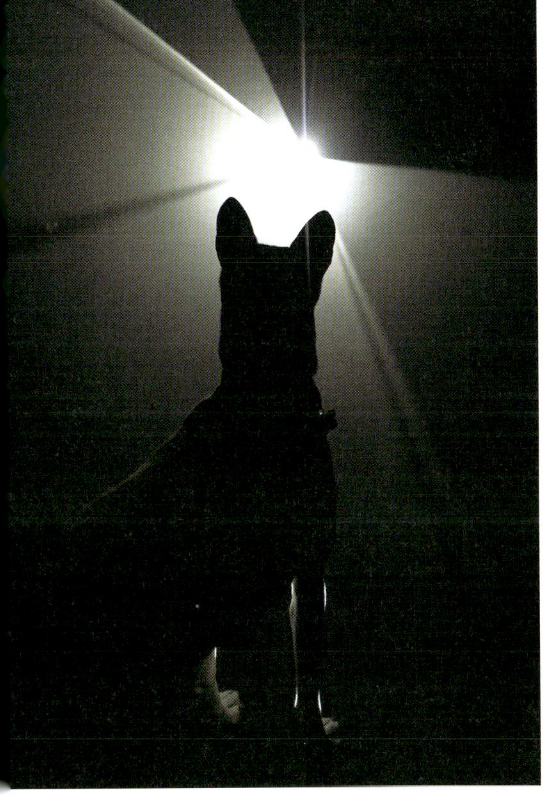

B

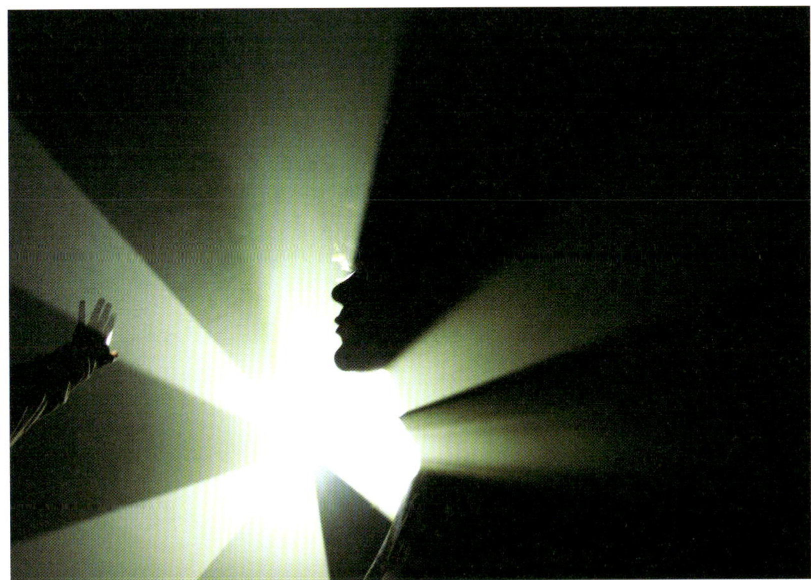

C

A. @pasagiae
B. @tommyvobot
C. @roanedwards
D. @eradf
E. @joshgreenspan

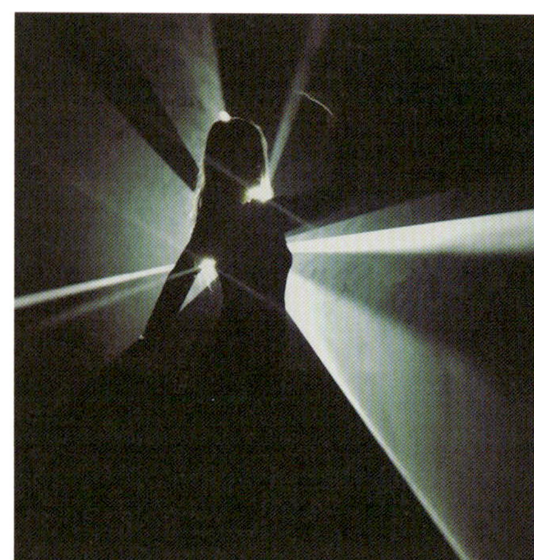

A

B

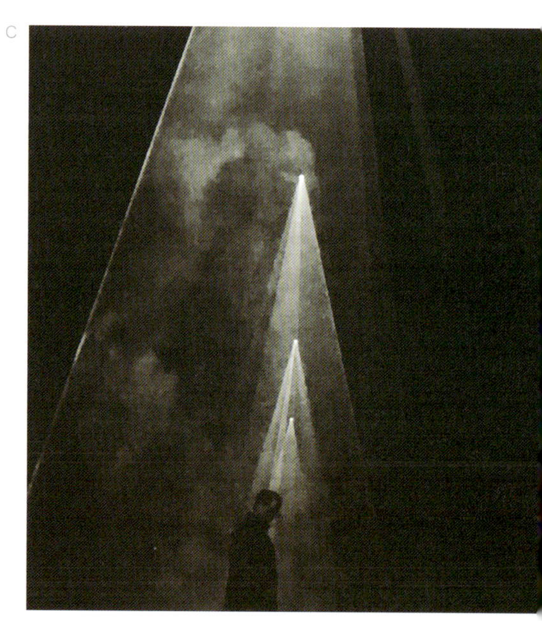

C

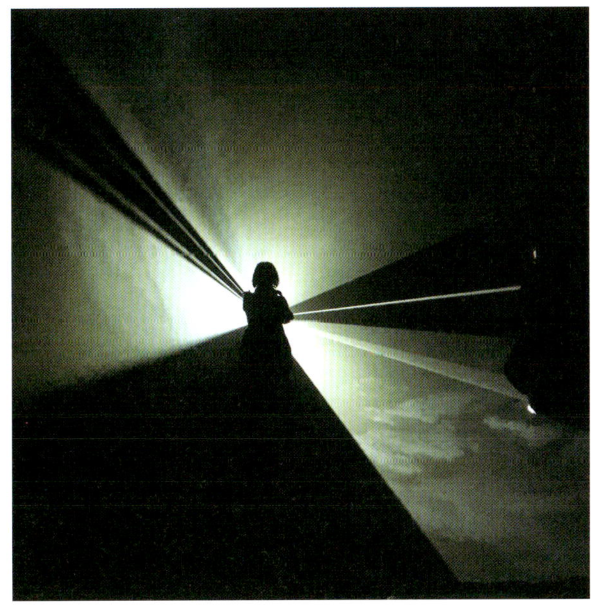

D

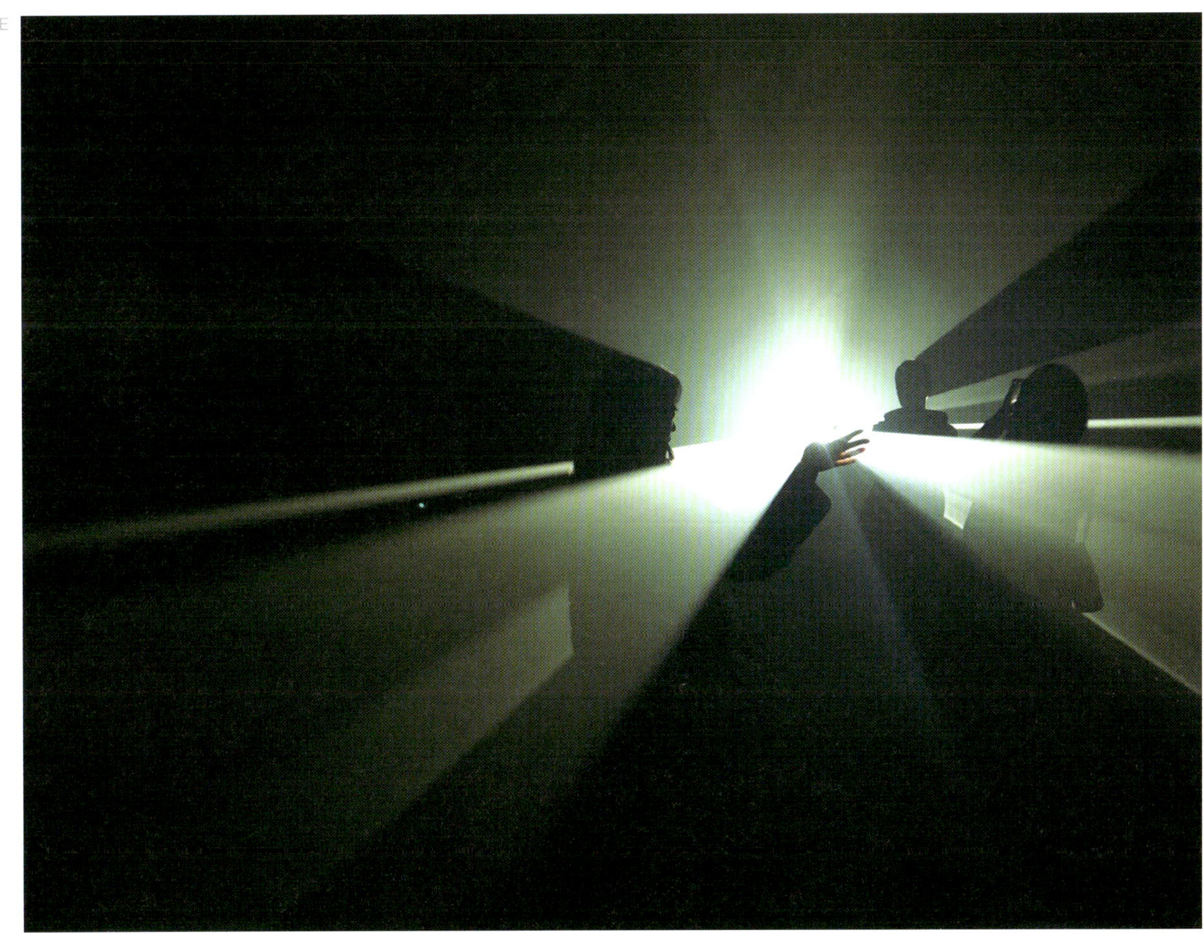

E

A. @bchasebchase
B. @koca_kola_inc
C. @pasagiae
D. @tommyvobot
E. @_s_v_e_v_a_16

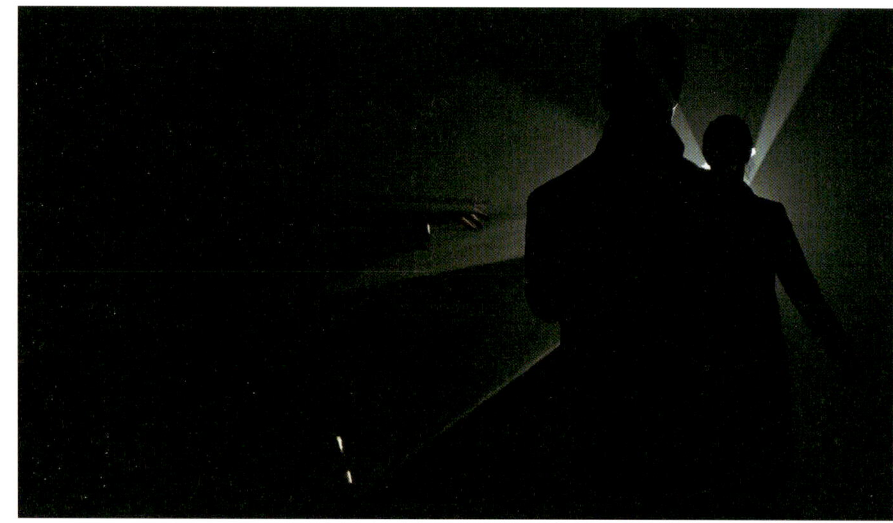

A

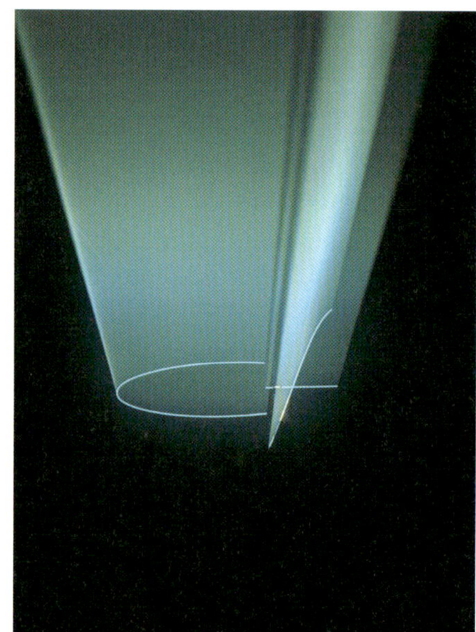

B

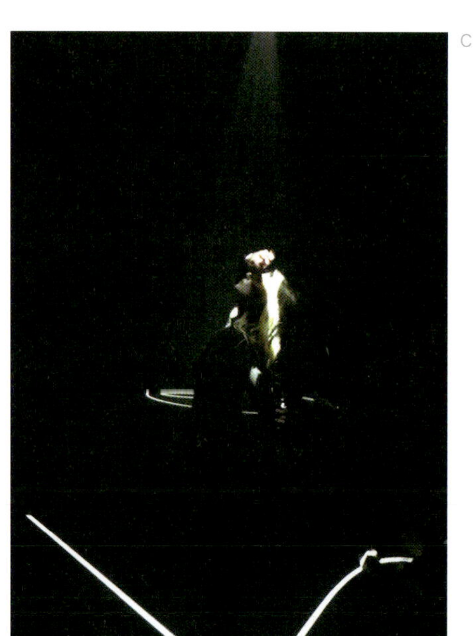

C

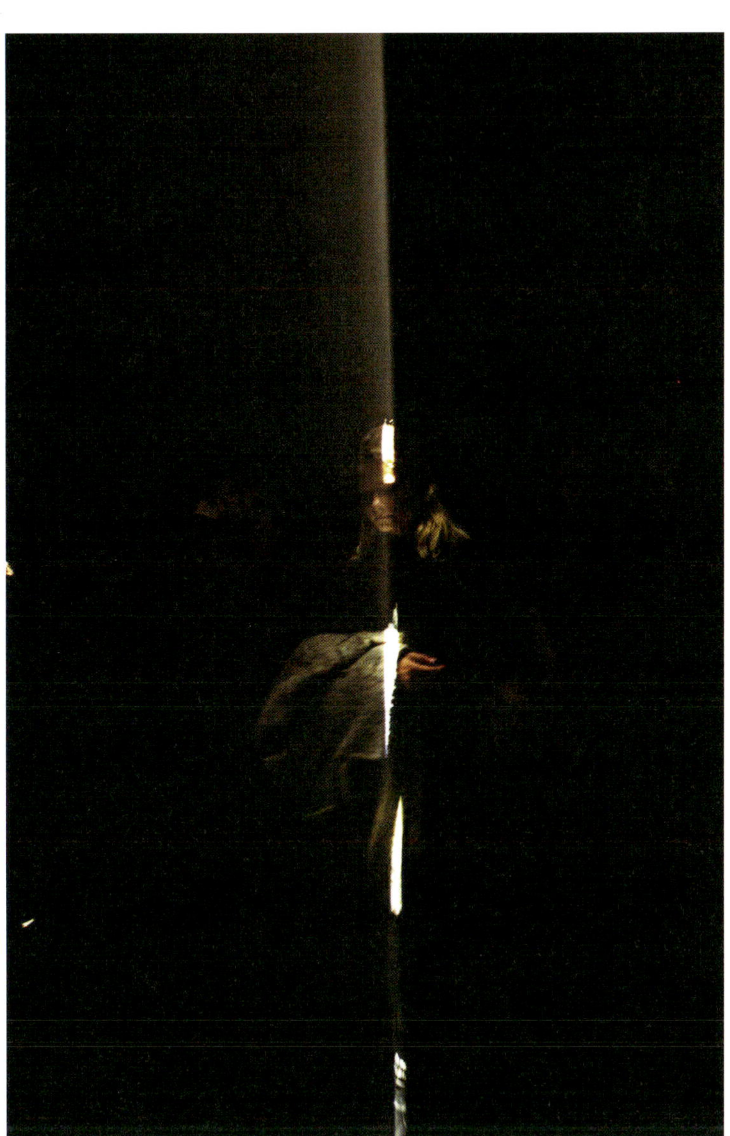

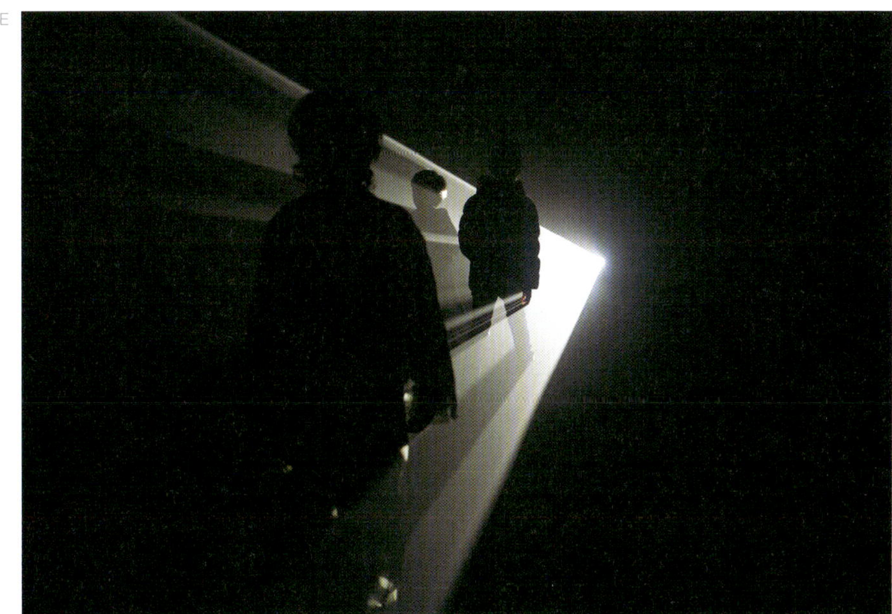

A. @pasagiae
B. @hamrahrama
C. @pasagiae
D. @ycsekmen
E. @bchasebchase

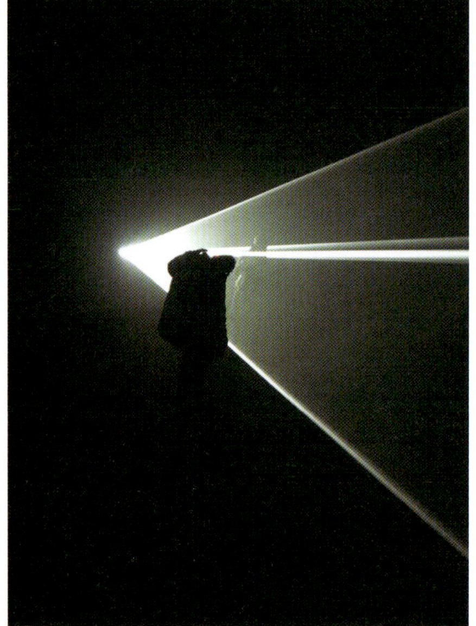

B

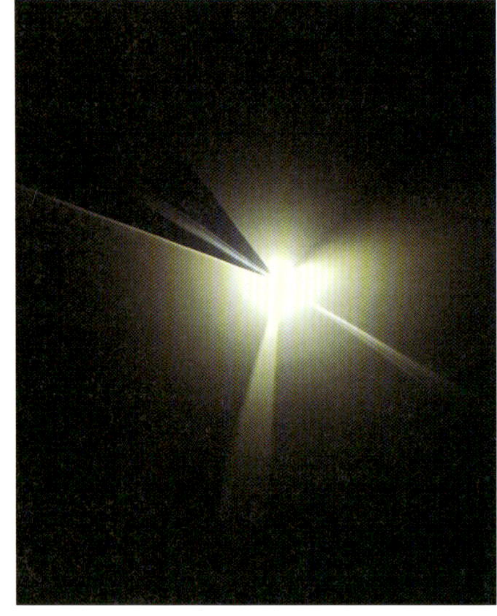

A

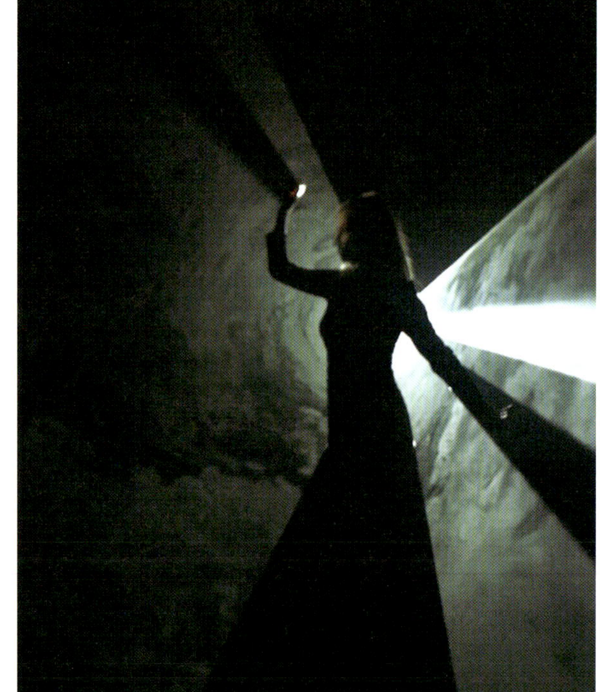

C

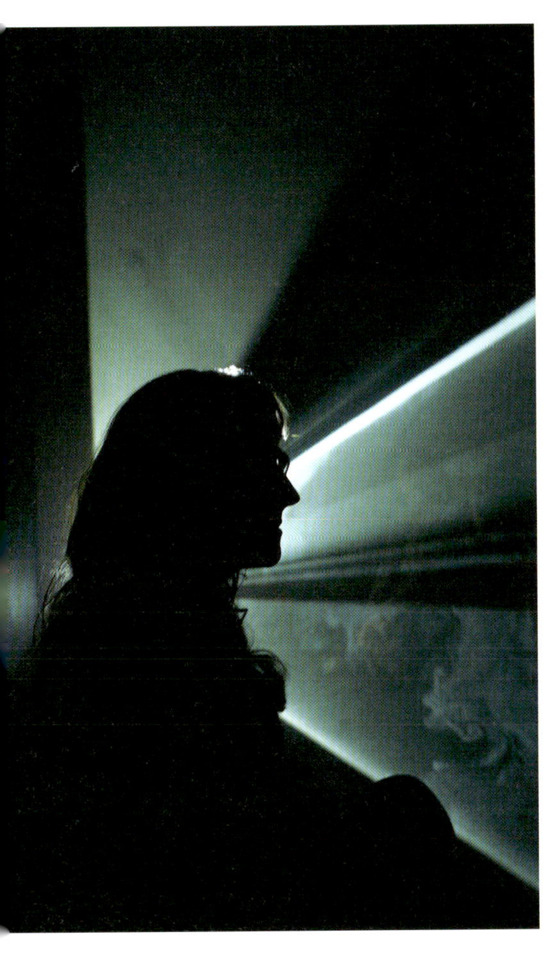

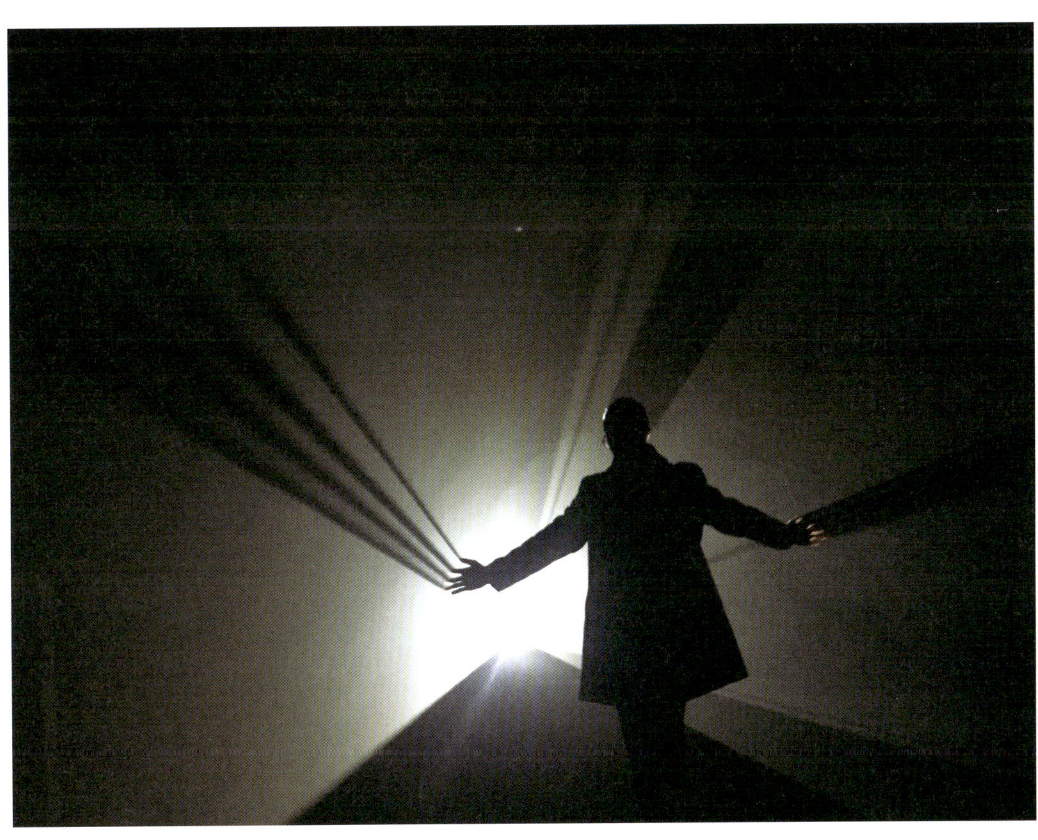

A. @pascalperich
B. @tommyvobot
C. @jayb.us
D. @arina_curly
E. @mudnuts

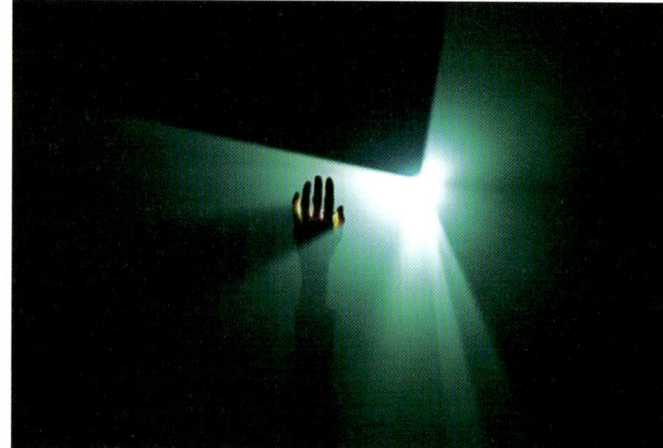

A

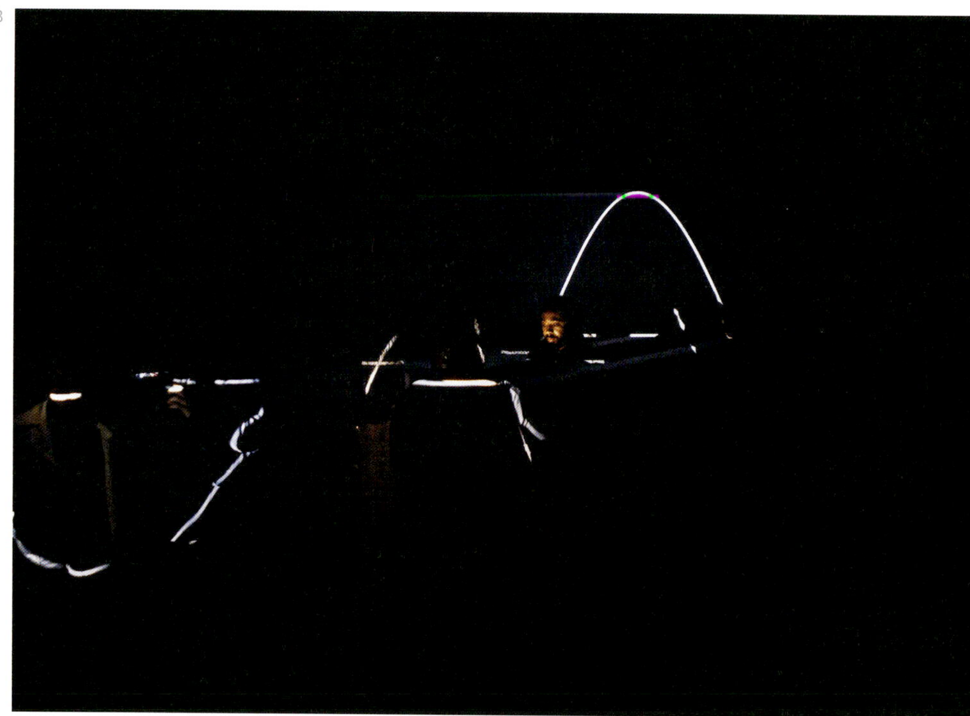

B

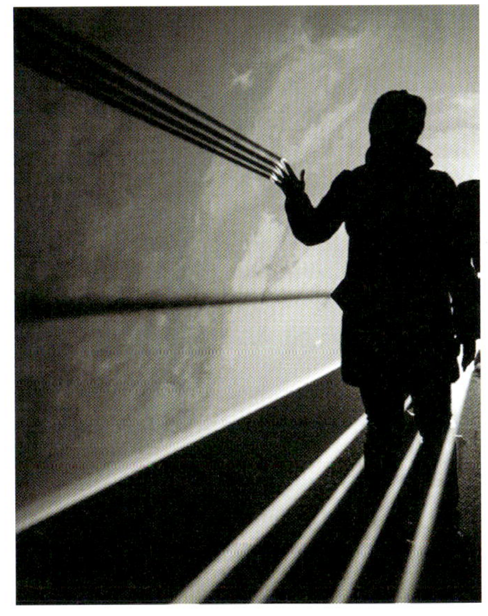

C

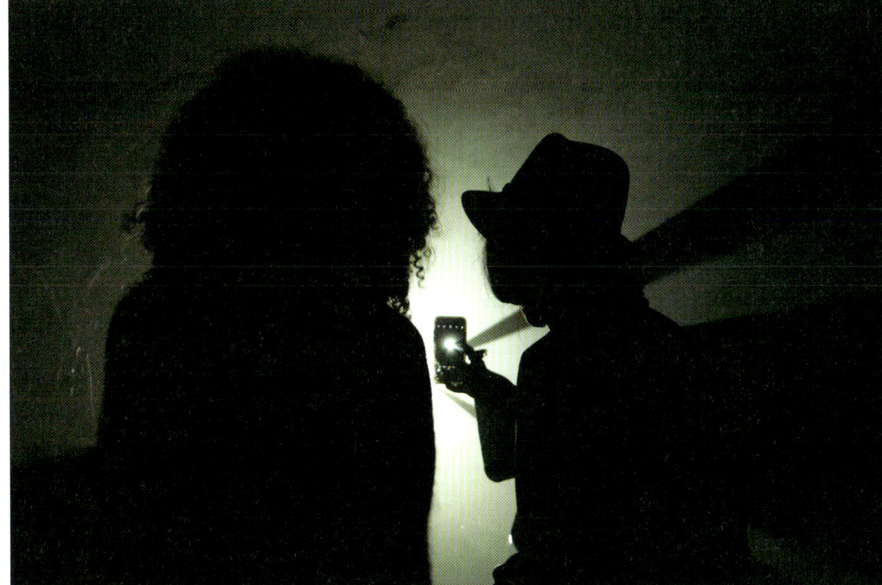

D

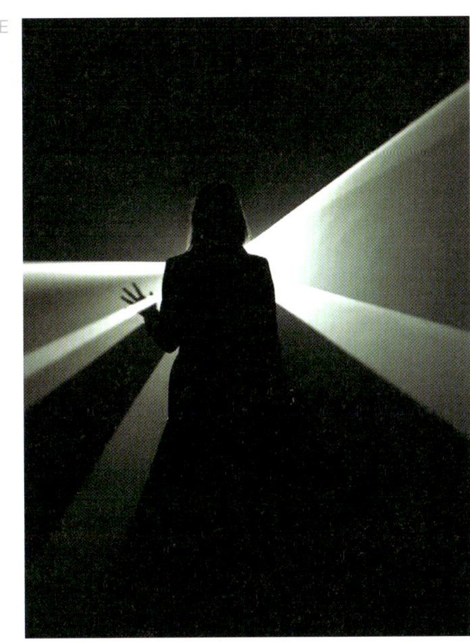

E

A. @xtinaedwards
B. @_s_v_e_v_a_16
C. @koca_kola_inc
D. @pascalperich
E. @pasagiae

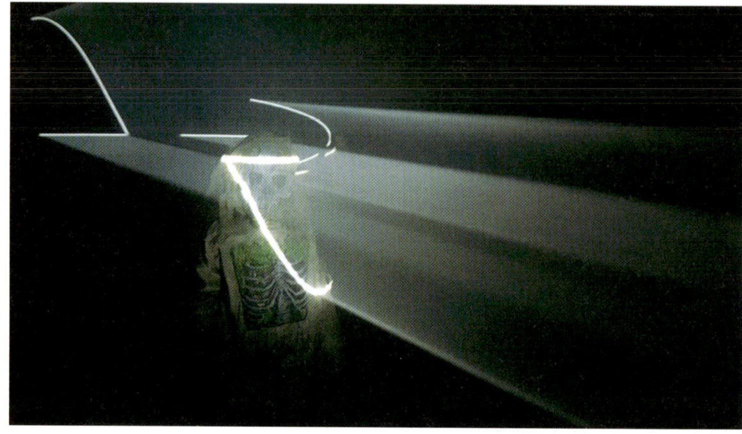

B

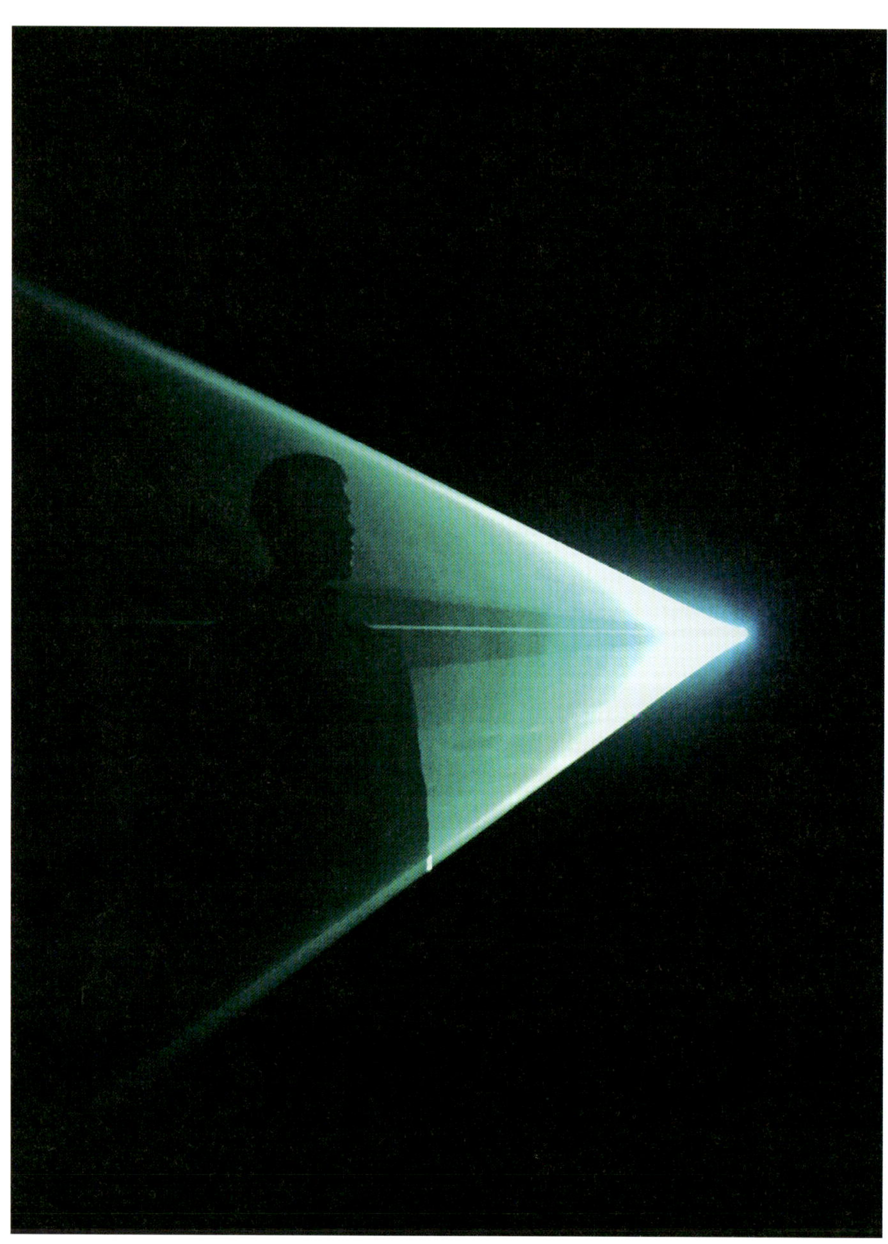

A

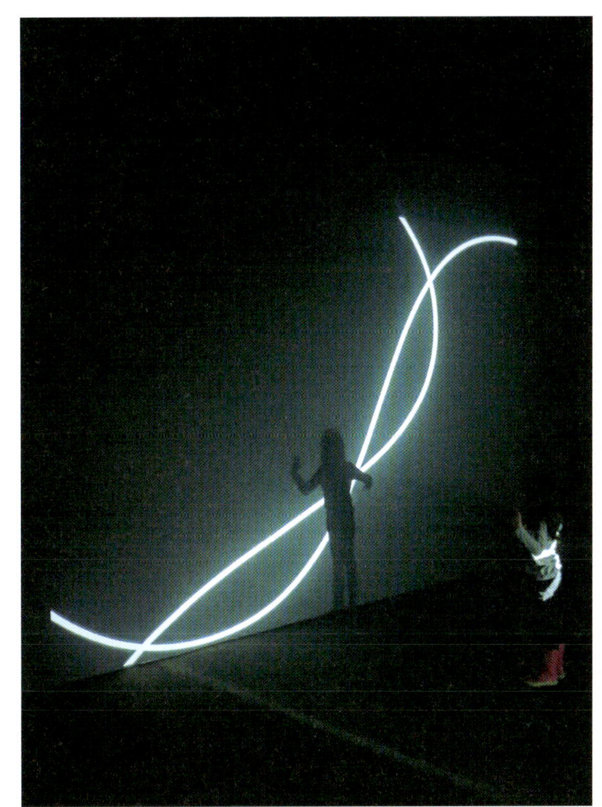

C

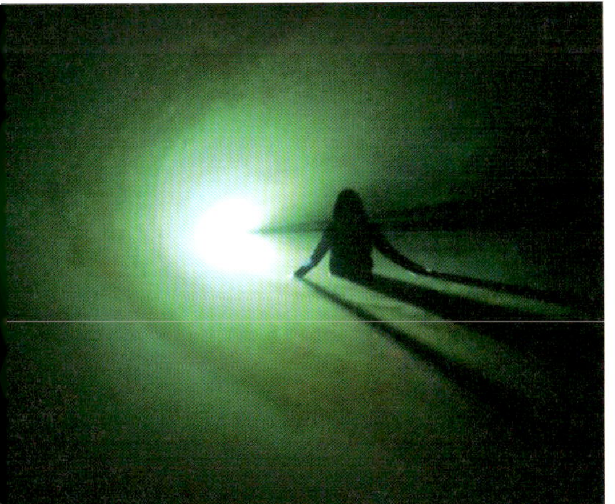

D

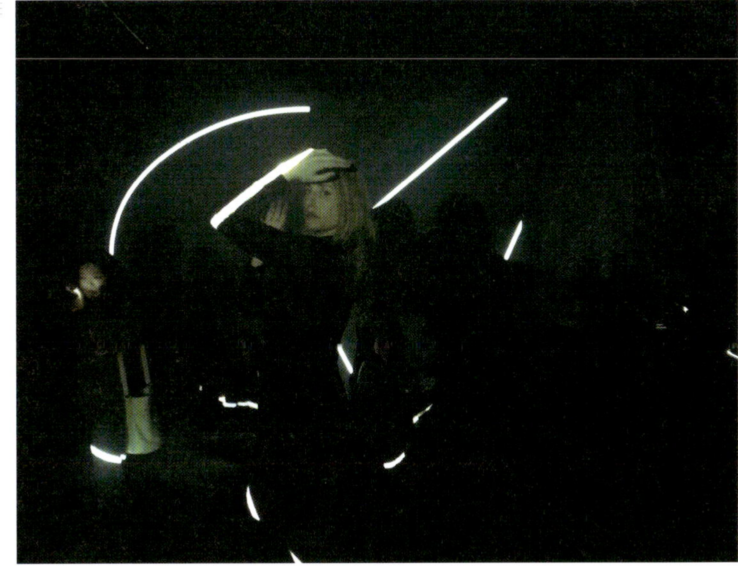

E

A. @joshgreenspan
B. @_reneecrowley_
C. @xin_liu_studio
D. @embonchi
E. @travisraustin

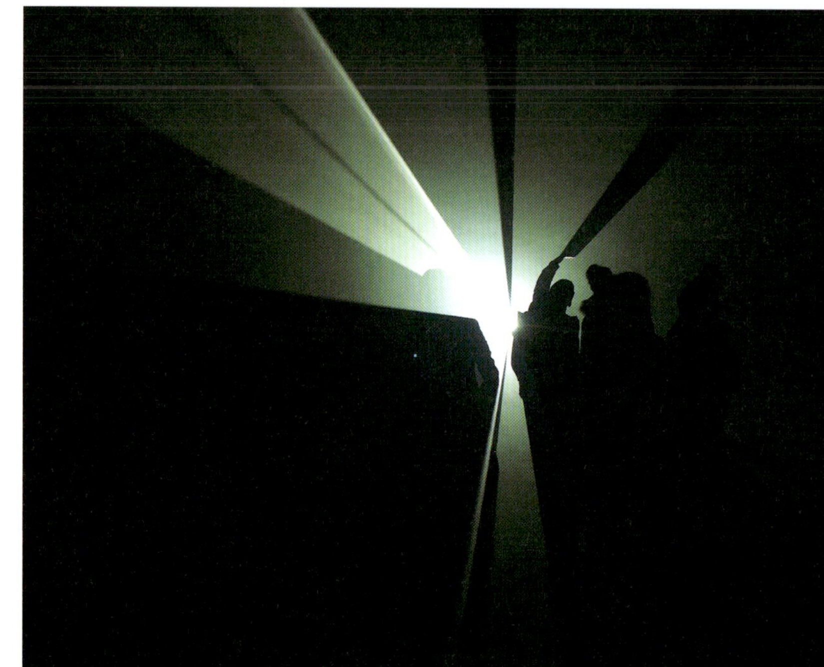

A

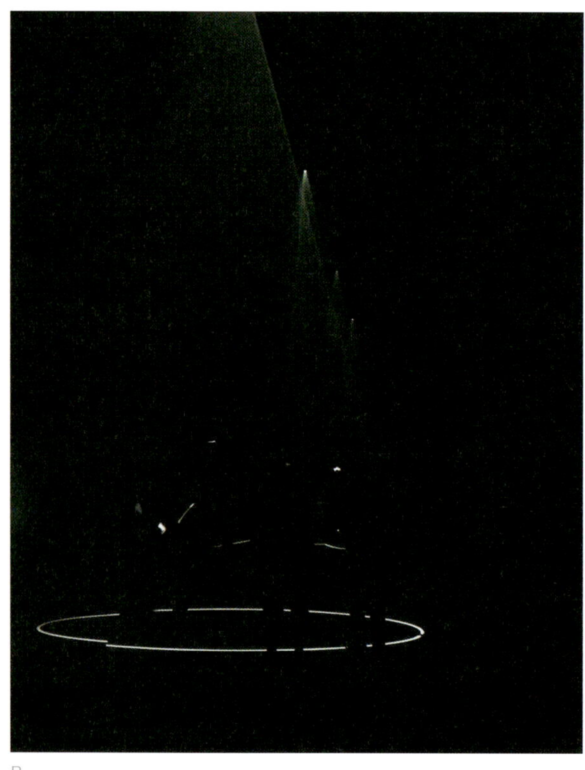

B

C

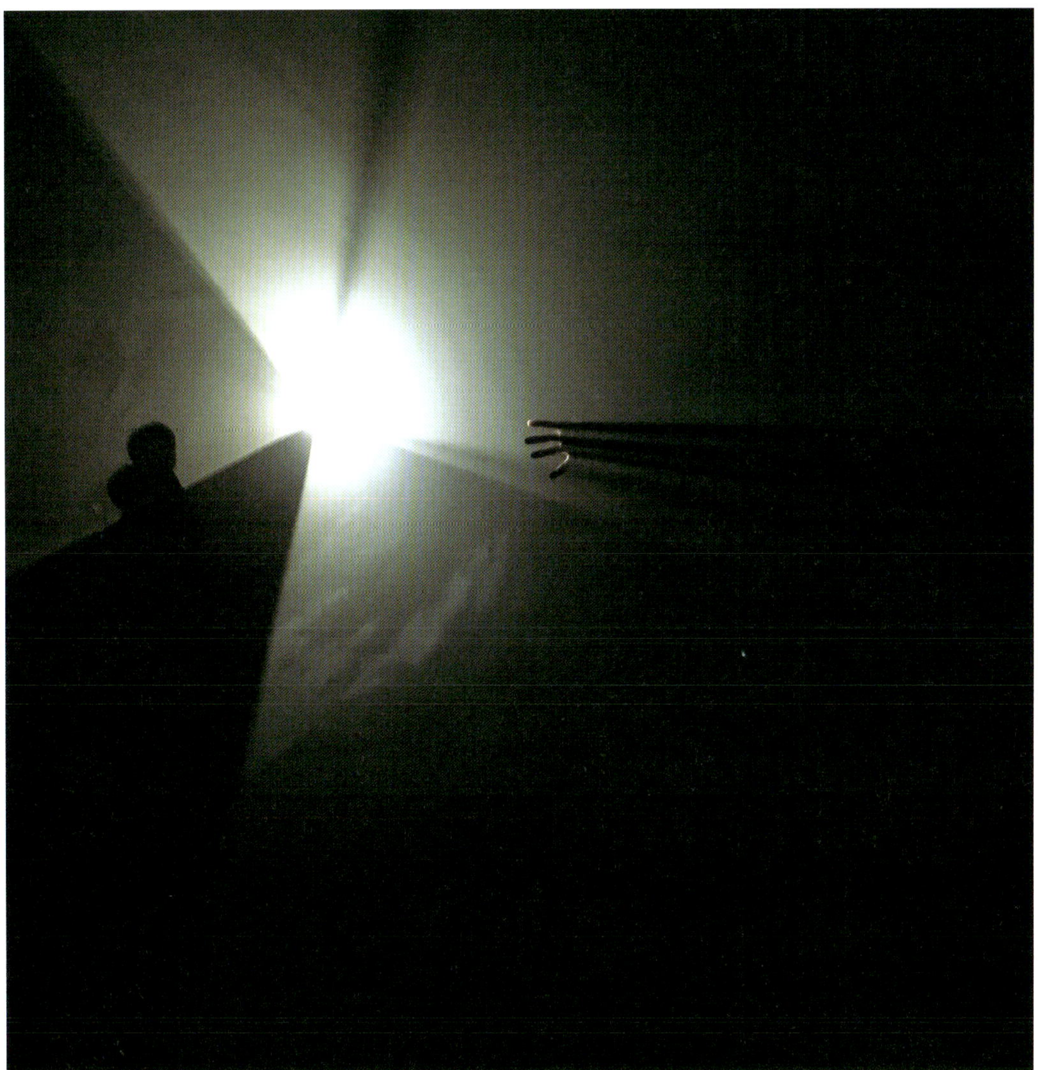

E

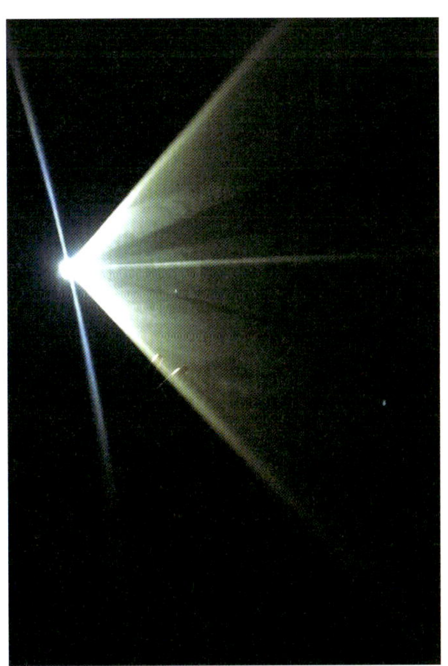

D

A.   @pascalperich
B.   @arina_curly
C.   @thehive
D.   @hamrahrama
E.   @koca_kola_inc.

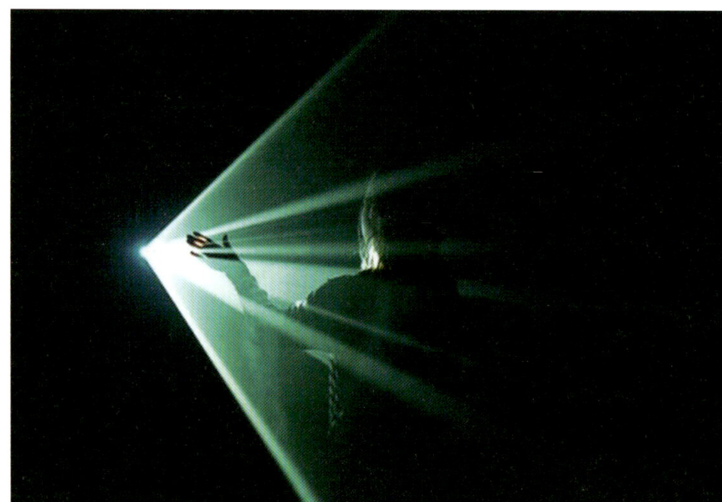

A

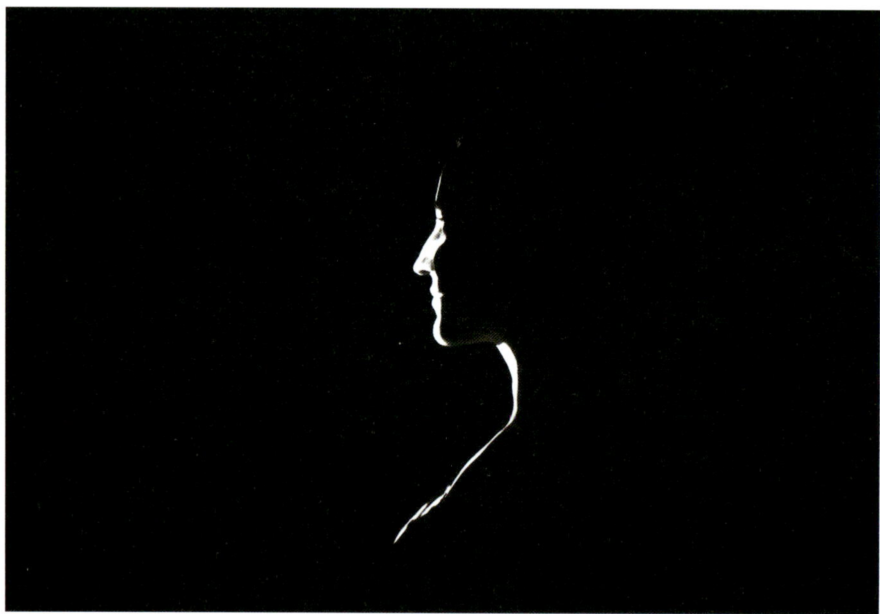

B

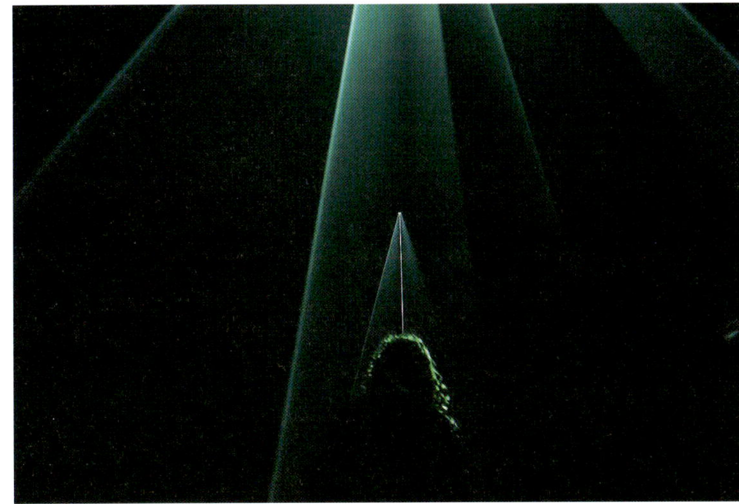

C

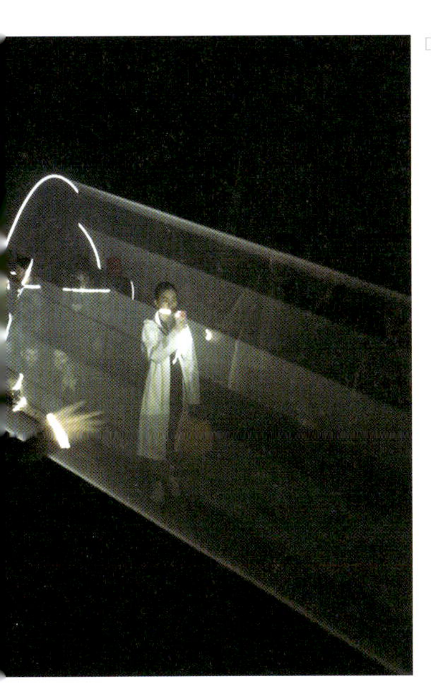

D

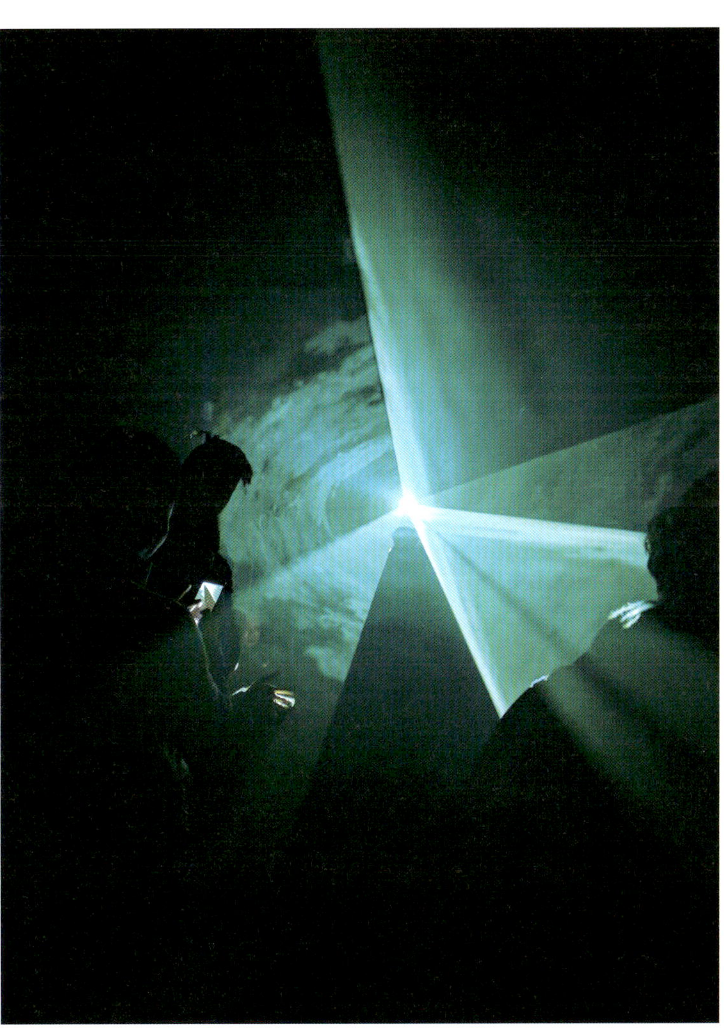

E

Anthony McCall. *Skirt (III)*, 2010.
Footprint sequence at 200-
second intervals, 2011.

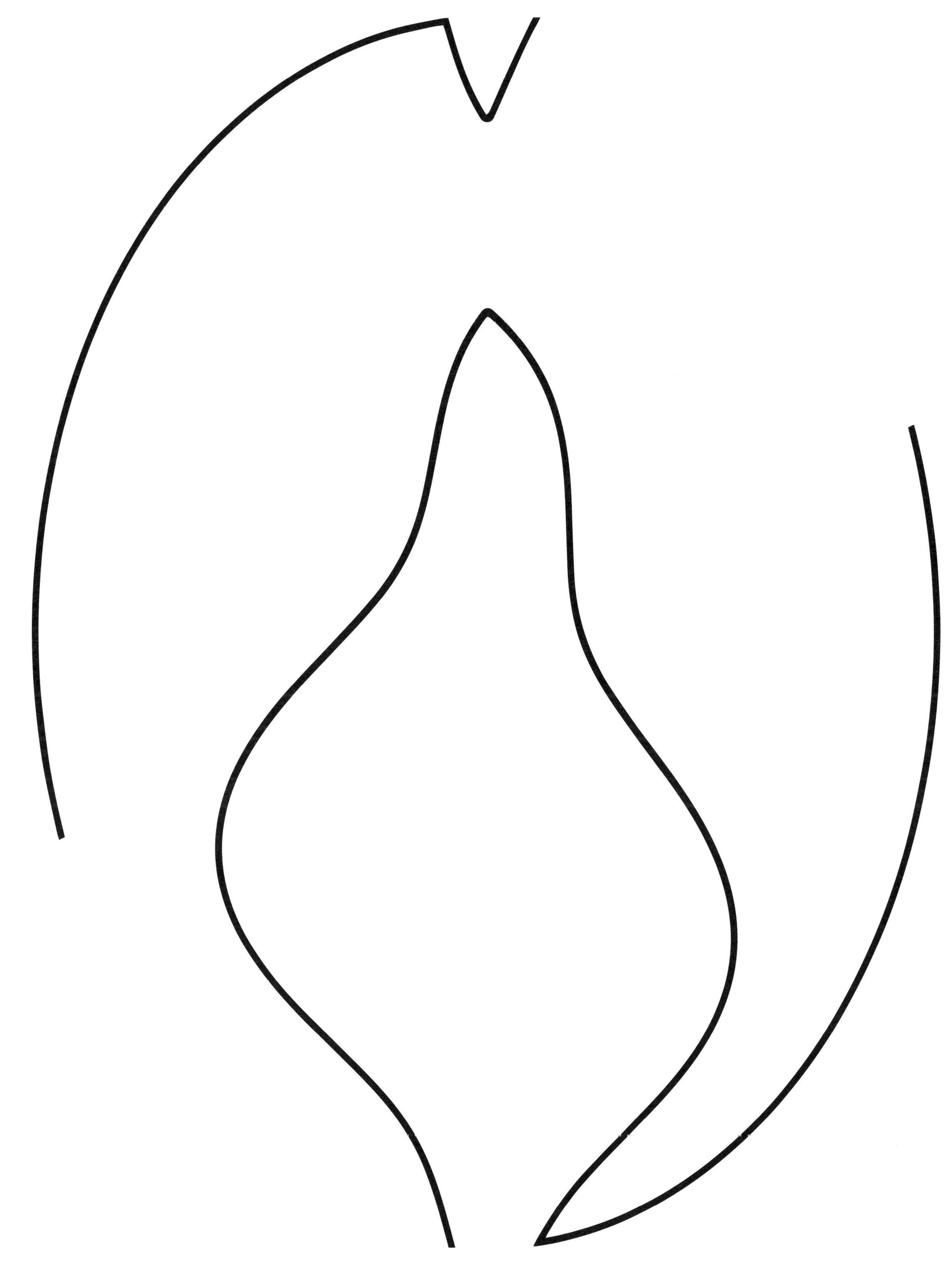

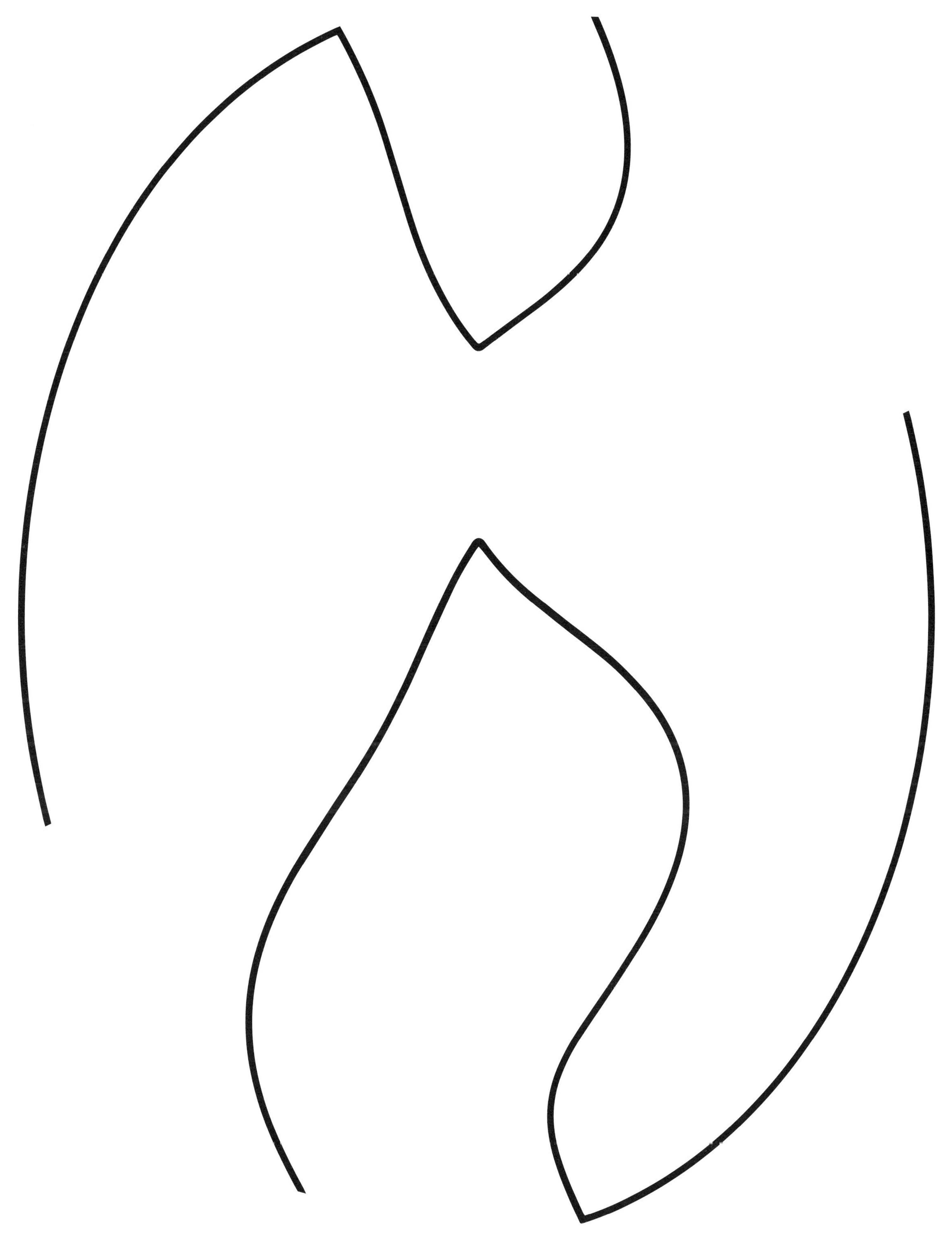

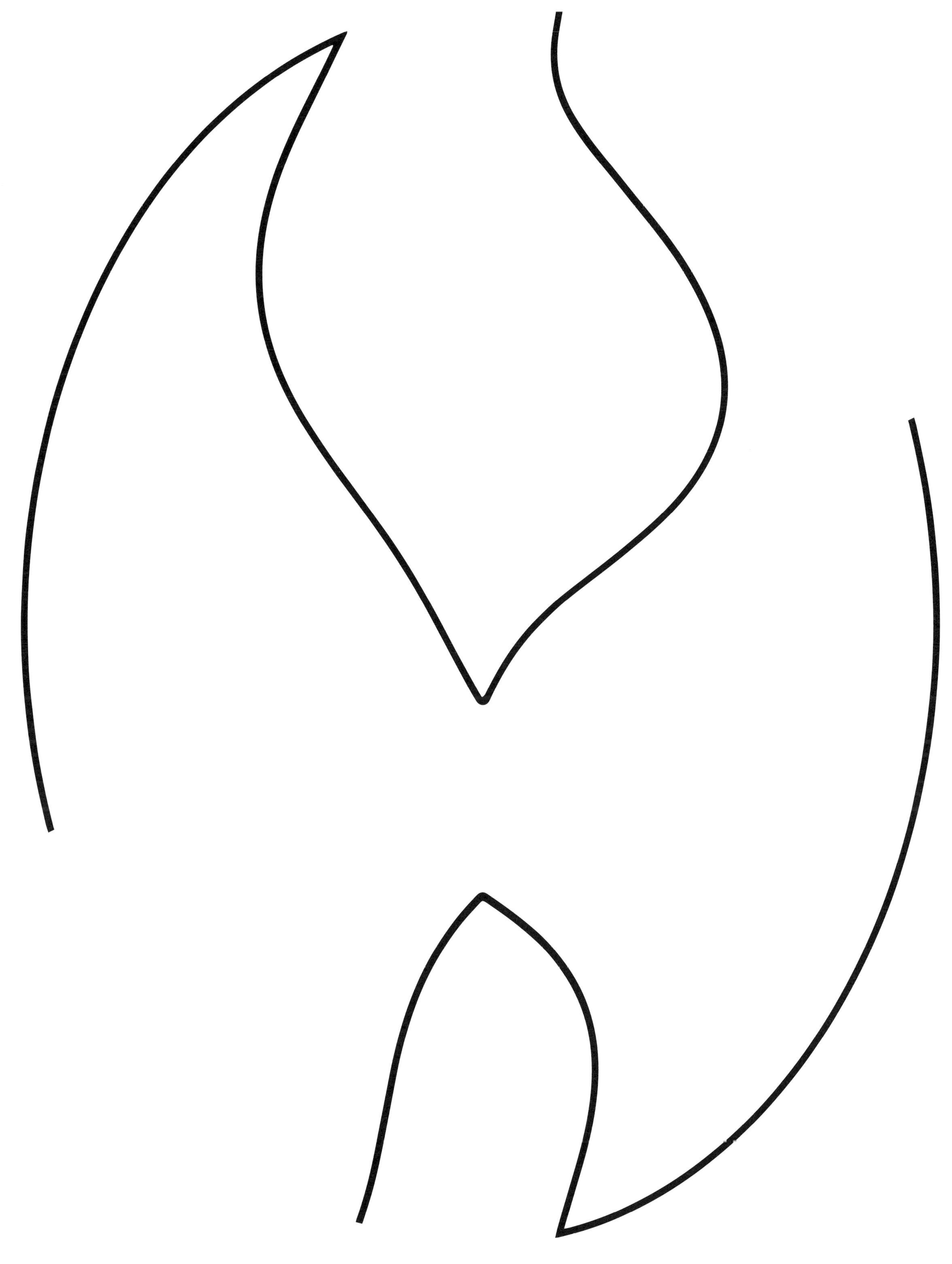

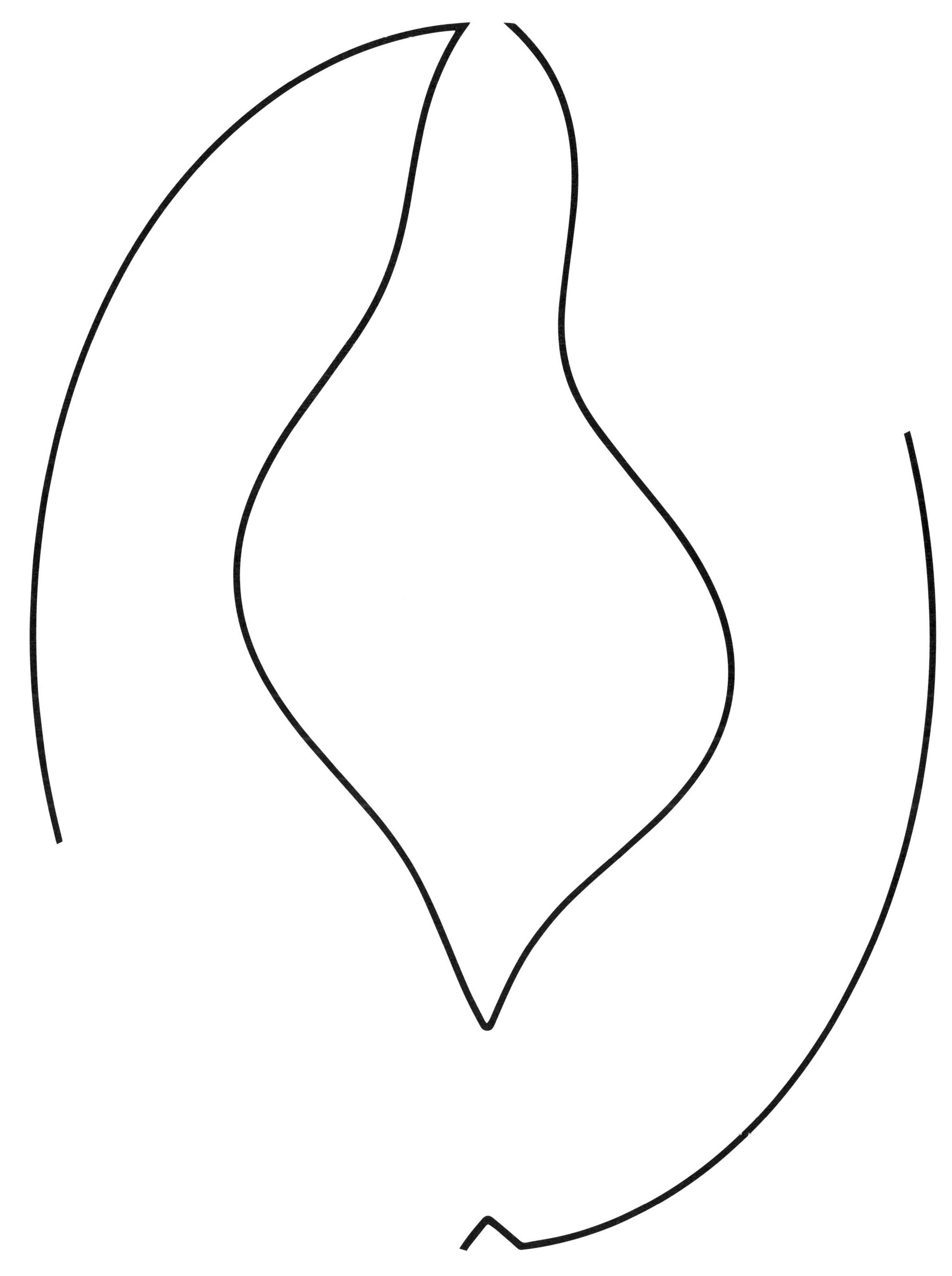

Musicians in Position

1. C. Spencer Yeh
    Violin & voice
2. Maria Chavez
    Turntable
3. David Grubbs
    Electric guitar
4. Sarah Hennies
    Vibraphone

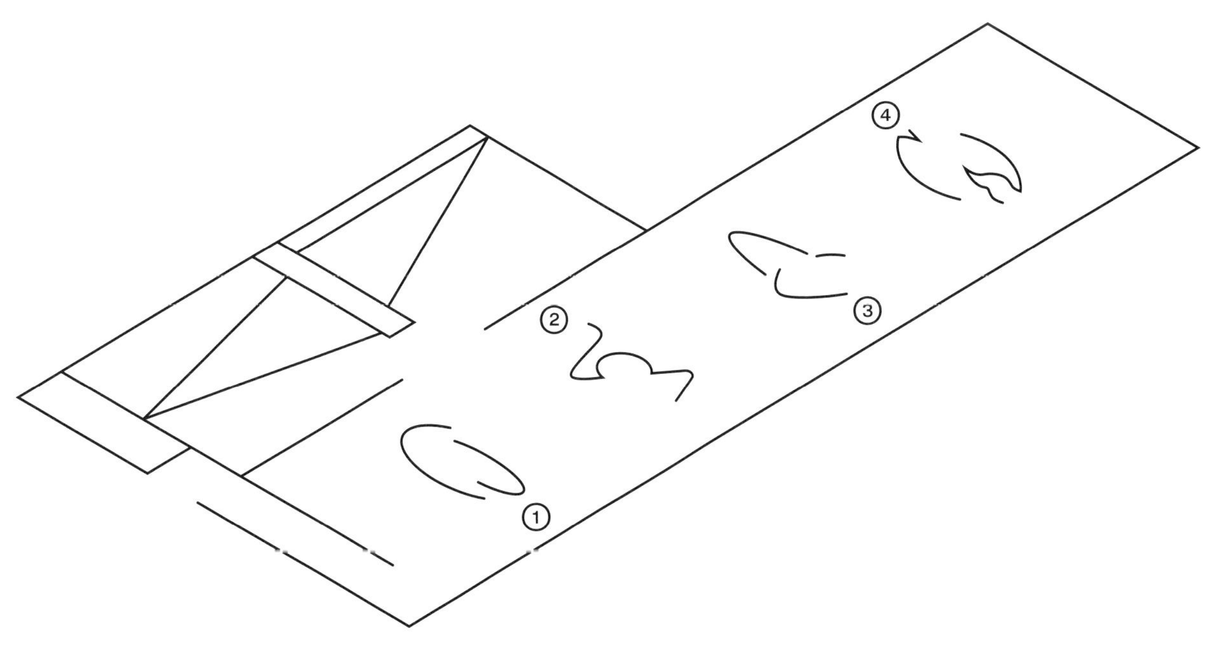

1. Susan Alcorn
    Pedal steel guitar
2. Nate Wooley
    Trumpet
3. Tomeka Reid
    Cello
4. Eli Keszler
    Drums & percussion

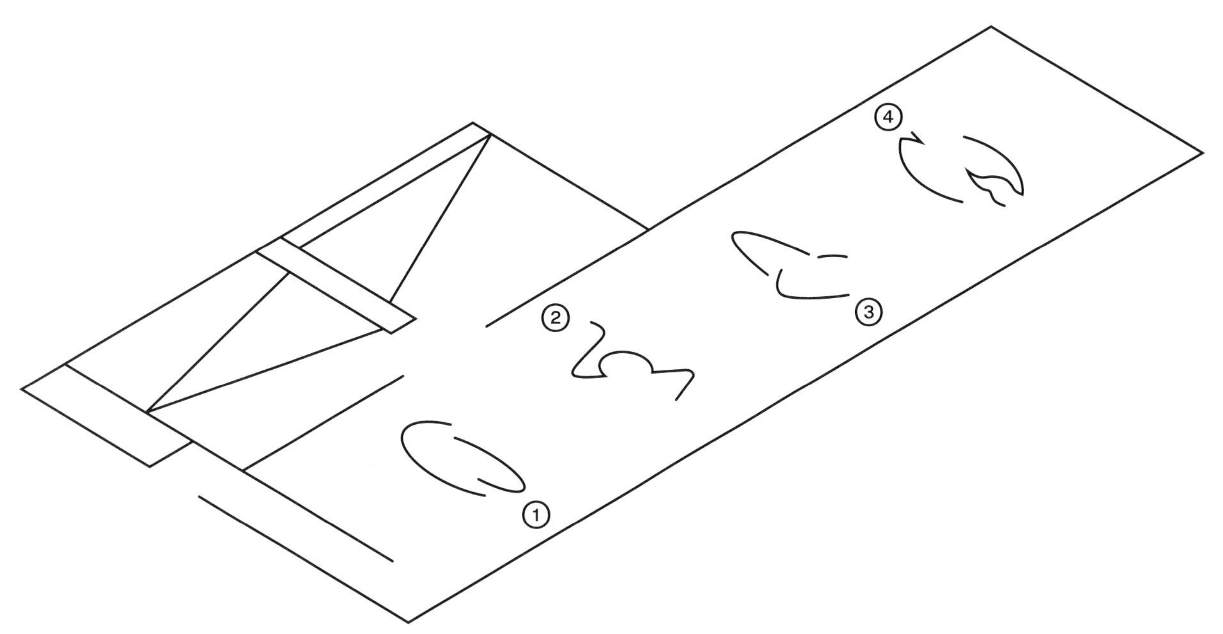

1. **Miya Masaoka**
   Mono chord, objects & koto, computer
2. **Ben Vida**
   Electronics
3. **MV Carbon**
   Cello, magnetic tape, & amplified object
4. **Che Chen**
   Woodwinds & tape machine

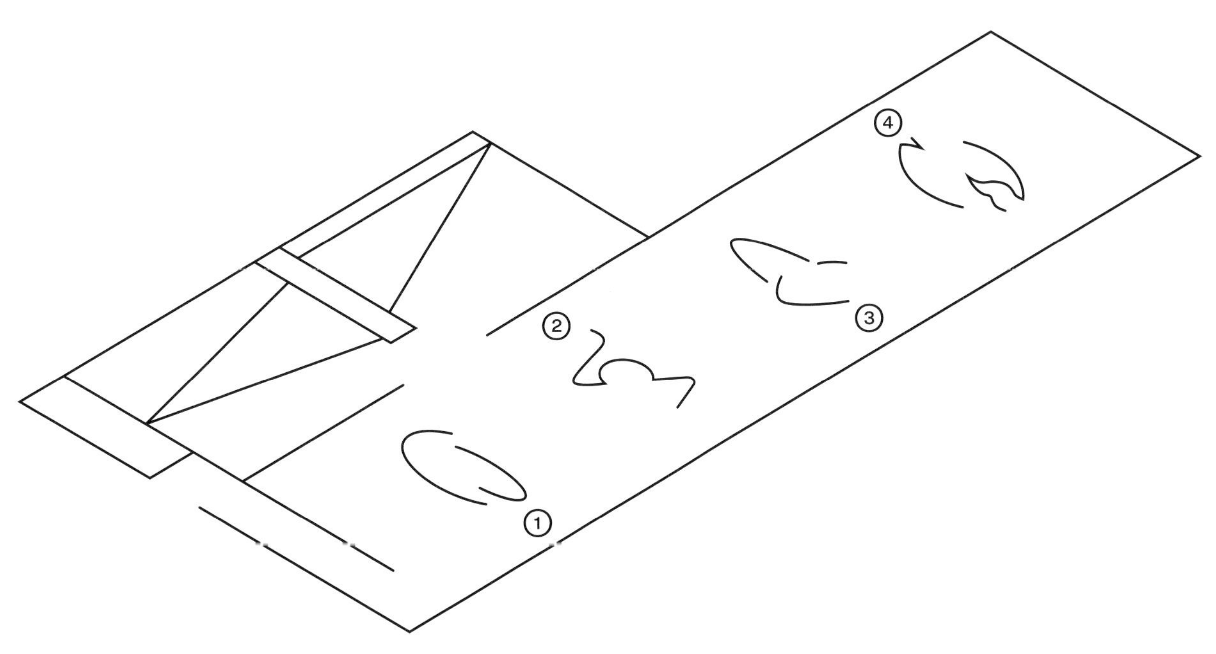

1. **Christopher McIntyre**
   Trombone & synthesizer
2. **Okkyung Lee**
   Cello
3. **Jules Gimbrone**
   Objects & electronics
4. **Yoshi Wada**
   Bagpipes & sirens

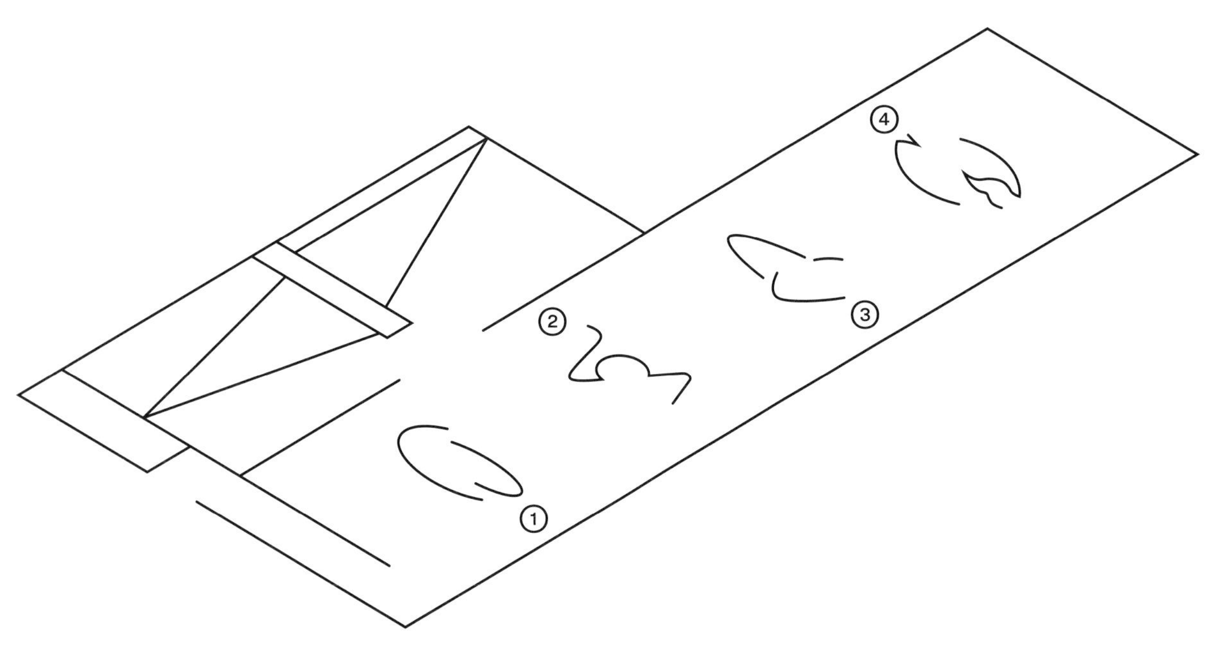

Musician Interviews:

Susan Alcorn, MV Carbon, Maria Chavez,
Che Chen, Jules Gimbrone, Sarah Hennies,
Eli Keszler, Okkyung Lee, Miya Masaoka,
Christopher McIntyre, Tomeka Reid, Ben Vida,
Yoshi Wada, Nate Wooley, C. Spencer Yeh

Walking in there and seeing the work relatively unoccupied, appreciating the serene vibe and look of the pieces without many people interacting with them—that's a real and beautiful experience. Because it was decided that I would be the first performer, in the front by where people would walk in, I wound up watching people have the experience that I myself had first walking in. People walked in and were struck by knowing that there was a performance going on and kind of seeing but not seeing the performers. At times you felt very much invisible. People would step right in front of you. People were so occupied with looking up that you expected them to run into one another.

We had a decision about having four solos for which the interaction was that we were all in the same room, playing to our respective sculptures, and that dictated to some degree how we would play—but it was something that you chose to move into and out of as well. There was uncertainty, but also a real respect for the situation; I performed in the first one, and we were a bit like the test group: "How many people can there be at the show?" On top of that, I was like the greeter for the series of performances. It was a very unique set of challenges, one that keeps you on your feet despite the whole vibe of just wanting to lie down.

The audience over the course of the exhibition's run trained themselves how to interact with the work and the space and the performances, and I sensed among certain people this aversion toward what had been described as "cuddle puddles." I thought it was really great the way this culture developed around it. We can't always guess what causes the lines around the block for certain artworks. For many people, their reaction is to take a picture of themselves with it, and then their friends react to it the same way. I really enjoyed what increasingly became this cultish behavior. It wasn't always at the expense of the performances, these globs of people either laying down amongst the work or huddled around the performers, but definitely listening.

I've always had a weird relationship with performance in the sense that it's a real challenge feeling that there are all these eyes on me, waiting for something to happen during the performance. So to be literally under the cover of darkness and to have the one audience member that I was playing to—that I was serenading—being the solid light work, there was an aspect of not being the focal point, and because of that being able to perform in ways that I've wanted to, but haven't always been able to. Audience members who weren't used to listening in certain ways found themselves being sensually forced to listen in new ways because bodies were relaxed, or taken out of the equation, or they were focused on the work. Sometimes in order to deeply listen you have to busy other parts of yourself so that they're not distracting you. It wasn't the responsibility of the improvisers to necessarily make those moments in time make sense as they would when typically performing improvisation. No one has to carry the moment, no one is auditioning for the improv all-stars. If the improvised material that I have is like liquid that trickles from one point to another, in this exhibition I could take that and vaporize it. Instead of pouring it or spilling it, you poof it in the air. It hangs there.

MARIA CHAVEZ

② 01.19.18

The thing that I keep thinking about, especially after a later studio visit with Anthony, is how the eye had to adjust to the light and how the stark contrast of this bright yet directional light in a black space coincided with how I noticed the audience listening. It takes time for the eyes to see everyone, and it took people time to hear where everyone was. I thought that was a beautiful parallel with the senses, and that's what made the concert series work for me. To have this sonic and visual parallel is something I've been thinking about as a sound artist, because a lot of my conceptual sound art practice is in trying to create sound installations that don't really focus on emitted sound. I find that emitted sound in sound art is very twentieth century. At first I thought this was just a concert for an art show, and then I realized that this is technically a sound art performance coinciding with a light sculpture that can also adjust to cinema, to sculpture. That kind of work to me is more interesting than spatial sound of, like, fifty speakers, where sound is just moving around. That to me is so old school, and really capitalist and classist. It's not just emitted sound that is sound art, it's also all of the ideas that surround sound: it's inner-ear phenomenology, it's how the vibrations can trigger things, it's so much more. I think it's really dangerous, especially in the twenty-first century and sound art for the art industry to just hold onto spatial sound or experimental performance practice as the only definition of sound art. For me it's not about the ego and being appreciated for it, it's about how I can take this opportunity and twist it, and make it more valuable for everyone, and more inclusive for the general public, and more challenging for myself as an artist. I think Anthony has a very similar approach.

When it was time to perform, volume was a huge concern. As an improviser with electronic equipment I have a lot of responsibility, and that's something that Pauline Oliveros and David Dove instilled in me early. The lesson that I learned is that I have the responsibility more so than acoustic performers in the space, because once I turn off my sound, my power, it sucks the room right out. I feel really confident about my improvisation practice when it comes to incorporating acoustic instruments, because that's how I started: I had to be aware of my responsibility early on, and I have been. That's something that Pauline taught me, that silence and the sucking out of a room from when you turn it off is actually more of a gesture than you performing. That blew my mind.

So when it was time to play in that space, there are high ceilings, but it's carpeted—and Sarah's over there, Spencer's here, and everyone is being emitted with power except for Sarah, and in a way I wished we had switched. That was something that I took into account as far as my deep listening skills were concerned: always try to sense her. Even if you can't hear her, always have a sense of her. Then of course being very selective. Do I need to exist here? Is it really necessary, or are the others creating enough of an environment where I can still wait? My approach was allowing everyone to have their interactive moments, allowing the space also—because it wasn't just us making sound, it was the audience, too, and they were making beautiful moments, random moments, too, and sometimes if someone was whispering I'd make a whispering noise, too, as if I was talking back.

DAVID GRUBBS

The weather was hellaciously weird on most of the evenings with events having to do with Anthony's exhibition, whether it was torrential rain, a snowstorm, or a nor'easter with an ice storm. And still, at 7:30 p.m. for each of the concerts, the musicians would be in place as the doors opened, and like clockwork an enormous crowd billowed in, people slowly filling the space while adjusting to the darkness, to the comparative hush, and to the spectacle of four of Anthony's vertical projection pieces. We were cocooned, everyone crowded into the cocoon. Once the audience filled the space, I can't recall being able to see Spencer, Maria, or Sarah. Several minutes into the performance, Sarah made the first sound: a single sustained pitch on the vibraphone that, at least from where I was positioned, hovered slightly above the noise floor of the walking and whispering. It tinged the darkness, gave it a marginally different hue. There were surprised greetings—folks literally running into one another in the dark—and quick snippets of conversation. In this

atmosphere, the ordinarily unremarkable sound of a needle hit-
ting vinyl had the power to make people jump, and I remember
thinking that a long thread connected Maria and Spencer, as at
times the two had a serendipitous flow centering on his voice
and her deciding to drop a recorded speaking voice into the
goings-on. Sarah often made the vibraphone seem as if it was a
kind of electric halo or improbably beautiful artifact of the room's
acoustics. I found myself from the start trusting the other three
performers' sensitivities, sensibilities, and skill, and also their
humor. There seemed no especial demand that musical conversations occur, and yet for long stretches they did, and were all
the more meaningful for not being compulsory.

The four musicians were placed just outside of the cones of
light, almost touching them but not quite, and as the contour of
the light projection sometimes moved toward my toes and sometimes away from them, I thought about that feeling of uncertainty
when you're at the beach and don't know whether the tide is
coming in or if it's going out. I managed to keep my feet dry.

I'm not sure whether it's easier for an audience member or a
performer to lose the sense of clock time. You might think that a
performer is more apt to get lost because of a heightened invest-
ment in the moment—maybe—but if you've spent years giving
performances that are often of a certain length, your muscle
memory will tell you when you've been gripping an instrument for
thirty minutes, and when it's been an hour. Still, there's often a
goal of obliterating one's sense of time, just as there's a desire to
mentally cover your tracks, to fool yourself into wondering, "How
did I get here?" It's a good sign when playing with others to arrive
at the no-place of "How did we get here?" I think I spent much
of the performance staring up at the light, not so much watching the drawing on the floor as it inched across people splayed
on the ground as I was tracking the veils and folds of light high
above the crowd, following it back to its source.

SARAH HENNIES   ④ 01.19.18

One of the first things that I noticed is that when I got there for
the soundcheck and it was empty, I felt very lucky that I got to
see it that way. I talked to Anthony about this, about how many
people were at the opening, and how many people were at the
performances, and it felt like a work that benefited from you
being in there by yourself. Just a second ago I found a photo that
I took right when I walked in the room, right when I very first got
there, and you can see maybe two people, and it had a really different feeling once it was full.

One of the things I remember that I told people about is that right before we started playing, and David was giving us our little pep talk, the first thing that he said was, "Now remember that these pieces don't need music." And it's kind of like, "Well... alright..." [laughter] I was thinking about that in terms of being a performer within a thing that exists on its own, and how that to me felt a little bit similar to being one of a crowd of people walking through a piece. It's different, but you're deciding what kind of interference you're going to cause within the thing, which is interesting to me. One of the things that surprised me about the performance—and I think that the rest of us had this too—is that I had a little group of people who laid down right in front of me, and just stayed there. That would not have been my instinct: to pick a spot and sit there, in this huge room with four different pieces. I don't have any deep thoughts about what that means—I was just surprised that it happened. I would have expected that people would have wanted to see what was on the floor, rather than bask in the light coming down on them, and I would have thought that people would want to move around.

Before people arrived, I had this idea that I would play in such a way that I would do a live improvisation using Anthony's piece like a score. A lot of what I was playing would be a single note that evolves over time, or maybe after several minutes a second note gets added. That seemed to me a great soundtrack for any of those four pieces of Anthony's. And then when people laid down on the floor, I was like, "Oh...I can't do this anymore." I could see the light moving in the air, but I couldn't see what it was anymore. I didn't play like that once I couldn't see the line on the floor, so it was more what I would do in a typical long improvisation, where I was responding to what was around me, but not so much the piece specifically. Once I couldn't see the piece on the floor, I was responding to more things than just the piece. It became an improvisation within a giant room with three other musicians and hundreds of people in which my sightline of the piece was obscured. That's how I would characterize the difference in playing when it was empty versus when it was full of people.

SUSAN ALCORN

The experience was bigger than life. It was a huge room. When it was dark, it was black, and when it was light, it was gorgeous white light. When people started coming in, it was like a happening from the sixties. The music was sort of in the background, because they were immediately confronted with these massive rays and subsequent pools of light. I'd be playing, and people would be coming in, putting their hands in and out of the light. When they started getting more used to everything, they began to walk around, and then when they started getting more comfortable in the space, they would sit down and listen to the music, or they'd continue walking around. In some ways it was a liberating experience as a musician—you're free basically to do whatever you want though somewhat constrained by sound, light, and geography. The night I performed, Eli Keszler was at the opposite side of the room, but I could hear him because... because he's a drummer. I could make out the shadows of Nate Wooley and Tomeka Reid, but musically it was often difficult to tell who was who because of the electronics—when an acoustic instrument no longer sounds like itself. The music was definitely a group effort. All of us were aware of each other, and musically we responded to each other. However, not being able to see each other, and hearing each other from what seemed like a distance while being intimately aware, it was like entering into a different world. I had no idea what I played that night; there were things that I never would have thought of otherwise. The experience wasn't just the music; it wasn't just the light sculptures; it wasn't just the darkness or the people who were there—it was everything in one. I imagine that's how most who were there would process it. The crowd was kind of like ghosts walking around in the darkness. Where I was playing was just outside one of those circles, and people would sit down inside the circle, and lie down, and listen to it and groove on it. The architecture of the space with the rays of light, the high ceiling, the walking shadows—that had an effect musically on my improvisation, an architectural sense. It seeped through. As the specifics recede from my memory, that evening is etched in my mind as one of the great experiences I've had as a musician. And like improvisation, it's there and then it's gone.

NATE WOOLEY

② 02.02.18

The thing that struck me most of all was the initial dichotomy between the light of Anthony's work and the darkness that I was in, and how that affected the music. The focus for me became the light of the sculpture that was in front of me and how it moved. I honestly didn't deal with people until they entered the space in front of me. The way it was set up with the four of us split out into this big room, and each in their own darkness with their own light, the whole thing became about geography for me. When I normally play it's so much about time, unfolding a narrative in a linear time. Especially with jazz music, you're unfurling a line that goes from point A to point B. Because I was in this blackness, next to this light—and the light was changing in time—I felt completely free to just exist in space without having to worry about time. To hear something come from Susan, it was not about responding to that, like you would normally in an improvised setting. Or hearing Eli or Tomeka, it was more about them in space, and then putting something else in space, and in the meantime there are these four other light beings that are almost taking the time away from you, so you can just exist in this thing—which is a really liberating way to play. That was a very special hour of a kind of communion, of being aware of music taking place in space. The meaning of the "simultaneous" part of it didn't dawn on me until we were doing it.

I tend to look down when I play, and there was a lot in the light as it hit the floor: what it inscribes, and how it moves. I was right up against the edge of it as it came out to its greatest depth, so there was a lot of watching that line get right up next to my foot, and then go back, and having different feelings about that: like stepping into the ocean, and having it recede. There was also an aggressive thing to it as you look at the full volume of light, seeing it come toward you and then move out, and I liked that, because I like to play aggressively. So I felt that there was a living, breathing, and not necessarily benign creature, and it's coming toward me and it's going away. When people would enter that, it was always a strange feeling, because I had relationships to it as an ocean or as another being, and then when someone would get inside it and lay down, it took me out of that, but in an interesting way—it's nice to be out of the metaphor, and to wonder how someone else is experiencing it.

I have been thinking more recently about translucence versus saturation with dynamics, and this has something to do with Anthony's work. Doing something that is ever-present but hardly noticeable because filmy—not cinematic, but filmy—versus making a sound that spreads throughout the space and takes up everything. A lot of that has to do with the technical aspects of the trumpet: those are two things that you can't easily do on the horn, and things that people don't do on the instrument. Trying to create something that feels translucent on the trumpet: no one does that. And the same is true of trying to get all of the overtones and to fill everything out. There is that thing in Anthony's work that I enjoy because it has volume, but it also has translucency, and there were moments when I was trying to do one or the other.

When we got there, we were trying to figure out where we were going to sit, and I believe it was Susan that was closest to the entrance, and then Nate, and then me, and then Eli. I couldn't see Susan. I could kind of see Nate, and I could kind of see Eli. I didn't know how the performance was going to go as far as how we were going to interact or if I was going to be able to hear the other people, or how I would be influenced by them—if I could hear them. I remember being a little nervous because there were people that would come up and be close to you or sit really close, and sometimes that gives me a bit of anxiety because I don't want to hit them with my bow. People get a little too close sometimes.

It was really cold that day, and then we entered this dark world. I may have been trying to play more with the other musicians instead of trying to be literal with the movement of the light. After a while, I just closed my eyes and tried to respond to the energy of the room. I was affected by the light because it set a tone. As far as the light was concerned, it was more like an energy thing: closing my eyes and trying to vibe off the crowd and what I could hear. I couldn't hear Susan that well, and also Nate didn't play that much. I was thinking, "You're closest to me, and I can't hear you!" I remember wondering what he was thinking—that's not a criticism—but it seemed that he didn't play a lot. I was trying to interact with him, because he was to my left, facing in the opposite direction, and Eli was to my right, and I could hear him more—not just because he was playing drums, but because he was more active, and Nate wasn't so much. I know myself; sometimes I can be a busy player, so I remember having space and thinking about pacing.

In those kinds of things, you always wish you could do it again, because you've just had a first experience and you're reacting, but that's part of it, too—you don't want to have something premeditated. That's the beauty of it. But you do think about how you would do it again.

Anthony McCall's idea of the light sculptures as being film, drawing, and sculpture—that idea manifests itself in the way that these performances unfolded. The musicians ended up taking on different structural roles than you would normally experience when playing with improvisers or working in an improvised-music context. So there ended up being moments where someone is creating a flat surface that takes on a sculptural quality, where it doesn't really move linearly. By "flat surface," I mean a sound that has very little contour to it, a limited frequency range, and a rhythmic stasis. It could be a drone, or I remember these noise textures that stayed flat, or squared off. In a more forward-facing improvised setting, with a proscenium set-up, it would be unusual for a musician to sustain something like that for, say, twelve minutes, while somebody else plays a much more detailed line. I think there's something about the staggering of the musicians in space: somehow that idea ends up rubbing off on the musicians. Also for the audience it's an unusual experience to walk up to a musician who you think is going to be very active, and nothing happens. They approach the musician and they're expecting some sort of flare or fireworks to go off, and instead they don't play, and the sound comes from across the room. It's a dispersed experience that you're not used to having in a musical setting. I love the idea that these sculptures can bring that out.

I could hear the other musicians, sometimes not as well as others, but there would be this beautiful counterpoint, sounds emanating in almost a four-part chorale. It's not a normal musical experience. There's a certain kind of energy you leave with when you play music, but this was different. Being a part of a sculptural body, it had a different aura. For me, having done my own projects that work with installation and performance, it's a feeling that I'm used to, but I think it's interesting that this configuration of pieces managed to do that without producing any sound. The pieces I've done have used installation as a kind of frame—the sounds act as a frame to stabilize the musical performance—but this is silent, and yet they produce some kind of cohesive music.

The thing I remember most vividly is the sensation of playing something very active—because I was playing the drums there's a kind of theatricality to it—and when I started playing, if there was more static material around me, people would turn around and go, "Oh, that's where the action is, I'll go check that out." And I might play for two minutes, then I would hear something from the other side of the room, and I would decide to drop to let something come out from Tomeka or Susan. People would still be approaching me, but I'd stop, and they'd sit there and wait for something to happen again. But they'd have to explore. It's an unusual thing to do in a musical performance. It's a hybrid space: observing music as a kind of installation. It makes sense to walk through it, because as you walk sound relationships change with the architecture, but this is a music that's typically very quick and has to do with a four-directional listening, and this is bypassing that.

MIYA MASAOKA

I thought about the architecture of the room. I was on one end, and people would walk and hear the sounds and music as they walked and stood, walked and stood. I thought about creating sounds that evolved over fifteen or twenty minutes, so when people cycled back the sounds would be changed, and offer a new experience. I thought about contrasting some of the sounds played by the other musicians, and creating a kind of filmic score with them in an unspoken manner, as we never discussed beforehand what we would do. I remember hearing that Anthony didn't want people to lie down, but keep walking. But people did lie down and stay and listen. People don't always do what is expected, or desired, but it ends up working out. Experientially, I thought about interrupting the acousmatic space and creating some dynamicism from what could be a more flat sonic space.

It was pitch black, so having different aspects of the senses being highlighted in the dark space was something that was completely new and removed from the musicians' point of view and the people experiencing it, because they didn't know what would be immediately obvious in a lighted room. The light itself was such an extraordinary presence that I think it affected all of us—I know that it did myself—psychically in a certain way, where whatever we chose to do musically or sound-wise had this other layer of how we were affected by the structures themselves. They felt like a presence—a supernatural, paranormal presence in the space.

I played electroacoustic koto, and I was focusing on different kinds of sounds that I thought would be somewhat of a companion to the structures of light: sustained sounds, or small loops, or musical or sound choices that would enhance the space. I could hear some of the larger sounds that would pierce the soundscape, and it was nice to be in a communal sense with the other musicians where we were playing together—but it was a very particular kind of improvising with the space and the musicians and the light, and because we were spaced out so far apart we were able to establish ourselves as an entity.

My focus continually changed. At different times I could hear what a particular musician was doing, and my focus was there. Then the audience would come in and interact with the solid light, and the focus would change. Sometimes it was packed, sometimes it was sparser, and at other times I would focus on what I myself was doing individually. I had some students who came up and talked to me during the show. I was playing and they were telling me what they were experiencing, because we were there for a lengthy period of time. There's a kind of mirroring that happens in the brain and these geometric shapes that are slowly changing and converging and reshaping themselves and evolving very slowly, as the shapes on the floor moved slowly. That was mirrored in the inner psyche, or inner psyches, of what to do musically; that had the effect of a source of power and almost like a score, even though there was nothing prescriptive about it, but it did feel score-like in the sense of slowly moving sounds that evolve over time. The fact that it was illumination had to do also with some kind of mirroring of the sonic sphere, illuminating points of sounds or moving that could be a companion to what was happening with the light.

BEN VIDA

A few years ago I was invited to play the "David Tudor" role in a staging of John Cage's *Musicircus*. It was clear from the outset that each participant would function as an independent yet unified element within the whole—and in that case the "whole" was a cacophony. What was unique about playing an elemental part in Anthony's installation was the absence of cacophony. It was a very still space, and one where it was possible for an audience member to recalibrate to a finer grain of sensing. Within that context I felt like our physical presence as performers became as important as the sounds we produced—we were deliberate bodies in that space. That's a different type of invitation, and I like that; it sets up a different set of expectations for myself as a performer.

I've found that these kinds of events have an ebb and flow musically where my focus is being drawn away from the playing by the absurdity of the situation, especially in a case like this were it was such a popular event; the physical proximity between the performers and audience becomes something to contend with, and that makes it an experience that is at once more intimate and more objectifying.

I'd performed solo at Pioneer Works before and found that, by way of really loud standing waves, I was able explore how weird and physical that space can be. For this event I had the chance to play with amplitude thresholds in a more communal manner that allowed for moments where I could overwhelm the space immediately around me with my own sound and then, dipping down into silence, receive Carbon, Miya, and Che's sounds from a distance, and I loved that spatialization—that was something I think the audience members were able to create for themselves through navigating the space.

For the performance I was playing a modular synthesizer through an amplifier, which is very different than playing a modular synthesizer through a P.A. system: it's much more of "one sound" instead of a sound world. It's like plugging a guitar into an amp. I have a long history of improvising on other instruments, and have only been improvising with the synthesizer for a few years. It is a different proposition since I am building a new system from the ground up each time I do it. I usually try to construct a simple system; I find that when the set-up is too complex it doesn't really lead to the best results. There's something special that happens in live performance and specifically with improvisation with the modular: there's less of a studio mentality of making corrections, of setting up a patch and then fiddling with it and editing, editing, editing. It's this very stream-of-consciousness, very linear thing, and so I find myself able to fall into unusual sound spaces that I would never arrive at in the studio, because I wouldn't allow something to travel through all of the permutations. In the studio there would always be a breaking point where I would then start again.

We had the luxury of being in the space before the performance. It was great to be in the installation in this more private way and walk through the different rooms and become seeded by the experience of the whole piece, and then for the performance having this more intimate relationship with the one element that you were placed in front of. In those moments becoming very receptive to the influence of the visual is such a pleasure, and in a strange way it pulls you out of your body a little bit. Performing is so much about being that lump of flesh right there in the performance space with everyone else, and this allowed for a much more ethereal interaction with the audience, the light, and the sound.

MV CARBON

③ 02.16.18

As one of the four soloists, I temporarily became a component of Anthony McCall's *Solid Light Works* natural habitat. We gathered to discuss our approach to form a whole sonic experience, which would be explored spatially within the exhibition. During our setup time it was completely dark, except for the sculptures, which exposed their form in hazy air. We assembled our instruments outside of the rays of light, in darker spots of the room, and tested out how our sounds traveled to each other. People flooded through the space and interacted with the sculptures as if they were communing with a new form of nature. They seemed inclined to run their hands through the beams of light and to feel the shape shift in the light and air. People weaved in and out of the darkness, discovering the sources of sound and light. I was drawn to the ambience, scale, and non-materiality of the work, which I feel highlights the alchemy of matter, form, perception, and illusion.

I used electric cello, amplified vessels, and oscillators, and manipulated my vocals through a reel-to-reel tape machine, which gathered and dispersed sonic remnants of the live space back into it. I was inclined to create sounds that felt submerged and organic. Che brought a tape machine as well and started the concert with airy sounds that traveled through the mist. With Miya's koto and electronics and Ben's modular synthesis, we created a rich range of frequency and texture. I think we all sonically meshed and were influenced by each other as well as by the environment Anthony created. The slowly shifting light made noticeable progress over time, as did our pace, rhythm, and mood. The hour seemed to go by in minutes.

④ 02.16.18

CHE CHEN

Pioneer Works' photos of the exhibition were so pristine, almost Euclidean—they look like ideas rather than a real situation— and so one thing that struck me getting there earlier in the day when the place was empty was how cold and damp it was because of the fog. Being there all day in that environment had a very different feeling than the images that I had seen. It was actually quite physical and a little bit unfriendly. It was February, and it was cold in there. It's interesting to see the difference between the documentation—and also having seen Anthony's work before in galleries—the cleanly executed concept, and seeing that unfold against the messiness of these concerts, of the situation, and the audience. Playing in that situation was unusual in so many different ways, especially being so far away from everyone. I like situations like that, where music is fulfill- ing some other kind of function besides just performance and the regular performer-audience relationship. Some people were paying very close attention to what the musicians were doing, and other people were not paying attention at all, or just social- izing, or just really lost in the lights—as they should be. I keep going back to this word, but there was a messiness that I liked about the situation.

As regards my approach, I had been playing bass recorder
a lot around then, getting ready for another piece I was playing
on, but it occurred to me that it might be good to bring something that wasn't so loud, even though it's a big space, and even
though I used an amp. Something that had a soft presence, and
also something that can't—at least in my hands—do too much at
once, because there are going to be four people and space is
a large part of this, so it eventually seemed like the right thing
to bring. It was interesting being spaced out like that, and really
having to focus if I wanted to hear what Miya was doing at the
other end. Just trying to think in that way: this very extreme
dynamic range of someone being twenty feet from you, or eighty
feet from you, and trying to think "How do I send something down
there?" or "How do I do something they can't hear?"

The immediate thing that the situation made me think of
was Cage and Cunningham, where two things are happening at
the same time, and one is not beholden to the other. On the one
hand, I was approaching it that way and not trying to think too
hard about any kind of relationship to the projection in front of
me. But at the same time, especially having to expand what I was
paying attention to so far into the room, trying to see and hear
everything in a diffuse way, having that kind of attention to the
room—in that sense I was very aware of the people and the lights
and Anthony's sculptures with people coming and going inside
of them. I tried not to be too distracting, to be a quiet presence
instead of a performative one.

One thing I appreciated about the concert was that I felt
that we did a good job at not being too reverential—that people
weren't being too polite. In a situation like this, there's some
temptation to be background music to what's happening, but
I felt that people were intuiting another way to be, and sometimes being loud and at other times falling back to nothing, and
I appreciated that there were dynamics to it, and an unfolding.
They're all great players, so I'm not surprised that happened,
but I'm happy that it did. There's a fine line. The sculptures exist
independently of the performers, and that encouraged the right
response from us.

CHRISTOPHER McINTYRE

① 03.02.18

My first memory of walking into the space was that there was
a real hush, a mental hush. I experienced Anthony's work in a
personal way that was less available once a couple of hundred
people were in the room. The setup period put me into a space of
just contemplatively sitting with my gear. I walked over and said

hello to my collaborators but then found myself naturally falling into an especially focused, mindful space. As soon as we all had our stuff together, it felt like the musical conversation had begun. It was such an evocative situation on all levels.

Having been to the space a number of times previously, including for two of the other concerts, I had already developed some concepts about what I thought made sense for my sound and equipment. When I finally arrived to perform, I tried to wipe away these preconceptions and start from scratch based on the work of the people I was playing with, to really consider their sound in that situation. In general, I was trying to be as responsive as possible while projecting my own images into the situation. There's a funny thing with the trombone where some players are really only interested in doing that singular thing: "I'm going to be as trombone-y as I can be." I felt that including the synthesizer was going to be the best way for me to find different pathways of interacting with the light pieces, and also to find a space with the other musicians. The trombone sound is so present: the second you go "pah," it's just right there. You can attempt to approximate "from nothing" but the tongue still has to go "bam" and make the sound happen, there's no avoiding that. So to have moments where I could use a potentiometer to enter the field little by little was a good counterbalance for me aesthetically.

It was difficult to acclimate on some levels. Each of us was lined up with a single piece of Anthony's, but regardless there were four of us making permeating sonic material. This fact necessitated finding a space to interact with one another, deciding when to cross the "soloist" line and when to stay behind it, when to play in duo with your assigned McCall piece versus in duos, trios, etc., with each other. That process of constantly shifting perspective was the essence of participating in these events, I think, for both the players and audience.

I experienced a constant flow of attention which was heavily influenced by what was happening around me physically, and by the dynamics of what I was playing. If I was droning on the synthesizer, I felt the changes in Anthony's piece more deeply. My solid light piece had two intersecting sections that would expand and contract and collapse on itself. I wouldn't say that I was doing any on-the-nose painting of that motion, but I did feel myself simulating it in a different time scale, growing and pulling back, sometimes in tandem with it. When only playing trombone, that same awareness of Anthony's piece expanding and contracting elicited melodic contour ideas rather than a droning texture. As the performance progressed, I found myself becoming more and more aware of the piece in its totality, the diffusion of its light and what that felt like. I would expand my sound as I felt more and more enveloped by it. Then I'd hear Okkyung doing something similar or somehow connected in that moment, and I'd tap into what she was doing in addition to my duo with Anthony's piece which would be overlapping. As much as I could, I attempted to have this type of subtle conversation with these moment-to-moment perceptions.

OKKYUNG LEE

② 03.02.18

Once I arrived, the room felt really quiet, because there were very few people walking around. There was one person already setting up, Chris McIntyre, who was close to the entrance. It felt subdued. Everbody was in a dreamlike state—it felt cozy and comfortable. I was a little concerned because of the carpet, but to see the lights coming down from the ceiling—even though it was white light, it created a certain sense of warmth. I was a little disappointed, actually, that I wasn't right under the light, because the musicians were a little off—we were staged along the wall— and I was jealous of the people who were walking in and out of the light, and I thought that would be a great way to interact. It was not easy to look around the room while I was playing, so I focused on the light right in front of me. In terms of sound, I remember it being rather quiet, not so resonant, but I was surprised that I was able to hear more than I expected. I asked for a monitor speaker to amplify myself a tiny bit, so I didn't have to strain myself. Once the people came in there were a lot of them, so I was a little worried, and again I was jealous that they got to be in the light. I rarely get nervous before performances these days, so there was a sense of excitement and "How am I going to navigate improvising with three other musicians that I can't hear that closely?" I decided to mainly interact with the light that was in front of me, and also to make sure that there was enough space. My musical choices were definitely based on the light and also how people interacted with it. How people walked in and out of it, looking up, looking down, going around. That was more of a guide than other musical cues I was getting. Most times I play with my eyes closed, so that was an interesting challenge: it wasn't like I was looking at the light all the time. I'd have my eyes closed for a moment and let the music pick up on its own, but because it started from the light it was still related to it. Musically it turned out more satisfying than I expected because everyone was respectful of the space, and I don't think it was necessarily about interacting with other musicians in a traditional sense of improvisation, but more like really feeling the space. I couldn't hear the room that well because of the carpet and so many bodies inside, but it felt like I was able to feel the room and leave enough space for the lights to be the main focus.

I often walk quite a bit while I'm playing. The typical musical set-up—the audience is passive and looking at the performer, and the performer is supposed to be just presenting it, and there's no direct sense of interaction—I try to break away from that mold and shake up the space between the performer and the audience. But with this performance I ended up sitting, and I didn't move at all. The light was enough to get people moving around the space. I didn't have to worry, I didn't have to be the one, because there was enough movement: the air was shifting, the sound was shifting. But I would like to be the only one in the room and to play with the lights. I got a little greedy.

JULES GIMBRONE

The first thing that I recollect is that when many people come into a room that's huge but covered in carpet, you don't really hear them approach. It's totally dark except for Anthony's projections. It's like you're on the savanna, and you're being hunted, but it's not scary. It's not exactly a savanna, but there's a cluster of people coming in that are going to pursue you, and you're just sitting there. It's a weird feeling that you don't usually have as a performer in the sense of the encounter, being a sitting duck and then this group of people approach you and approach the forms of light. It wasn't a stalking in a bad sense; it was an inviting into this space that had been ordained as exceptional because of the lighting and the carpet and because of us being placed there in anticipation of something happening. So there was a lot of anticipation in the beginning moments. That's why I'm talking about being hunted.

I had brought two of my glass vessels and created a stereo field with them. They were spread out about four feet apart from one another in front of me. On a table to the left of me was my tape delay, an analog mixer, a microphone, my pitch-shifter box, and maybe a distortion pedal. I thought about whether I was going to bring my computer, and what that would signify. Because of the light from that I decided not to bring it, and to go all-analog which was kind of a risky choice because you couldn't see so well, so I also had lights on the mixer. The glass vessels had water in them, and I had mirrors lining the space between them. The vessels were perched on top of two rubber squares that I use in my sculptural forms. I also had my loop machine so that I could record things and have them play through. The whole idea was that at different points, while sound was coming through the vessels, I was going to pour out the liquid from one into the other, thus creating changes in overtone, and the whole timbre of the sound would change depending on the amount of liquid, literally kind of pouring a sound into another thing. Which involves the ability to see, which I didn't have, so it was a weird choice.

The audience was coming up and wanting to be close to the objects, and I could create a performance for them, or not—and they'd have to start listening to other people. It was interesting because I couldn't see the other musicians. I could only see the audience. There was a tension with giving the audience what they want. If there are thirty people in front of you, they want you to do something. At one point I was in the middle of playing, and this guy came up to me and started asking questions about what I was doing: "Are those microphones on the glass vessels?" And I was like, "What's happening here?" I turned to him and said, "I'm performing," and he backed away.

YOSHI WADA

④ 03.02.18

This was quite an unusual experience for me. The space had a very high ceiling, and Anthony McCall's light projection was mysterious and amazing. We did a small rehearsal on the performance day, and that gave me a positive feeling, and I became familiar with the space layout. At the performance time, I was waiting to come out to play bagpipe, and I didn't get a cue and so it had a little delay, but was fine. Pioneer Works' space is huge, and sometimes I couldn't hear the other players. Anthony's work was impressive, and I watched his light work during the performance.

I chose to play bagpipe and then added sirens and alarm bells to give unusual sound effects. I was walking around when playing bagpipe, and it gave a good edge to it.

I liked Pioneer Works' space quite a lot, but never depended on the space. I improvised a lot of things during the performance, and I like it that way. What I liked about the sound of the space is that it's ambient and mysterious—it became a good opportunity for me to experiment.

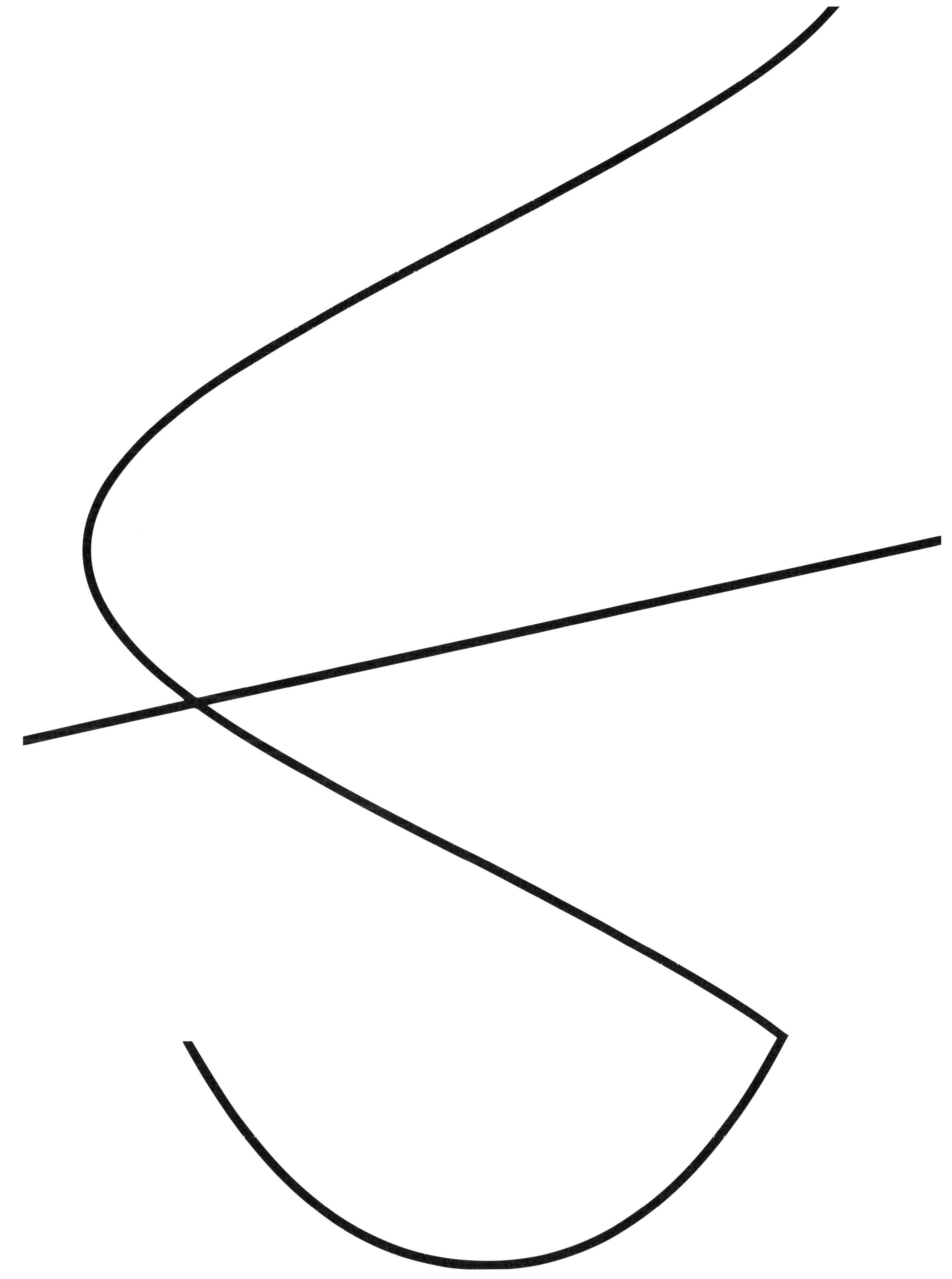

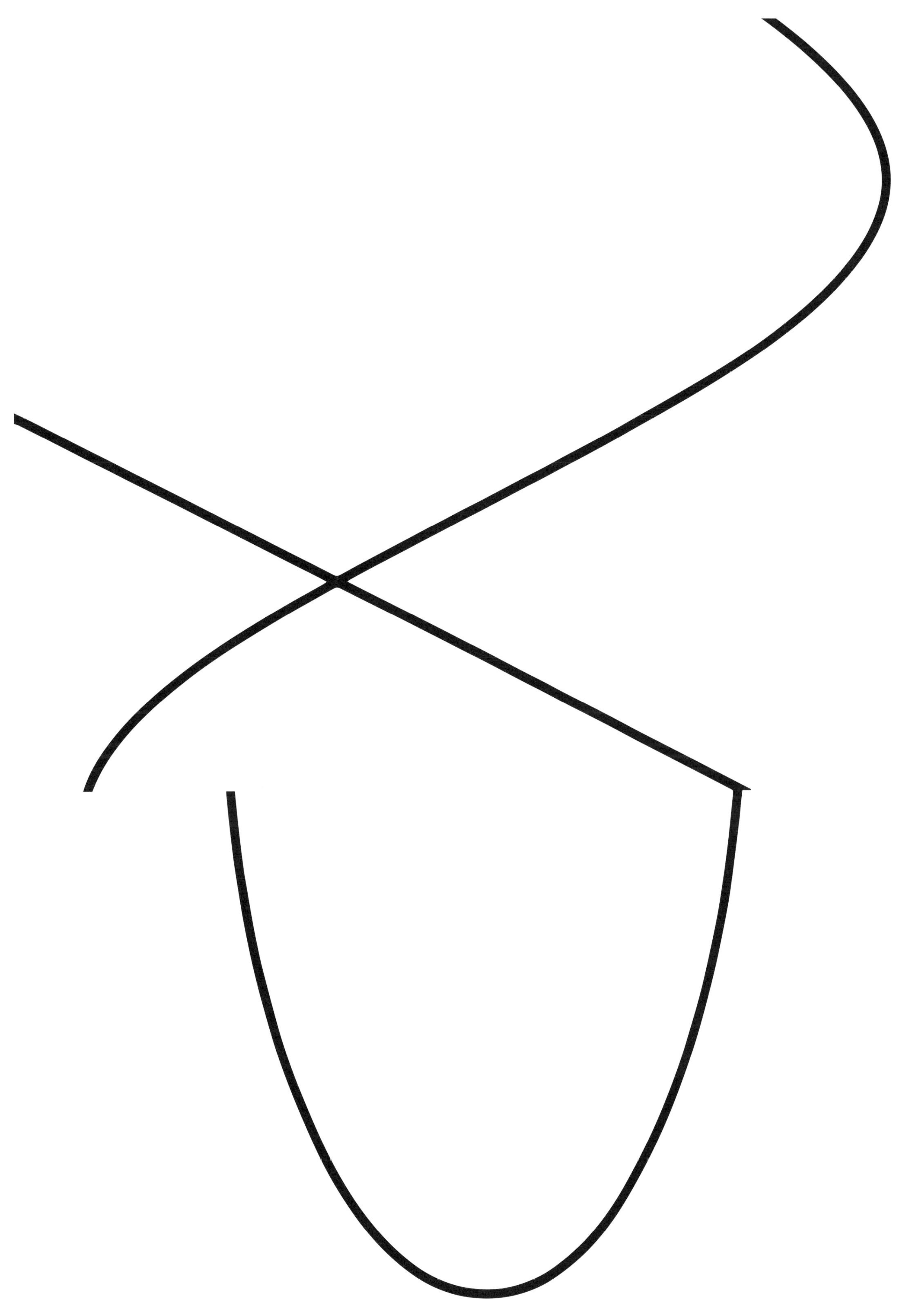

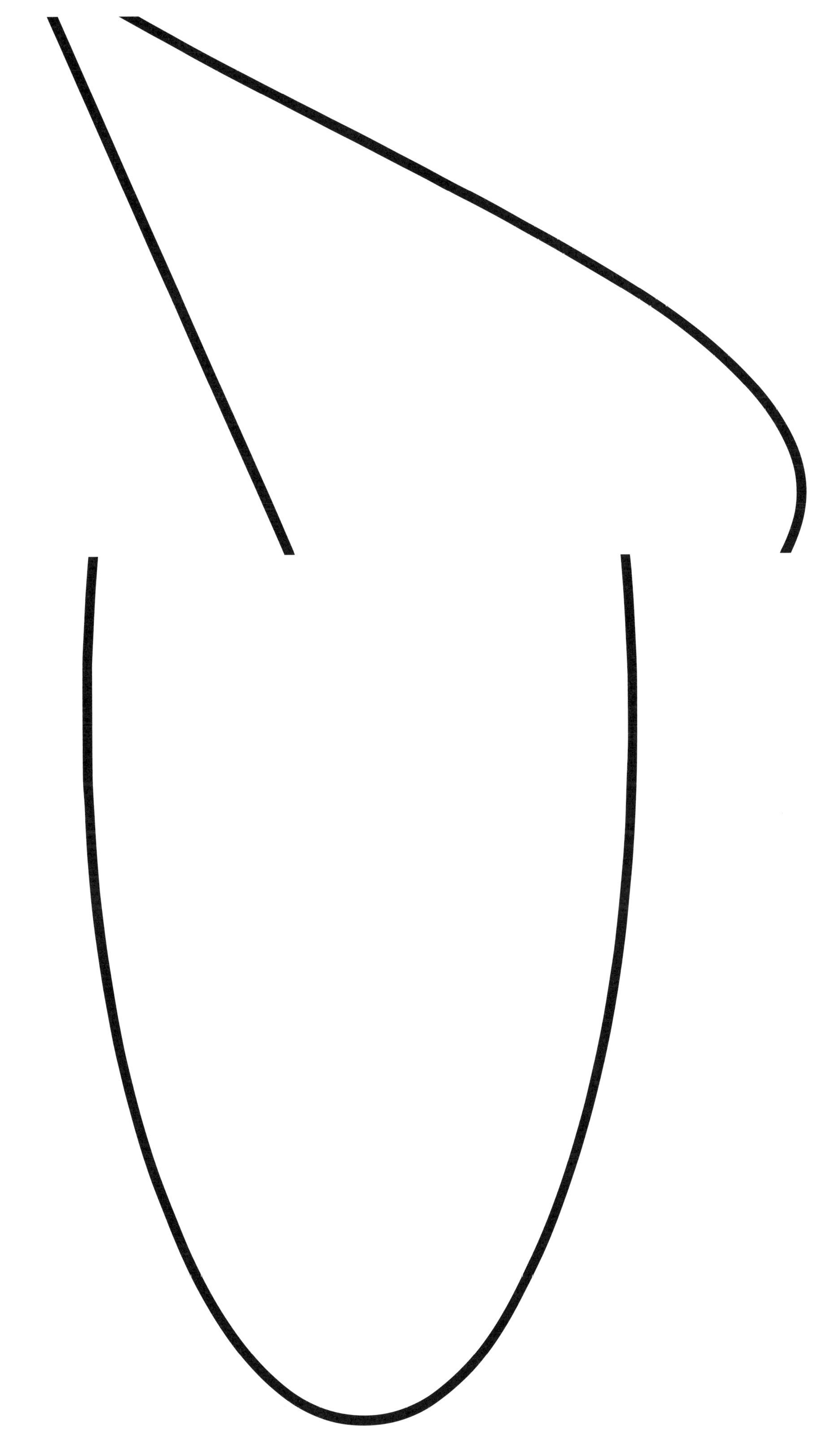

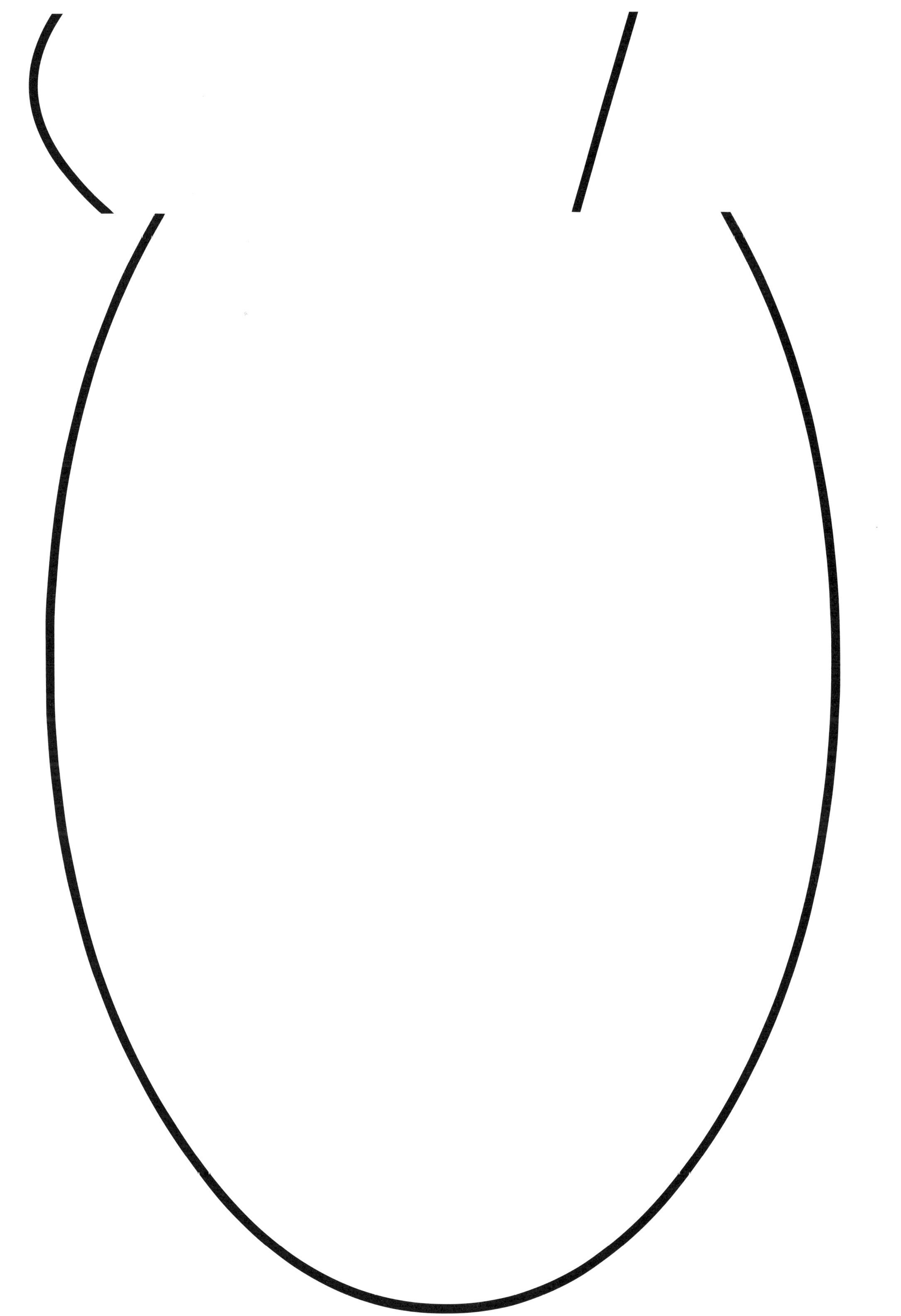

Works in the Exhibition

Horizontal	Vertical
You and I, Horizontal (2005) Media player, QuickTime movie file, video projector, haze machine. 50-minute cycle.	*Meeting You Halfway* (2009) Media player, QuickTime movie file, video projector, haze machine. 15-minute cycle.
Doubling Back (2003) Media player, QuickTime movie file, video projector, haze machine. 30-minute cycle.	*Breath (III)* (2005) Media player, QuickTime movie file, video projector, haze machine. 15-minute cycle.
	You and I (II) (2010) Media player, QuickTime movie file, video projector, haze machine. 16-minute cycle.
	Skirt (III) (2010) Media player, QuickTime movie file, video projector, haze machine. 12-minute cycle.

Susan Alcorn
One of the world's premier exponents of her instrument, Susan Alcorn has taken the pedal steel guitar far beyond its traditional role in country music. Having first paid her dues in Texas country and western bands, she began to expand the vocabulary of her instrument through her study of twentieth-century classical music, visionary jazz, and world musics. In 2017 she received the Baker Artist Award and in 2018, along with saxophonist Joe McPhee, the Instant Award in Improvised Music.

MV Carbon
MV Carbon's work cross-connects multimedia performance, painting, installation, and music composition. Her signature vocal style employs the use of magnetic reel-to-reel tape manipulation, and she applies extended techniques to cello and creates rhythmic meshes through the amplification of vessels, gongs, and crafted resonant objects. Her current work embodies the communicative cognition and endurance of biological feedback and consciousness.

Swagato Chakravorty
Swagato Chakravorty is a Ph.D. candidate in History of Art, combined with Film and Media Studies, at Yale University. He is broadly interested in practices of screening and spectatorship from the nineteenth century through the present day, and his work examines this in the contexts of decolonial theory and practices, archival and institutional spaces of art, and the global discourse of contemporary art.

Maria Chavez
Maria Chavez, born in Lima, Peru and based in New York City, is best known as an abstract turntablist, conceptual sound artist, and DJ. Her improvised solo turntable performance combines recorded sounds from vinyl records with the electro-acoustic sounds of vinyl and needle in various deteriorating phases, and her conceptual sound installation practice tends to be site-specific.

Che Chen
Che Chen is a musician/multi-instrumentalist (guitar, contrabass, woodwinds, percussion, etc.) based in Queens and Stonybrook, New York. Chen studied visual art before turning his attention to sound/music; his primary interests include modal and free improvisation, tuning theory (just intonation), and the psychoacoustic properties of tones, repetition, rhythm, and duration.

Jules Gimbrone
Jules Gimbrone is an artist and composer who creates fragile corporeal sound and sculptural ensembles that highlight the differentiations between modes of perceptual acquisition—specifically visual and sonic—within complex and precarious arrangements of subjects and objects. Combining materials into synesthetic, immersive, aural, and haptic environments, Gimbrone investigates how sound travels through space, bodies, and language as a way of exploring hidden or sublimated gendered systems.

David Grubbs
David Grubbs is Professor of Music at Brooklyn College and The Graduate Center, CUNY. He has released fourteen solo albums and is the author of *Records Ruin the Landscape: John Cage, the Sixties, and Sound Recording* (2014); *Now that the audience is assembled* (2018); and *The Voice in the Headphones* (2020), all published by Duke University Press.

Sarah Hennies
Sarah Hennies is a composer based in Ithaca, New York whose work is concerned with a variety of musical, sociopolitical, and psychological issues including queer and trans identity, love, intimacy, psychoacoustics, and percussion. She is primarily a composer of solo and chamber works, but is also active in improvisation, film, performance art, and dance. In 2017 she premiered the groundbreaking work *Contralto*, a film exploring transfeminine identity that uses aspects of "voice feminization" therapy as artistic material.

Branden W. Joseph
Branden W. Joseph is the Frank Gallipoli Professor of Modern and Contemporary Art at Columbia University. He is the author of *Random Order: Robert Rauschenberg and the Neo-Avant-Garde* (MIT Press, 2003); *Beyond the Dream Syndicate: Tony Conrad and the Arts after Cage* (Zone Books, 2008); *The Roh and the Cooked: Tony Conrad and Beverly Grant in Europe* (August Verlag, 2012); and *Experimentations: John Cage in Music, Art, and Architecture* (Bloomsbury, 2016).

Eli Keszler
Eli Keszler is a New York-based artist, composer, and percussionist. He has recorded, performed, and exhibited throughout the world.

Okkyung Lee
Okkyung Lee is a cellist, composer, and improviser. Since moving to New York in 2000, she has worked in disparate contexts as a solo artist and collaborator with creators in a wide range of disciplines. A native of South Korea, Lee has taken a broad array of inspirations—including noise, improvisation, jazz, Western classical, and the traditional and popular music of her homeland—and used them to forge a highly distinctive approach.

Miya Masaoka
Miya Masaoka is a composer and artist based in New York City. Classically trained, her work operates at the intersections of sound, temporality, and perception. She is Associate Professor and Director of the Sound Art Program at Columbia University. Her interconnected artistic practices include notated composition, hybrid acoustic-electronic performance, new Noh music, spatialization, and sonifying the behavior of plants, brain activity, and insect movement.

Anthony McCall
Anthony McCall is a New York-based artist. His solid light works have been shown in numerous solo exhibitions including Serpentine Gallery (London, 2007), Hangar Bicocca (Milan, 2009), Hamburger Bahnhof (Berlin, 2012), and Pioneer Works (Brooklyn, 2018). He has also been represented in historical surveys such as *The Expanded Screen: Actions and Installations of the Sixties and Seventies* (mumok, Vienna, 2003) and *Dreamlands: Immersive Cinema and Art, 1905-2016* (Whitney Museum, New York, 2016).

Christopher McIntyre
Christopher McIntyre's primary artistic activity is performing on trombone and electronics in various musical contexts (from improvisative to interpretive) within the protean New York City community. He also makes compositional work for various media and forces, experimenting with recorded and synthesized sound and using transformational structures to create a narrative of evolving sonic states. He is the director of Brooklyn's TILT Brass, teaches contemporary brass chamber music at Mannes School, and frequently performs in groups such as Either/Or, SEM Ensemble, and Ne(x)tworks, among many others.

Tomeka Reid
Tomeka Reid has emerged over the last decade as one of the most original, versatile, and curious musicians in Chicago's jazz and improvised music community. Reid has been a key member of ensembles led by legendary reedists such as Anthony Braxton and Roscoe Mitchell, as well as a younger generation of visionaries including flutist Nicole Mitchell, singer Dee Alexander, and drummer Mike Reed. Reid released her debut recording as a bandleader in 2015 with the eponymous recording by the Tomeka Reid Quartet.

Ben Vida
Ben Vida is a composer, improviser, and artist based in New York. He co-founded the minimalist quartet Town & Country and has produced solo records under the moniker Bird Show. His recordings of electronic music have been released by Shelter Press, PAN, and Kranky, among many others. His current work examines the aural threshold between verbal sense and nonsense through text-based compositions scored for vocalists, electronics, and ensemble. Vida teaches in the Sonic Arts MFA program at Brooklyn College, CUNY.

Yoshi Wada
Yoshi Wada is a composer and artist associated with the downtown New York experimental arts scene of the last fifty years. Wada was born in Kyoto, Japan, studied sculpture at the Kyoto University of Fine Arts, and moved to New York in the late 1960s. In the early 1970s, Wada began building homemade musical instruments and writing compositions for them based on his personal research in timbre, resonance, and improvisation with the overtone series.

Nate Wooley
Nate Wooley is an interpreter, improviser, and composer whose work exists at the conjuncture of contemporary classical, jazz, noise, and electronic music. While a large part of his work has consisted of solo improvisation and composition, he has collaborated with Anthony Braxton, Éliane Radigue, Annea Lockwood, Yoshi Wada, Christian Wolff, Wadada Leo Smith, and others. He is the editor of the journal *Sound American*.

C. Spencer Yeh
C. Spencer Yeh is recognized for his interdisciplinary activities and collaborations as an artist, improviser, and composer, as well his music project Burning Star Core. His video works are distributed by Electronic Arts Intermix, and Yeh volunteers as a programmer and trailer editor for Spectacle Theater, a microcinema in Brooklyn. Recent exhibitions and presentations of work include *Shocking Asia* at the Empty Gallery (Hong Kong) and "Two Workaround Works Around Calder" at the Whitney Museum.

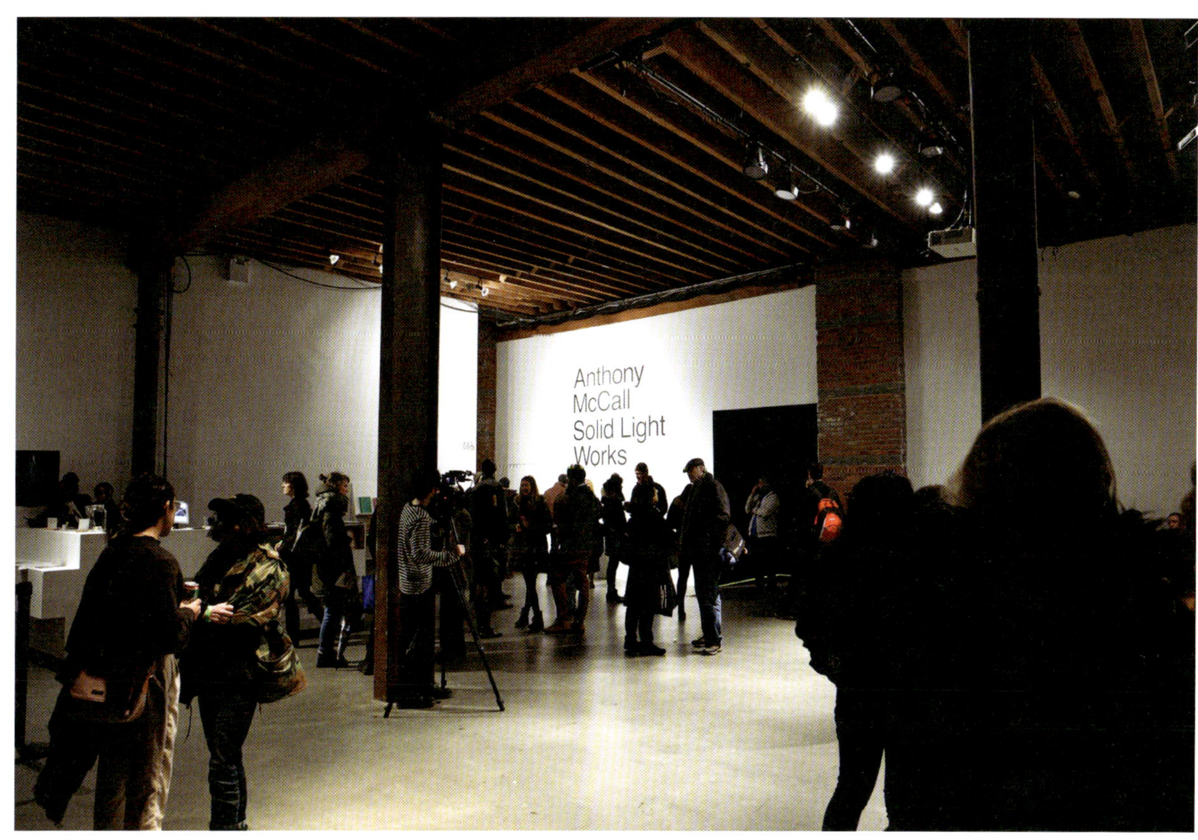

Anthony
McCall
Solid Light
Works

ACKNOWLEDGMENTS

Anthony McCall
My immense gratitude goes to Dustin Yellin and Gabriel Florenz of Pioneer Works for their unflagging resolve to bring *Solid Light Works* to their unique spaces and to realize the exhibition flawlessly. I would like to thank my collaborator David Grubbs, who created such an eloquent structure for the *Four Simultaneous Soloists* performances, as well as introducing fifteen extraordinary musicians for whom I have great admiration and owe much thanks. Thanks are due to my studio manager Nicole Wittenberg, who tenaciously oversaw every detail of the exhibition; to my unparalleled studio assistant and archivist Lauren Nickou; to developers Oleg Ivanov and Eric Mika, who over the years have brought their creative intelligence and clarity to the programming of the solid light works. My appreciation to art historians Branden W. Joseph and to Swagato Chakravorty; and to Sean Kelly and Janine Cirincione at Sean Kelly Gallery for their support throughout the development of the exhibition.

David Grubbs
I would like to thank Cathy Bowman, Emmett Bowman-Grubbs, Swagato Chakravorty, Camille Drummond, Gabriel Florenz, Katie Giritlian, Jennie Gottschalk, Branden W. Joseph, Daniel Kent, Dustin Yellin, all of the participating musicians, and everyone at Pioneer Works whose skill, ingenuity, and open-mindedness made this project such a pleasure. Warmest thanks are due to Anthony McCall, among the most rewarding collaborators with whom one could hope to work.

COLOPHON

Published on the occasion of the exhibition *Anthony McCall: Solid Light Works*, January 12–March 11, 2018 at Pioneer Works. Curated by Gabriel Florenz.

Edition of 2000
Pioneer Works Press, 2019

Pioneer Works Press
159 Pioneer St.
Brooklyn NY 11231
Pioneerworks.org

Pioneer Works builds community through the arts and sciences to create an open and inspired world.

Pioneer Works is a non-profit 501(c)(3).

Pioneer Works Press publishes a range of projects that explore new ways of thinking, and seeks to advance the dissemination of knowledge and art through publication and recorded sound. Through our imprint, bookstore, and annual Press Play publishing and music fair, we seek to demonstrate that publication is essential to accessing the arts beyond the institution, and that it is a foundation of all creative practice.

Pioneer Works programs are made possible by the generous support of our board of directors, grants, and donations.

All rights reserved including rights of reproduction in whole or in part in any form. © 2019 Pioneer Works Press and the contributing authors.

Every reasonable attempt has been made to identify owners of copyright. Errors or omissions will be corrected in subsequent editions.

Text copyright 2019
Anthony McCall
David Grubbs
Swagato Chakravorty
Branden W. Joseph

Publication copyright 2019
Pioneer Works

Editors
Anthony McCall
David Grubbs

Founding Artistic Director and Curator
Gabriel Florenz

Associate Curator
Vivian Chui

Design Director
Daniel Kent

Design Assistance
Anna Feng

Publishing Coordinator
Katie Giritlian

Publishing
Camille Drummond
Mary Thompson

Copy Editor
Alison Gore

Typeface
Helvetica Now

Paper Stock
Sirio Color Nero, 290 gsm
Arctic Volume White, 150 gsm

Printed in Belgium by die Keure

ISBN
978-1-945711-09-1

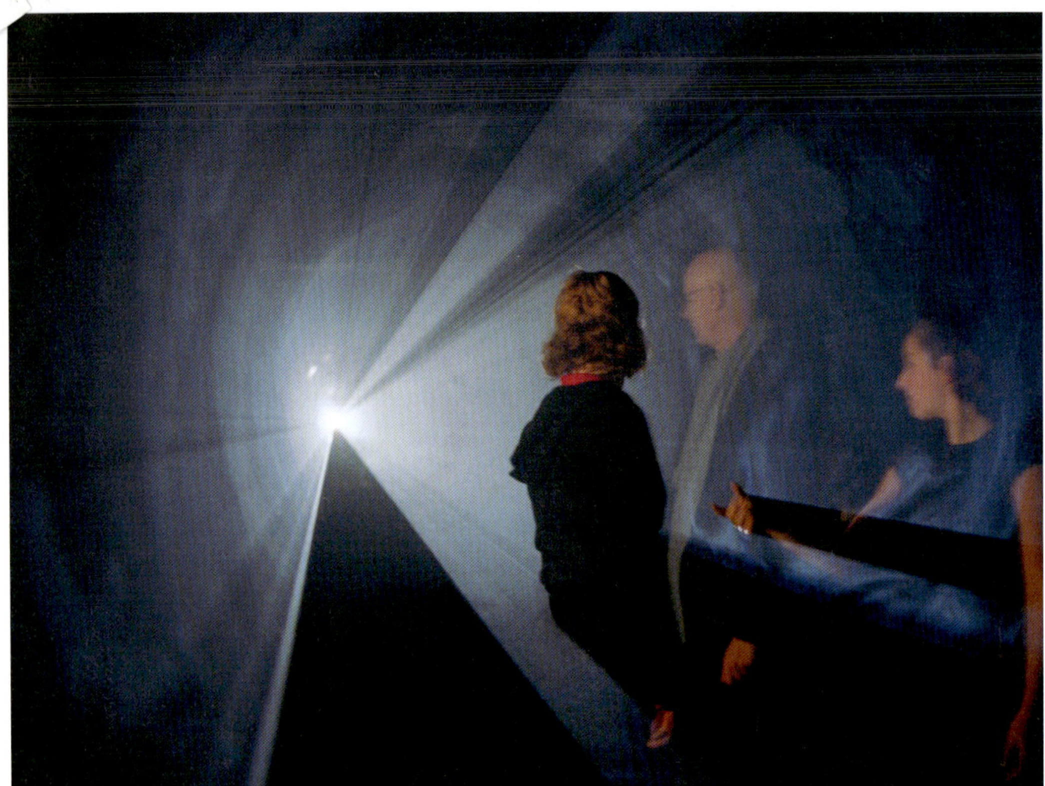

Anthony McCall. *Line Describing a Cone*, 1973. Installation view, Whitney Museum of American Art, New York, 2001.